Effective Leadership for School Improvement

D0974381

In a complex and multi-layered world, the conventional idea of great leadership being the result of the efforts of a single individual is rapidly becoming redundant. This book takes up the challenge of finding an alternative method of leadership in educational contexts, and looks at how this can help achieve sustained improvement in schools.

The authors acknowledge that there are no simple solutions to school improvement. They argue that the effective leaders of the future will be those who are able to share responsibility, build positive relationships and offer stakeholders – teachers, parents and students – an opportunity to work together to improve their schools.

The book is based around four key areas of concern: the changing context of leadership; leadership and school improvement; building leadership capacity; and future direction and implications. In each Part, the authors discuss current theories and issues, and put forward alternative ideas and perspectives.

This book will make valuable reading for headteachers, principals, deputies and other senior teachers, particularly those undertaking leadership qualifications and training. It will also interest postgraduate students and school governors.

Alma Harris is Professor of School Leadership and Director of the Leadership, Policy and Improvement Unit at the Institute of Education, University of Warwick. **Christopher Day** is Professor of Education and Co-Director of the Centre for Teacher and School Development at the School of Education, University of Nottingham. **Mark Hadfield** is a Senior Lecturer in Professional Development and School Improvement at the School of Education, University of Nottingham. **David Hopkins** is Director of the Standards and Effectiveness Unit at the Department for Education and Skills. **Andy Hargreaves** is Professor of Educational Leadership and Change at the University of Nottingham, and Professor in the International Centre for Educational Change at the Ontario Institute for Studies in Education, University of Toronto. **Christopher Chapman** is a Research Fellow at the Institute of Education, University of Warwick.

School Leadership series

Series editors: Brent Davies and Linda Ellison

Strategic Direction and Development of the School
Brent Davies and Linda Ellison

School Leadership in the 21st Century
Brent Davies and Linda Ellison

Effective Change in Schools
Chris James and Una Connolly

Effective Leadership for School Improvement

Alma Harris, Christopher Day,
Mark Hadfield, David Hopkins,
Andy Hargreaves and
Christopher Chapman

RoutledgeFalmer
Taylor & Francis Group

LONDON AND NEW YORK

First published 2003 by RoutledgeFalmer
II New Fetter Lane, London EC4P 4EE

Simultaneously published in the USA and Canada
by RoutledgeFalmer
29 West 35th Street, New York, NY I000I

RoutledgeFalmer is an imprint of the Taylor & Francis Group

© 2003 Alma Harris, Christopher Day, Mark Hadfield,
David Hopkins, Andy Hargreaves and Christopher Chapman

Typeset in Palatino and Gill by BC Typesetting, Bristol
Printed and bound in Great Britain by
MPG Books Ltd, Bodmin

British Library Cataloguing in Publication Data
A catalogue record for this book is available from the British Library

Library of Congress Cataloging in Publication Data
A catalog record for this book has been requested

ISBN 0–4I5–24223–I (pbk)
ISBN 0–4I5–30046–0 (hbk)

Contents

Contributors

Christopher Chapman is a Research Fellow at the Institute of Education, University of Warwick. His current research interests focus on the areas of leadership and school improvement particularly in challenging and low-performing schools. He is involved with several research projects including 'Building the Capacity for Improvement' and 'Leadership in Schools facing Challenging Circumstances', both funded by the National College for School Leadership. Most recently, he is engaged in a large-scale research project funded by the Department for Education and Skills looking at teacher effectiveness.

Christopher Day is Professor of Education and Co-director of the Centre for Teacher and School Development at the School of Education, University of Nottingham. He has worked as a schoolteacher, teacher, educator and local authority adviser. Professor Day is Co-director of the International Successful School Leaders Project and Co-ordinator and Director of the VITAE Project (a four-year study of teachers' work, lives and their effects on pupils). He is editor of *Teachers and Teaching: Theory and Practice*, and co-editor of *Educational Action Research*. He is a Board Member of the International Council for Teacher Education (ICET). In addition to the *International Handbook of the Continuing Professional Development of Teachers* (Open University Press, 2002) his recent publications include *Leading Schools in Times of Change* (Open University Press, 2000).

Mark Hadfield is a Senior Lecturer in Professional Development and School Improvement at the School of Education, University of Nottingham. He has published widely on the themes of leadership and school improvement. His most recent research work has focused upon developing leadership capacity for the National College for School Leadership. His work also encompasses a wide range of social justice issues and he has recently published an anti-racist manual for schools. He is currently researching risk-taking with groups of young people.

Andy Hargreaves is Professor of Educational Leadership and Change at the University of Nottingham, England and Co-director of and Professor in the International Centre for Educational Change at the Ontario Institute for Studies in Education of the University of Toronto. He is the author and editor of more than twenty books in the fields of teacher development, the culture of the school and educational reform. His book *Changing Teachers, Changing Times* received the 1995 Outstanding Writing Award from the American Association of Colleges for Teacher Education. Among his other recent books are *Teaching In the Knowledge Society* (2003) and (with Lorna Earl, Shawn Moore and Susan Manning) *Learning to Change: Teaching Beyond Subjects and Standards* (Jossey-Bass, 2001). He initiated and coordinated the editing of the *International Handbook of Educational Change* (Kluwer, 1998) and is founding editor-in-chief of the *Journal of Educational Change* (published by Kluwer). Andy is holder of the Canadian Education Association/Whitworth 2000 Award for outstanding contributions to educational research in Canada.

Alma Harris is Professor of School Leadership and Director of the Leadership, Policy and Improvement Unit at the Institute of Education, University of Warwick. She has published extensively on the theme of leadership and school improvement and her latest books include *School Improvement: What's in it for Schools?* (RoutledgeFalmer, 2002), *Leading the Improving Department* (David Fulton Press, 2002) and (with Nigel Bennett) *School Effectiveness and School Improvement: Alternative Perspectives* (Cassell, 2001). Her most recent research work has focused upon effective leadership in schools facing challenging circumstances and the relationship between teacher leadership and school improvement. She is currently working with the National College for School Leadership in a research and development capacity.

David Hopkins is Director of the Standards and Effectiveness Unit at the Department for Education and Skills. Prior to this appointment, Professor Hopkins was Dean at the University of Nottingham, Chair of Leicester City Partnership Board and a member of the Governing Council of the National College for School Leadership. He has published extensively on the themes of school development, change and improvement and has an international reputation for his research and writing. His latest books include *A Teacher's Guide to Classroom Research*, 3rd edition, *Improving the Quality of Education for All* and *School Improvement for Real*. He has also recently co-edited *The International Handbook of Educational Change* and co-authored *Models of Learning: Tools for Teaching*, 2nd edition. He is also an experienced mountain guide and has climbed many of the world's most famous mountain ranges.

David Jackson was a highly successful headteacher and is currently Director of Research and School Improvement at the National College for School Leadership, based at the Jubilee Campus of the University of Nottingham. The Group is committed to inquiry-based models of leadership and has established Research and Development Programmes in five key areas: Successful Leadership in Urban and Challenging Contexts; Networked Learning Communities; Building Capacity for School Development; New Visions for Early Headship; and Learning from Best Practice Worldwide.

Acknowledgements

The authors of this book have been fortunate to work together on a variety of research projects involving schools and teachers across many countries. Their work has been influenced by the insights and challenges offered by those working in schools on a daily basis. We would like to acknowledge and thank all the teachers and headteachers we work with who continue to enthuse, inform and inspire our research. It is their contribution that makes all the difference.

The authors would also like to thank Brent Davies and Linda Ellison for including this book in their series and to the publishers for their unending patience.

Introduction

Alma Harris

> It remains that the superhero images of leadership will not work. In tomorrow's schools success will depend upon the ability of leaders to harness the capacity of locals, to enhance sense and meaning and to build a community of responsibility.
>
> (Sergiovanni, 2001: 55)

> I would like to put forward the revolutionary idea that all teachers can lead. If schools are going to become places where all children and adults are learning in worthy ways, all teachers *must* lead.
>
> (Barth, 2001: 85)

There is a growing recognition in the increasingly complex contexts of educational change and accountability that deep and sustained school improvement will depend upon the leadership of the many rather than the few. There is a groundswell towards leadership as empowerment, transformation and community-building and away from the 'great man' theory of leadership. As Heifetz (1994) suggests 'instead of looking for saviours we should be calling for leadership that will challenge us to face problems for which there are no simple, painless solutions – problems that require us to learn new ways' (21). Similarly, Fullan (2001: 2) proposes that 'charismatic leaders inadvertently do more harm than good because, at best, they provide episodic improvement followed by frustrated or despondent dependency'. Consequently, there is a powerful argument for looking at alternative ways of leading, looking for competing theories of leadership and challenging the orthodoxy that equates leadership with the efforts of one person.

This book aims to present alternative perspectives and views about leadership and school improvement. It is not a book that subscribes to conventional, rational leadership theory or a book that endorses leadership traits and tricks. Instead, it aims to present some of the real challenges, contradictions and complexities that surround leadership and school improvement. It argues that effective leaders in schools will be those who are able to build collaborative cultures through generating positive relationships. It endorses the view that effective leaders are those who build the capacity for improvement through working collaboratively and through building professional learning communities within and between schools. It suggests that effective leaders have a shared vision for their school and that this can only be realised if teachers work together as a learning community.

Building a learning community or a 'community of practice' is increasingly accepted as being the critical element in school improvement. Sergiovanni (2001) contends that 'developing a community of practice may be the single most important way to improve a school'. A wealth of research evidence reinforces this position and highlights that successful schools build communities that are inclusive and value, above all, individual development and achievement. Building the capacity for school improvement therefore necessitates paying careful attention to how relationships in schools are fostered and developed (Harris and Chapman, 2001). It also suggests a form of leadership that is, as Sergiovanni (2001) suggests, 'ideas-based', where locating the source of authority for leadership is in the quality of ideas rather than position or role. As ideas and common commitments are shared in the school, so is leadership, and teachers, parents and students share the responsibility for school development and change.

One of the most congruent findings from recent studies of effective leadership is that authority to lead need not be located in the person of the leader but can be dispersed within the school in between and among people (MacBeath, 1988; Day et al., 2000; Harris, 2002). In this sense leadership is separated from person, role and status and is primarily concerned with the relationships and the connections among individuals within a school. This form of leadership is one where individuals 'feel confident in their own capacity, in the capacity of their colleagues and in the capacity of the school to promote professional development' (Mitchell and Sackney, 2000: 78). It also implies that 'teachers are participants in decision-making, have a shared sense of purpose, engage in collaborative work and accept joint responsibility for the outcomes of their work' (Lambert, 1998: 11).

This alternative image of leadership is one of empowering people to understand, rather than solve, the problems that they face. It is, as Sergiovanni (2001) proposes, largely concerned with the 'lifeworld' of the school rather than the 'systemworld', where attention is focused upon developing social, intellectual and other forms of human capital rather than concentrating upon achievement of narrow, instrumental ends. It is a form of leadership premised upon the leadership capability of the many rather than the few and is centrally concerned with building the capacity for organisational growth and change. Inevitably this mode of leadership challenges the conventional orthodoxy of the single, individualistic leader suggesting instead a form of leadership that is distributed, instructionally focused and ultimately teacher-owned (Harris *et al.*, 2001).

The main purpose of this book is to explore, elucidate and reflect upon the relationship between leadership and school improvement. The central argument of the book is that new and alternative approaches to leadership are required if schools are to improve and change. The book suggests that deep and sustained educational reform can only be achieved if leadership in schools becomes principally concerned with maximising social and academic capital. It also proposes that school improvement is more likely to occur where leaders build the capacity for change and development, where they invest in teachers and teaching and where they empower others to lead (Harris, 2002). Schools that are improving are 'learning communities' that cultivate a deep culture of teaching and learning. Effective leadership for school improvement, therefore, should be principally concerned with building the capacity and creating the conditions to generate improvement and, most importantly, to sustain improvement over time.

Structure of the book

The book is divided into four parts each reflecting a different dimension of the relationship between effective leadership and school improvement. Part I considers the current context of school leadership and provides an overview of the main theoretical positions within the contemporary leadership field. The first chapter offers an analysis and interpretation of dominant leadership theory and highlights the limitations of these various traditions and positions to adequately represent or describe current leadership practices. Chapter 2 charts the implications for leadership development for heads in relation to the different theoretical positions and highlights some of the limitations of the current modes of professional development. The chapter reinforces the importance of reflection in leadership practices that promote school improvement. It concludes by raising some questions and posing some challenges about the future professional development of school leaders.

Part II considers alternative contemporary views of leadership, particularly those that are directly associated with school and classroom improvement. Chapter 3 considers instructional leadership and argues that leadership should focus upon learning and that leaders should be primarily concerned with improving the quality of teaching and learning. By taking an instructional focus, leadership in this chapter is viewed as primarily concerned with creating the optimum conditions for teaching, learning and classroom improvement. It proposes a style of leadership that is consistent with raising levels of student achievement and leaders that are able to focus on teaching and learning and building professional learning communities. Chapter 4 looks at the relationship between teacher leadership and school improvement. It suggests that when teachers are empowered to lead there is greater potential for collaboration and mutual learning. This theme is reinforced in Chapter 5 in the broader discussion of capacity-building. Here distributed leadership to teachers, parents and students is viewed as a key to school improvement. The chapter argues that building social capital and fostering distributed leadership are central to building the capacity for school improvement.

Part III moves away from theory generation to theory-testing by utilising the findings from recent empirical work focused upon effective leadership for school improvement. Chapters 6 and 7 concentrate on the potential of the idea of 'capacity' to support school leaders in critically reflecting upon the nature of school leadership and improvement. Both chapters focus upon the practical aspects and implications of 'capacity-building'. They draw heavily upon practitioners' views about capacity-building and offer insights into how well this idea resonates with schools and what messages are emerging about this particular view of school improvement. Chapter 8 offers a case study of school improvement in difficult and challenging circumstances. Drawing upon empirical evidence from a study commissioned by the National College for School Leadership, the chapter highlights the processes and practicalities of school improvement. The stages of improvement are outlined and the particular approach to leadership adopted is illuminated. The chapter suggests that building the capacity for school improvement will necessitate investing in teacher leadership and distributing decision-making responsibilities throughout the school.

Part IV is concerned with the future directions and implications for leadership in schools of the future. Chapter 9 focuses upon successful leadership in the twenty-first century and offers some challenges and possibilities for school leadership in changing and complex times. Chapter 10 reflects upon the future of schooling in the knowledge society. The chapter suggests that an emphasis upon performance and standards is unlikely to produce the kinds of teaching and learning required for a rapidly changing world. It concludes by arguing that creating professional learning communities promises a way of securing longer-term, sustainable school improvement but that this will only be achieved through empowering teachers to lead school development and change.

Commentary

As schools face continuous pressure to raise standards and to improve performance there will be increased demands for approaches to school improvement that work most effectively. This will inevitably mean focusing upon the leadership practices that foster sustained improvement and positive change in schools. The central message of this book is that effective leadership for school improvement will require quite radical changes in structures to allow people to collaborate both within and across schools. It will necessitate relinquishing belief in the 'superhuman' leader and replacing it with an image of a school where all teachers and students have leadership potential and capability. It will require a range of leadership approaches at different times. Schools are likely to cope with change in turbulent times more readily by generating leadership capacity of the many rather than the few. In short, it means a fundamental reconceptualisation of leadership as a form of social capital which, if distributed or shared, has the greatest potential to contribute to sustained school development and improvement.

References

Barth, R. (2001) *Learning by Heart*, San Francisco, Jossey-Bass.

Day, C., Harris, A., Hadfield, M., Tolley, H. and Beresford, J. (2000) *Leading Schools in Times of Change*, Milton Keynes, Open University Press.

Fullan, M. (2001) *Leading in a Culture of Change*, San Francisco, Jossey-Bass.

Harris, A. (2002) *School Improvement: What's in it for Schools?*, London, Routledge.

Harris, A. and Chapman, C. (2001) 'Democratic Leadership for School Improvement in Challenging Contexts', paper presented at the International Congress on School Effectiveness and Improvement, Copenhagen.

Harris, A., Day, C. and Hadfield, M. (2001) 'Headteachers' Views of Effective School Leadership', *International Studies in Educational Administration*, 29(1): 29–39.

Heifetz, R. (1994) *Leadership without Easy Answers*, Cambridge MA, Harvard University Press.

Lambert, L. (1998) *Building Leadership Capacity in Schools*, Association for Supervision and Curriculum Development, Alexandria, Virginia, USA.

MacBeath, J. (ed.) (1998) *Effective School Leadership: Responding to Change*, London, Paul Chapman Publishers.

Mitchell, C. and Sackney, L. (2001) *Profound Improvement: Building Capacity for a Learning Community*, Lisse, Swets and Zeitlinger.

Sergiovanni, T. (2001) *Leadership: What's in it for Schools?* London, RoutledgeFalmer.

Part I

The changing context of leadership

Chapter 1

The changing context of leadership

Research, theory and practice

Alma Harris

Introduction

Leadership is currently in vogue. Across many Western countries, there has been a renewed emphasis upon improving leadership capacity and capability in the drive towards higher standards. Governments around the world are involved in the business of educational reform. Improving the micro-efficiency of the school has been viewed as a means of addressing some of the macro-problems of the state and society (Macbeath, 1988: 47). The pressure upon schools to raise achievement has resulted in reduced teacher autonomy and increased demands for higher performance. Even though there are few certainties about the ability of educational policy to secure higher performance from the educational system, the arguments for investment in education remain powerful and compelling.

While the education challenges are considerable and the route to reform is complex, the potential of leadership to influence pupil and school performance remains unequivocal. It has been consistently argued that the quality of headship matters in determining the motivation of teachers and the quality of teaching which takes place in the classroom (Eraut, 1994; Hargreaves, 1994; Hargreaves and Fullan, 1998; Day *et al.*, 1998). Researchers of school effectiveness and school improvement have long argued the importance of leadership in schools:

> Leadership helps to establish a clear and consistent vision for the school, which emphasises the prime purposes of the school as teaching and learning and is highly visible to both staff and students.
>
> (Sammons *et al.*, 1997: 199)

The importance of leadership in securing sustainable school improvement has been demonstrated in both research and practice (Harris and Bennett, 2001). Similarly, leadership is highlighted as a key constituent in school and departmental effectiveness (Sammons *et al.*, 1997; Harris, 1999). Consequently, from a policy maker's perspective, school leaders are viewed as holding the key to resolving a number of the problems currently facing schools. This has led to a major investment in the preparation and development of school leaders across many countries and has proved a main impetus for the establishment of the National College for School Leadership in England.[1]

Yet the belief in leadership as a panacea for raising standards is not without its critics. Anti-leadership proponents emerge sporadically. Most recently, anti-leadership arguments have begun to emerge most forcefully in the work of Lakomski (1998, 1999) who claims that there is no natural entity or essence that can be labelled 'leadership'. It is Lakomski's (1999) view that leadership research has yielded a mass of largely inconclusive results and has demonstrated that leadership means different things to different people in different contexts. In response to Lakomski's position, Gronn (2000) has suggested that the fact that researchers have provided inconclusive results is not a sufficient argument for jettisoning the concept of 'leadership' altogether. He argues that leadership is still needed but that a fundamental reconceptualisation of the nature of leadership within organisations is overdue (Gronn, 2000).

If we accept that leadership is a meaningful and useful construct, the question remains: what does effective leadership look like? There are a number of conceptual understandings about leadership which offer some relevant insights into effective practice. Riley (2000: 47) suggests that:

- there is no one package for school leadership, no one model to be learned and applied regardless of culture or context, though leadership can be developed and nurtured;
- school leadership is more than the effort of a single individual;
- school leadership is not static;
- school leaders do not learn how to do leadership: they are often rule breakers and are willing to change in response to new sets of circumstances.

The view of school leadership outlined above encompasses both mobility and fragility. It is based on the assumption that schools are constantly changing and that the challenge for school leaders is to respond to the school's inner life as well as to the external context. The evidence from the international literature demonstrates that effective leaders exercise an indirect but powerful influence on the effectiveness of the school and on the achievement of pupils. It shows that effective school leaders exercise both professional and political leadership and are able to draw on their past experience to respond to new situations.

Hallinger and Heck (1996) found that there were four areas in particular in which the leadership of the headteacher influenced the school. The first was through establishing and conveying the purposes and goals of the school. A second area of leadership influence was through the interplay between the school's organisation and its social network. A third was through influence over people and the fourth was in relation to organisational culture. While their review of the literature highlighted the centrality of the leader in terms of organisational change and development, it also revealed the complex and sometimes contradictory messages within the leadership field.

One such contradictory message concerns the way in which leadership is simultaneously romanticised and de-romanticised. If one subscribes to trait theories of success, then leadership is largely concerned with personal characteristics, much more than effort or skill. The notion of the 'superhead' is caught up in an interpretation of leadership as an inherent set of qualities, as someone with charisma and personal power.

As Fullan (2001: 1) notes:

> Charismatic leaders inadvertently often do more harm than good because at best they provide episodic improvement followed by frustration or despondent dependency. Superhuman leaders also do us another disservice: they are role models who can never be emulated by large numbers.

In sharp contrast, the literature is also replete with guidance about 'how to lead', suggesting that there is a generic set of leadership skills and a common body of knowledge that any potential leader can access. This inevitably leads to different interpretations and understandings of the term 'leadership' and to competing leadership theories.

Whatever the limitations of the existing research base, in the last decade or so there has been renewed interest in the leadership field and a resurgence of research activity in this area. The need to take account of successful leadership in action has been recognised and there are more studies emerging that embrace the moral, professional and emotional dimensions of leadership. This chapter encompasses the contemporary views of leadership and outlines a range of theoretical perspectives concerning leadership. Its main purpose is to provide an overview of the current research findings concerning school leadership and to provide a theoretical context and reference point for the chapters that follow.

The changing context of leadership

The current focus on leadership stems from the need to cope with discontinuous and accelerating change. Educational development over the last decade has been framed by a socio-political context characterised by growing consumerism, a developing knowledge revolution, increased globalised and intensified competition, increasing global turbulence and the growing use of regulatory power as a frame for business practice (Law and Glover, 2000). The development of the quasi-market in education together with increased choice and diversity has dramatically altered the role of the head-teacher:

> whether we like it or not, under new public sector management, there are emerging irreconcilable goals for schooling. On the one hand there are those who are pushing schools to operate like businesses, and to pursue the educational equivalent of profit maximisation. On the other hand, schools are ultimately concerned with the development of students who are not only employable, but also autonomous, responsible, moral individuals who are effective members of society.
>
> (Dempster and Mahoney, 1988: 137–8)

There is evidence that a significant number of headteachers have welcomed many of the post 1988 reforms and the possibilities brought by the quasi-market and delegated management. However, there have been problems as well as opportunities created by the new market environment. The language of reform has undoubtedly redefined the role of the school leader as 'chief executive' or 'managing director' (Caldwell and Spinks, 1992; Sergiovanni, 1992; Leithwood *et al.*, 1999). This has led to a dramatic shift in the way school leadership is construed and interpreted:

> A process of ideological transformation is occurring in contemporary English society in which education is regarded as a commodity; the schools as a value-adding production unit; the headteacher as chief executive and managing director; the parents as consumers; and the ultimate aim of the whole enterprise to achieve a maximum value-added product which keeps the school as near to the top of the league table of success as possible . . . Contemporary headteachers are therefore expected to 'market the school', 'deliver the curriculum', and to 'satisfy the customers'.
>
> (Grace, 1995: 21)

In the early 1990s effective headteachers could be characterised in four main ways. Firstly, they were responsible for defining the mission of the school and setting goals. These goals emphasised traditional student achievement and were widely shared both within and outside the school. Secondly, they were responsible for managing the routine functions within the school organisation that supported teaching and learning: for example, managing resources, time, the curriculum and staff. Thirdly, headteachers were required to promote a professional learning climate by establishing high expectations and standards of student behaviour. Finally, headteachers were expected to develop a strong culture at the school that included a safe and orderly work environment, staff collaboration and cohesion. In short, the tendency at this time was to place the burden for improvement upon the headteacher as the individual 'strong leader' within the organisation.

In the current context the role of the leader is primarily characterised as coping with change and coping with complexity. Heads now work with a number of reform paradoxes:

- an increase in independence in the management of schools alongside increasing dependence upon curriculum, monitoring, assessment and inspection frameworks imposed by government;
- a performance and results orientation which has the potential to create divisiveness;
- new forms of accountability which are intended to enhance effectiveness, but which simultaneously increase workload and bureaucracy;
- new imposed curriculum certainties which reduce teachers' abilities to recognise and act upon differentiated student need;
- increased attention to cognitive challenge which reduces attention to emotional need (Day et al., 2000).

It has been suggested that 'the headteacher more than anyone else has the capacity to bring about such a release of energy and potential and even more importantly, a belief in the school's potential to succeed' (National Commission on Education, 1996: 335). The current activities of school leaders are shaped by the need to manage change and cope with complexity:

> The contemporary school leader must be politically astute, a successful professional entrepreneur, a skilled mediator and an effective agent of change. Therefore, the bases of power now are sound knowledge of how organisations function, interpersonal relations, group dynamics, personal management and people's value sets.
>
> (Day et al., 2000)

Research has shown that the growth in the external scrutiny and monitoring of schools has created its own sets of tensions (Day et al., 2000). Headteachers now find themselves positioned uneasily between those outside of schools instigating and promoting changes and their own staff within school who will ultimately have to deliver them. Even when not caught directly between these groups headteachers can find themselves trying to offer leadership in a context where their teachers' performance is being set against that of colleagues in other departments or even nearby schools.

These 'internal drivers' for change can be characterised as a complex mixture of school-based factors, i.e. the institutional needs and wants which provide the impetus for the school's development. Some of these internal drivers are 'givens' in that they would exist irrespective of the type of leadership approach adopted. Other internal drivers are 'constructed' by leaders within the school by their commitment to a particular vision, values framework or strategies of management. The 'external drivers' arise from policy interventions and edicts that require compliance. Increasingly headteachers, and those around them, are aware of being caught between these two sets of drivers:

> Changes are externally imposed so that the head must interpret incoming documents before she can inform the staff. The speed with which those changes have had to be introduced means that she has had little time to motivate staff and she is finding it increasingly difficult to justify imposing yet more demands for change. It also makes it more difficult to see things through – she has had to learn to delegate more of the responsibility for managing change.
>
> (Day *et al.*, 2000)

Headteachers who are used to being proactive rather than reactive have had to learn how to deal with a more or less constant flow of initiatives. They now have to demonstrate their leadership by the selection of which initiatives they take on, the relative support which they provide for their implementation, their knowledge of how others are tackling new initiatives and how well they can adapt initiatives that are forced on them to their particular circumstances. Within the United States and Canada, a changing pattern of headship is also discernable. Viewed initially as administrators, by the late 1980s school principals had assumed the role of instructional leaders. Today, their primary role is that of change agent within their organisations. As Fullan (1998: 16) points out, 'if the principal does not lead changes in the culture of the school, or if he or she leaves it to others, it normally will not get done'.

This view of leadership that places an emphasis upon the individual power of the leaders is one that has dominated much of the literature. This individualism, which may be typified as a belief in the 'power of one', is grounded in the assumption that effective performance by an individual, group or organisation is dependent upon someone with the right leadership skills and abilities. The definition and interpretation of the 'right' skills and abilities vary widely within the literature and reflect a range of different leadership theories.

Leadership theory

Leadership in education has generated an enormous amount of interest among researchers and practitioners. Most of the literature on leadership is derived from North American and European sources and, it has been suggested, reflects an overreliance upon commercial and business views of leadership. Yet, despite a large research base, the search for a singular theory of leadership has proved to be somewhat futile. Sergiovanni (1992: 2) notes that 'after fifty years of steady work, social science can tell us little about the subject'. As Law and Glover (2000: 4) note: 'We must acknowledge the centrality of professionalism, reject the quick fix prescription and accept that there are no ready made or universally applicable theories we can simply pull off the shelf.'

The research on leadership has produced a bewildering array of findings and the endless accumulation of empirical data has not resulted in any clear understanding of leadership. In 1959 Bennis wrote:

> Of all the hazy and confounding ideas in social psychology, leadership theory undoubtedly contends for the top nomination. Probably more has been and less is known about leadership than any other topic in the behavioural sciences.
>
> (Bennis, 1959: 259)

The study of leadership has tended to dwell upon issues of style and levels of decision-making, assessing the consequences of their variations for organisational effectiveness and improvement. As a consequence, the literature is full of competing theories and counter-claims that make any attempt at generating a single, overarching theory impossible. Sergiovanni (1992) suggests that there are two main failures within the leadership literature: firstly, its reliance upon a view of leadership as behaviour rather than action; secondly, its overemphasis upon bureaucratic, psychological and technical rational authority.

Fullan (1996) has suggested many of the new theories fail to provide robust examples and insights, which in turn can be linked to powerful concepts. He argues that more work needs to be done to develop a meaningful action-based theory of leadership. While there are examples of such work emerging (e.g. Day et al., 2000; Leithwood et al., 1999), the existing leadership literature is still dominated by theory that is premised upon a rational and technicist perspective.

West et al. (2000: 32) suggest that thinking about leadership falls into a number of phases – as follows:

- initial interest in the personal qualities and characteristics of 'successful leaders' which result in personality or trait theories of leadership;
- increasing focus on what it is that leaders actually do – are there some behaviours and approaches that are consistently associated with successful leadership? Such inquiries support the development of behavioural theories of leadership;

- growing awareness that task-related and people-centred behaviours may be interpreted quite differently by different groups and in different contexts, prompting explanation of how the particular context might be best accounted for within a general theory, and resulting in a variety of situational approaches to leadership;
- most recently, emphasis upon the links between leadership style and the culture of the organisation – a notion of leadership as transformational – having the potential to alter the context in which people work.

This last phase has been at the forefront of the research and writing concerning educational leadership in the past decade. The debate between transactional and transformational leadership has dominated both policy and practice in different countries. In countries where the systems of command and control are in place there has been an interest in and focus upon transactional leadership. In countries where decentralisation has occurred, there has been renewed interest in transformational leadership and more democratic leadership approaches.

Transactional leadership

Transactional leadership theory dominated the attention of those within the leadership research field until the early 1980s. Implicit in this theoretical position is a crudely abstracted leader–follower dichotomy, in which leaders are superior to followers and followers depend on leaders. In this way leadership consists of doing something for, to and on behalf of others. It is also premised upon tasks being delegated to the followers and followers completing these tasks. This form of leadership is one that emphasises procedures and hard data to inform decision-making. Based upon an exchange of services for various kinds of rewards that the leader controls, the role of the transactional leader is to focus upon the purposes of the organisation and to assist people to recognise what needs to be done in order to reach a desired outcome.

Despite extensive research and writing on the theme of transactional leadership, its value has been drawn more and more into question. It is clear that as a theory of leadership it fits well with well-recognised models of 'task' and 'maintenance' management models (Adair, 1983). It is also a rational form of leadership that is premised upon leadership equating with the management of systems and processes rather than the management of people. In approaching school development and improvement, transactional leadership would be primarily concerned with promoting structural rather than cultural change.

The transactional leadership or management approach is concerned largely with structures, emphasising organisational purposes rather than people. This style of leadership is people- rather than organisation-orientated and requires a leadership approach that transforms the feelings, attitudes and beliefs of others. The role of the transactional leader is to focus upon the key purposes of the organisation and to assist people to recognise what needs to be done in order to reach the desired outcomes.

If the parameters for success are well defined, transactional leaders can be very effective. Where conformity rather than creativity is the norm, then transactional methods tend to be most appropriate. West *et al.* (2000: 33) suggest that 'transactional leadership approaches, therefore, seem best suited to static school systems and communities'. In contrast, schools that are dynamic require a leadership approach that will promote and sustain organisational change and development.

Transformational leadership

The seminal work of Burns (1978) provided a competing and compelling alternative theory to transactional leadership. He distinguished between transactional and transformational leadership and argued that most leaders use transactional management rather than transactional leadership. Since the work of Burns (1978) there has been an increasing emphasis upon the links between leadership and the culture of the organisation (Dalin, 1996). This has led towards a view of leadership as transformational, having the potential to alter the cultural context in which people work. This transformational leadership perspective focuses on the moral values and value-laden activities of a leader and how these are disclosed to other colleagues (Duignan and Macpherson, 1992).

Blase (1989) argues that leaders acting in this mode try to use power with or through other people, rather than exercising control over them. It is this perspective that leads Hodgkinson (1991) and Sergiovanni (1992) to describe leadership as a 'moral art' rather than a technical science. Implicit in this view is also the notion of shared or devolved leadership activity where leadership activity is not chiefly the preserve of the headteacher.

Transformational leaders not only manage structure but they purposefully impact upon the culture in order to change it. At its most basic level, to transform essentially means to change, so in this respect any leader who brings about change could be viewed as transformational. However, in the leadership literature the term 'transformational' has a more precise definition. It is concerned with relationships and engagement of individuals. In contrast to transactional leadership, transformational leadership entails a change in the leader–follower relationship for mutual benefit and good (Leithwood, 1999). Leithwood *et al.* defines transformational leadership as including charisma, inspirational motivation, intellectual stimulation and individualised consideration.

Burns (1978) describes transformational leadership as concerned with 'exploring conventional relationships and organisational understandings such that there is involvement between persons in which leaders and followers raise one another to higher levels of motivation and morality'. Proponents of transformational concepts such as Peters and Austin (1985) see the leader as a 'cheerleader, enthusiast, wanderer, dramatist, coach, facilitator, builder'. These views are endorsed by Kouzes and Posner (1987) who identify in their research that the ability to inspire, challenge and to enable others to act is a fundamental part of transformational leadership. Leithwood (1999) suggests that the transformational leader pursues the continuous professional development of teachers and builds the capacity for learning within the school.

A recent overview of the research relating to transformational leadership has suggested that taken at face value, transformational leadership is strongly related to positive perceptions of the headteacher's effectiveness, organisation level effects and student effects (Leithwood *et al.*, 1999). Burns (1978) describes transformational leadership as being concerned with exploring conventional relationships and organisational understandings through involvement and participation.

Leithwood *et al.* (1999) propose that transformational leadership in schools may be identified by a number of core leadership activities:

- setting directions (includes vision-building, goal consensus and the development of high performance expectations);
- developing people (includes the provision of individualised support, intellectual stimulation and the modelling of values and practices important to the mission of the school);
- organising (culture-building in which colleagues are motivated by moral imperatives and structuring, fostering shared decision-making processes and problem-solving capacities);
- building relationships with the school community (1999: 39).

These behaviours have been shown to encourage teacher collaboration, to increase teacher motivation and to improve teachers' self-efficacy. There is evidence to demonstrate a positive relationship between such transformational leadership approaches and school improvement. This has been shown to involve the building of school cultures or promoting culture behaviours that contribute directly to school improvement (Leithwood *et al.*, 1999). Culture-building by transformational leaders includes behaviours aimed at developing school norms, values, beliefs and assumptions that are student-centred and support continuing professional development.

Some of the behaviours utilised by transformational leaders to strengthen the school culture include reinforcing with staff norms of excellence for their own work and the students and assisting staff to clarify shared beliefs and values and to act in accord with such beliefs and values.

Post-transformational leadership

A recent study into effective headship in the UK has posited a new theoretical position on leadership that has been labelled 'post-transformational' (Day *et al.*, 2000). The two most important aspects of this form of leadership are that, firstly, effective leaders are constantly and consistently managing several competing tensions and dilemmas; and, secondly, effective leaders are, above all, people-centred:

> Managers know that people make the critical difference between success and failure. The effectiveness with which organisations manage, develop, motivate, involve and engage the willing contribution of the people who work in them is a key determinant of how well those organisations perform . . . employee commitment and positive 'psychological contact' between employer and employee are fundamental to improving performance.
>
> (Patterson *et al.*, 1997: vii–viii)

This form of leadership starts not from the basis of power and control but from the ability to act with others and to enable others to act (Blackmore, 1989; Shakeshaft, 1996): 'Effective leaders must have the ability to read and adjust to the particular context or set of circumstances they face. In this respect, their leadership behaviour is contingent on context and situation. The choices that they make relate directly to their own beliefs, values and leadership style.'

Within post-transformational leadership it is recognised that the capacity of leaders to make a difference depends upon their interpretation of and responses to the constraints, demands and choices that they face. Caldwell and Spinks (1998) argues that effective leaders must know how to span boundaries in order to promote information and resource control. At the same time as they negotiate the constraints of internal and external environments, they must capitalise on the many opportunities for making choices.

Centrally important in post-transformational leadership is the cooperation and alignment of others to the leaders' values and vision with those of the leader. As Bhindi and Duigan (1996) suggest:

> Authentic leaders breathe the life force into the workplace and keep the people feeling energised and focused. As stewards and guides they build people and their self esteem. They derive their credibility from personal integrity and 'walking' their values.
>
> (1996: 29)

This model of leadership incorporates, but is more than, what Stoll and Fink (1996) have termed 'invitational leadership'. Effective leaders tend to be reflective, caring and highly principled people who emphasise the human and emotional dimensions in preference to managerial requirements. They place a high premium upon personal values and are more concerned with cultural rather than structural change. Implicit within the post-transformational approach to leadership is a residing concern with sharing power with others and where leadership is viewed as having a moral purpose (Sergiovanni, 1992).

Moral leadership

Most recently, leadership studies have focused upon values and moral purpose. Writers have talked about the moral craft of leadership (Sergiovanni, 1992, Tom, 1984); the roles of leaders in creating a 'community of learners' (Barth, 1990, Senge, 1990) and the capacities of leaders to 'make a difference' through their ability to 'transform' (Sergiovanni, 1995) or 'liberate' (Tampoe, 1998). Sergiovanni suggests that when transformative leadership is practised successfully 'purposes which may have initially seemed to be separate, become fused' (1995: 119).

Implicit in the idea of moral leadership is stewardship whereby people and institutions entrust a leader with certain obligations and duties to fulfil and perform on their behalf: in other words, the means by which leaders can get the 'necessary legitimacy to lead' (Sergiovanni 1992: 124). Servant leadership is premised upon providing purpose for others and in giving certainty and direction to those who may have difficulty achieving it for themselves. Similarly Grace (1995) suggests the link between moral authority and servant leadership as being primarily concerned with the service of others and the service of ideals:

> Leadership in general must maintain an ethical focus which is oriented towards democratic values within a community. This has to do with the meaning of ethics historically – as a search for the good life of a community . . . Ethics here refers to a more comprehensive construct than just individual behaviour; rather it implicates us and how we as a moral community live our communal lives.
>
> (Grace, 1995: 55)

Fullan (2001: 14) argues that moral purpose is about both 'ends' and 'means', at its 'loftiest, moral purpose is about how humans evolve over time, especially in relation to how they relate to each other'. The best leaders tend to be those that create powerful learning communities and are able to integrate the intellectual, emotional and spiritual. They recognise the importance of core values and that organisational performance is largely dependent on the beliefs people hold and how they work together. In this sense leadership is a form of social capital that can be increased through investment in the development of others.

Pedagogical or instructional leadership

Pedagogical leadership is a model of leadership that places an emphasis upon the development of the school through the development of others. Sergiovanni (1998) describes 'pedagogical leadership' as a form of leadership which invests in capacity-building by developing social and academic capital for students and intellectual and professional capital for teachers. He argues that this model differs from the existing bureaucratic, visionary and entrepreneurial leadership theories that dominate the literature because it is concerned with adding value by developing various forms of human capital.

As teaching and learning environments have changed in response to new challenges, so the importance of teachers' continuing professional development has been recognised as being a crucial element in effective schools. In America, Barth has called upon heads to become 'head learner' in their school (Barth, 1990; Barth, 1996), creating a community of curriculum leaders, maintaining high expectations of staff and students and exercising authority through quality control (see also Southworth, 1995; Ainscow and Southworth, 1995). Such a leadership style has been shown to facilitate staff development and has enhanced feelings of professional worth.

Effective leaders aim to build 'learning-enriched' schools for staff as well as pupils through pedagogical leadership which is 'fuelled by a vision of possibilities. Their vision leads to a sense of the drama being played out everyday in the school. It is a drama of becoming a people, learning how to participate, how to negotiate, how to forgive, how to celebrate heroic ideals' (Starratt, 1993: 57). In this respect, leadership is as much about developing the self as it is about capacity-building in others.

A definition of leadership in terms of instruction tends to be much more focused and specific than many other conceptions of leadership in education. Elmore (2000: 14) suggests that 'the skills and knowledge that matter in leadership are those that can be connected to, or lead directly to, the improvement of instruction and student performance'. Where leadership is instructional it is dispersed to those who have the most influence over teaching and learning. Distributed leadership means allocating responsibility and authority for the guidance and direction of instruction to others. The influence of the subject or department leader on instructional and school improvement is well established in the literature and they constitute an important focus for distributed leadership (Harris, 2001).

Commentary

This brief overview of the leadership field has highlighted how leadership is being redefined to encompass notions of distributed or devolved leadership practice. While distributed leadership is not a new idea it resonates with the contemporary view that large-scale improvement is unlikely to be achieved by traditional command and control leadership approaches. An emerging consensus suggests that action among people with a shared desire for improvement and a collective responsibility for achieving that improvement is more likely to result in sustained improvement. Fullan (2001: 2) notes: 'Deep and sustained reform depends on many of us, not just on the very few who are destined to be extraordinary.'

This image of leadership is one of mobilising people to understand the problems they face and to tackle these problems together. Implicit within this interpretation is a need to develop, foster and enhance relationships among people within the organisation. This can only be achieved if leaders demonstrate emotional sensitivity and intelligence in their interactions with others. Fullan (2001: 71) notes that 'people have always needed emotional intelligence, but in complex times people need it in spades'. As the challenges facing leaders in schools become increasingly complex over the next decade, it is possible that the best leaders will be judged on how they manage their feelings and the feelings of others, rather than how they manage systems or structures. The evidence points towards a reconceptualisation of leadership practice that is fundamentally concerned with building relationships and harnessing the capacity of those within the school to create the conditions for sustained school improvement.

Note

1 The National College for School Leadership is located at Nottingham University.

References

Adair, J. (1983) *Effective Leadership*, London, Pan.

Ainscow, M. and Southworth, G. (1995) *School Improvement: A Study of the Roles of Leaders and External Consultants*, mimeo, University of Cambridge Institute of Education.

Barth, R.S. (1990) *Improving Schools from Within: Teachers, Parents and Principals Can Make the Difference*, San Francisco, Jossey-Bass.

Barth, R.S. (1996) 'Building a Community of Learners', paper prepared for California School Leadership Center, 1996.

Bass, B.M. and Avolio, B.J. (1993) 'Transformational Leadership: A Response to Critiques', in M.M. Chemers (ed.), *Leadership Theory and Research Perspectives and Directions*, San Diego, Academic Press.

Bass, B.M. and Avolio, B.J. (1994) *Improving Organisational Effectiveness through Transformational Leadership*, Thousand Oaks, CA, Sage.

Bennis, W. (1959) 'Leadership Theory and Administrative Behavior: The Problem of Authority', *Administrative Science Quarterly*, 4(2): 259–301.

Bhindi, N. and Duignan, P. (1996) 'Leadership 2020: A Visionary Paradigm', paper presented at Commonwealth Council for Educational Administration International Conference, Kuala Lumpur.

Blackmore, J. (1989) 'Educational Leadership: A Feminist Critique and Reconstruction', in J. Smyth (ed.), *Critical Perspectives on Educational Leadership*, London, Falmer.

Blase, J. (1989) 'The Micropolitics of the School: The Everyday Political Orientation of Teachers toward Open School Principals', *Educational Administration Quarterly*, 24(4): 377–407.

Block, P. (1993) *Stewardship: Choosing Service over Self-Interest*, San Francisco, Berrett Koehler.

Burns, J.M. (1978) *Leadership*, New York, Harper and Row.

Caldwell, B.J. (1997) 'Rethinking the Work of School Leaders in an Age of Change', paper presented to the 6th National Conference in Educational Research, University of Oslo, Norway, 20–22 May, 1997.

Caldwell, B.J. and Spinks, J.M. (1988) *The Self Managing School*, Lewes, Falmer Press.

Caldwell, B.J. and Spinks, J.M. (1992) *Leading the Self-Managing School*, London, Falmer Press.

Carr, W. and Kemmis, S. (1986) *Becoming Critical: Knowing through Action Research*, London, Falmer Press.

Dalin, P. (1996) *School Development*, London, Cassell.

Day, C., Hall, C. and Whitaker, P. (1998) *Developing Leadership in Primary Schools*, London, Paul Chapman.

Day, C., Harris, A., Hadfield, M., Tolley, H. and Beresford, J. (2000) *Leading Schools in Times of Change*, Milton Keynes, Open University Press.

Deal, T. and Peterson, K. (1990) *The Principal's Role in Shaping School Culture*, Washington, DC, US Department of Education, Office of Educational Research and Improvement.

Dempster, N. and Mahoney, P. (1998) 'Ethical Challenges in School Leadership', in J. MacBeath (ed.), *Effective School Leadership*.

Duignan, P.A. and Macpherson, R.J.S. (1992) *Educative Leadership: A Practical Theory for New Administrators and Managers*, London, Falmer Press.

Elmore, R. (2000) *Building a New Structure for School Leadership*, Washington, DC, Albert Shanker Institute.

Eraut, M.E. (1994) *Developing Professional Knowledge and Competence*, London, Falmer Press.

Fullan, M. (1993) *Change Forces: Probing the Depths of Educational Reform*, London, Falmer Press.

Fullan, M. (1996) 'Leadership for Change', in K. Leithwood, J. Chapman, D. Corsan, P. Hallinger and A. Hart (eds), *International Handbook of Educational Leadership and Administration*, vol. 2, Dordrecht and London, Kluwer.

Fullan, M. (1998) 'Leadership for the Twenty First Century: Breaking the Bonds of Dependency', *Educational Leadership* 55(7): 6–10.

Fullan, M. (2001) *Leading in a Culture of Change*, San Francisco, Jossey-Bass.

Grace, G. (1995) *School Leadership: Beyond Education Management*, London, Falmer Press.

Gronn, P. (2000) 'Distributed Properties: A New Architecture for Leadership', *Educational Management and Administration* 28(3): 317–38.

Hallinger, P. and Heck, R.H. (1996) 'The Principal's Role in School Effectiveness: An Assessment of Methodological Progress, 1980–1995', in K. Leithwood, J. Chapman, D. Corsan, P. Hallinger and A. Hart (eds), *International Handbook of Educational Leadership and Administration*, vol. 2, Dordrecht and London, Kluwer.

Hargreaves, A. (1994) *Changing Teachers, Changing Times: Teachers' Work and Culture in the Postmodern Age*, New York, Teachers College Press.

Hargreaves, A. and Fullan, M. (1998) *What's Worth Fighting for Out There*, New York, Teachers College Press.

Harris, A. (1999) *Teaching and Learning in the Effective School*, London, Arena Press.

Harris, A. (2001) 'Department Improvement and School Improvement: A Missing Link?', *British Educational Research Journal*, 27(4): 477–87.

Harris, A. and Bennett, N. (eds) (2001) *School Effectiveness and School Improvement: Alternative Perspectives*, London, Cassell.

Hodgkinson, C. (1991) *Educational Leadership: The Moral Art*, Alban, State University of New York Press.

Kouzes, J.M. and Posner, B.Z. (1987) *The Leadership Challenge*, San Francisco, Jossey-Bass.

Law, S. and Glover, D. (2000) *Educational Leadership and Learning: Practice, Policy and Research*, Buckingham, Open University Press.

Leithwood, K.A. (1992) 'The Move towards Transformational Leadership', *Educational Leadership*, 49(5): 8–12.

Leithwood, K. (1995) 'Leadership for School Restructuring', in K. Leithwood, J. Chapman, D. Corsan, P. Halliger and A. Hart (eds), *International Handbook of Educational Leadership and Administration*, vol. 2, Dordrecht and London, Kluwer.

Leithwood, K. and Jantzi, D. (1990) 'Transformational Leadership: How Principals can Help Reform Cultures', *School Effectiveness and School Improvement*, 1(4): 249–80.

Leithwood, K., Jantzi, D. and Steinback, R. (1999) *Changing Leadership for Changing Times*, Buckingham, Open University Press.

MacBeath, J. (ed.) (1998) *Effective School Leadership: Responding to Change*, London, Paul Chapman.

National Commission on Education (1996) *Success against the Odds: Effective Schools in Disadvantaged Areas*, London, Routledge.

Patterson, M.G., West, M.A., Lawthom, R. and Nickell, S. (1997) *Impact of People Management Practices on Business Performance*, London, Institute of Personnel and Development.

Peters, T. and Austin, N. (1985) *A Passion for Excellent*, New York, Collins.

Reynolds, D., Bollen, R., Creemers, B., Hopkins, D., Stoll, L. and Lagerweij, N. (1996) *Making Good Schools: Linking School Effectiveness and School Improvement*, London, Routledge.

Sammons, P., Thomas, S. and Mortimore, P. (1997) *Forging Links: Effective Schools and Effective Departments*, London, Paul Chapman Publishing.

Senge, P. (1990) *The Fifth Discipline*, New York, Doubleday.

Sergiovanni. T.J. (1992) *Moral Leadership: Getting to the Heart of School Improvement*, San Francisco, Jossey-Bass.

Sergiovanni, T.J. (1995) *The Principalship: A Reflective Practice Perspective*, Boston, Allyn and Bacon.

Sergiovanni, T. (1996) *Leadership for the Schoolhouse*, San Francisco, Jossey-Bass.

Sergiovanni, T.J. (1998) 'Leadership as Pedagogy, Capital Development and School Effectiveness', *International Journal of Leadership in Education*, 1(1): 37–47.

Shakeshaft, C. (1996) *Women in Educational Administration*, Newbury Park, Unwin.

Southworth, G. (1995) *Talking Heads: Voices of Experience*, Cambridge, University of Cambridge Institute of Education.

Southworth, G. (1996) 'Improving Primary Schools: Shifting the Emphasis and Clarifying the Focus', *School Organisation*, 16(3): 263–80.

Stoll, L. and Fink, D. (1996) *Changing our Schools: Linking Schools Effectiveness and School Improvement*, Buckingham, Open University Press.

Tampoe, M. (1998) *Liberating Leadership*, London, The Industrial Society.

Tom, A. (1984) *Teaching as a Moral Craft*, New York, Longman.

West, M., Jackson, D., Harris, A. and Hopkins, D. (2000) 'Leadership for School Improvement', in K. Riley and K. Seashore Louis (eds), *Leadership for Change*, London, RoutledgeFalmer.

West-Burmham, J. (1997) *Managing Quality in Schools* (2nd edn), London, Pitman Publishing.

Chapter 2

The changing learning needs of heads

Building and sustaining effectiveness

Christopher Day

Introduction

This chapter focuses upon headteachers' learning needs in leading and managing schools in times of change and challenge. Interestingly, there are still few studies which focus upon the career development and thus the learning or non-learning lives of headteachers; and what few there are tend to be small-scale narratives. For example, in Canada, Daresh (1987) found, not surprisingly, that the first year of headship is typically full of frustration and anxiety. In an American study of twelve high-school principals, Parkay *et al.* (1992) speculated that principals' expectations about school change become more realistic as their experience increases. In England, Weindling and Earley (1987) recommended that new head-teachers needed to receive special attention and support from their peers. In a study of junior schools (age 7–11), also in England, Mortimore *et al.* (1988: 276) found that such new headteachers were generally associated with less effective schools. These and other school-effectiveness and improvement studies, however, do not focus explicitly upon identifying development phases of heads.

We know from a range of leadership research – not least those that focus upon life histories – that principals' identities are shaped by their learning trajectories (Sugrue and Furlong, 2001: 29). We know also from research on teachers' lives that such learning trajectories are not smooth. Indeed, they are likely to be fragmented and discontinuous (Huberman, 1995) and do not always result in positive responses. Recent research by Ribbins (1998), Möller (2001), Sugrue (1996), and Moos (2001) has used life-history approaches in studying headteachers' professional lives and identities in England, Norway, Ireland and Denmark and revealed the complexities of their work and development. It is quite likely, then, that, although heads indisputably are concerned centrally with the betterment of teachers in order that they (the teachers), who are the most important asset in the learning and achievement of students, may provide the best learning oppor-tunities, they (the heads) are likely to have learning and achievement needs which are equally complex. If they are unmet, then effectiveness is likely to be, at best, only 'good enough'.

Chris Hodgkinson, a Canadian Professor of Educational Administration and Public Administration, wrote of values, morals and ethics as being at the very heart of leadership. He identified four knowledge imperatives: (1) know the task; (2) know the situation; (3) know the followership; (4) know oneself. It is this last 'moral injunction' which relates closely to the empirical research on successful school leadership described later in this chapter:

> This extends above and beyond the organisation, and before and after, as well as during, the leader's commitment to it. Morality in its highest sense is a progressive discovery of one's will; of the truth that one has a will and can manifest it in the world through other people and other wills. Morality is the reconciling of this will with the ethics to which one chooses to subscribe . . . for the administrator (headteacher) . . . there is an added charge and a greater responsibility because all organisations and all politics involve the exercise of power over others. If the blind are not to lead the blind, nor the sleeping to lead those who are even deeper asleep, then the leader must have vision, must become more conscious.
>
> (Hodgkinson, 1991: 153–4)

The emotional nexus occupied by teachers and leaders is of particular importance in times of change and reform (Beatty, 2001) and so it is perhaps no accident that over the last decade there has been an increasing interest in the significance of emotions in headteacher leadership, and in particular their relationship to transformational (Leithwood and Jantzi, 1990) and moral (Hodgkinson, 1991; Sergiovanni, 1992) leadership which are themselves widely regarded by researchers as being the *sine qua non*s for successful schools. It is not the remit of this chapter to explore the research as it relates to leadership. Others have done so (Beatty, 2001; Hargreaves, 2002). However, it has been suggested that today's effective leadership skills, like those in teaching, depend partly upon the understanding of emotions in self and others and the ability to manage these. The claim that 'emotional intelligence' (Goleman, 1995) accounts for more than 85 per cent of exceptional performance in top leaders (Hay Group, 2000) is not supported by research. However, whilst urging caution to such extreme claims, recent empirical research provides preliminary evidence for the relationship between emotional intelligence and effective leadership:

> those leaders who rated themselves as paying special attention to the achievement and development needs of subordinates (individualised consideration) also rated themselves as more likely to monitor and manage emotions both within themselves and others.
>
> (Palmer *et al.*, 2001: 8)

Furthermore, there is growing evidence from case-study and life-history research in Norway, Denmark and the UK into headteachers' identities that Hargreaves's (1998) research on the emotional politics of teachers' work supports the claim that leadership is, fundamentally, about emotions (Biott and Spindler, 2001; Möller, 2001; Moos, 2001); that

1   Leading is an emotional practice.
2   Leading and learning involve emotional understanding.
3   Leading is a form of emotional labour.
4   Leaders' emotions are inseparable from their moral purposes and their ability to achieve these purposes.
5   Leaders' emotions are rooted in and affect their selves, identities and relationships with others.
6   Leaders' emotions are shaped by experiences of power and powerlessness.
7   Leaders' emotions vary with culture and context (Hargreaves, 1998: 319).

So it is important to consciously examine the various 'selves' of the leader. It is a close and detailed knowledge of these – the leader as educator, person, manager, etc. – that may, for example, cause one to speculate on the prevailing underlying models of human nature which may be present, implicitly or explicitly, in the management's structures and school and departmental cultures. At the risk of oversimplifying, do these illustrate, for example, McGregor's theory X or Y? In the former, the average human being is seen as having an inherent dislike for work and will avoid it if possible. Because of this most people must be coerced, controlled, directed and threatened with punishment so that they will work towards the organisation's goals. In the latter, physical and mental work are as natural as play. If they are satisfying, people will exercise self-direction and self-control towards an organisation's goals if they are committed to them. Commitment is a function of rewards and the best rewards are ego satisfaction and self-actualisation. The average person can learn to accept and seek responsibility and avoidance of this is a learned not inherent characteristic; and creativity, ingenuity and imagination are widespread among people and do not occur in only a select few (McGregor, 1960: 33–57). However, to move to a far more personal level:

> Analysis in itself is merely academic if not complemented by right action which, in turn, may depend upon adequate emotional control on the part of the leadership . . . The leader is expected to perceive the total organisational situation in a clear-eyed and cool-headed way. This is an obligation of perspective and affect control which is quite apart from the leader's personal complex of interests. Value analysis itself presupposes this . . .
>
> (Hodgkinson, 1991: 139)

Hodgkinson goes on to discuss the obstacles to emotional control, a theme adopted and elaborated more recently by Hochschild (1993), Goleman (1995), Hargreaves (2002) and others.

Such work recognises that reflection is not always a comfortable process and that often the very idea of change – a regular consequence of reflection – is threatening. Indeed, 'emotions such as frustration, depression, love, shock, elation, hatred and fear interacted with cognitive components', throughout the reflective processes in one study of Canadian teachers (D'Andrea, 1986: 258).

Effective principals

The literature on effective principals suggests that they are 'transformative', rather than 'transactional' (Burns, 1978), 'invitational' rather than 'autocratic' (Stoll and Fink, 1996), 'empowering' rather than 'controlling' (Blase and Anderson 1995). There are relatively few empirical studies of principals in action over time which attempt to map their own development phases and few also which examine their work from the viewpoints also of their teachers, students and other stakeholders. One of the key strands to emerge from recent research on successful school leadership in England (Day *et al.*, 2000) is their engagement in reflection which is values-based and which emanates not only from their need to engage in contingency-related system maintenance and problem-solving situations but from key sets of personal and professional values which underpin, inform and drive their agendas for learning and achievement. The findings from this research resonate with other recent studies of highly effective business leaders and principals in England (Tampoe, 1998; T.T.A., 1998). These found that successful leaders are both strongly driven by sets of personal values (religious, spiritual, humanistic) which create a 'passionate conviction' to build, implement and continually monitor a vision by means of feedback from stakeholders inside and outside the organisation, and are able to manage a number of tensions and dilemmas which arise from the competing interest groups which represent the internal and external contexts in which they work.

In a recent critical overview of the literature, values and purpose combined with intra- and interpersonal knowledge have been identified as central to effective leadership (Leithwood *et al.*, 1999). Empirical research into what leader behaviours would best suit current and future generations of people in organisations of various kinds, conducted with one thousand 'followers' in business (Tampoe, 1998) identified also that leadership skills and behaviours were driven by beliefs and trust in self and others.

Headteachers' learning careers

There are few other careers which start during mid-life. This inevitably provokes questions concerning development. For example how does personal

practical knowledge grow after achieving headship? Are there developmental phases in headteachers' careers? If so, what do they look like and
do they follow an even trajectory? What are the influences of life-related
stages on the professional development of headteachers' careers and their
effectiveness?

In a recent piece of research (Day and Bakioglu, 1996) the opinions of 305
teachers in the Midlands region of England were elicited by questionnaire.
The questionnaire was based on previous research in which Weindling
and Earley (1987) investigated differences in opinions between newly
appointed headteachers and experienced headteachers. One hundred and
ninety-six questionnaire responses were received, a response rate of
64.2 per cent. After analysing the responses a sample of 29 of these headteachers were then interviewed.

The majority of headteachers had over eight years of experience (46 per
cent). There were more headteachers with one to three years' experience
(28 per cent) than there were headteachers with four to eight years (26 per
cent). The majority of respondents were over 46 years of age (64 per cent).
Those under 45 years of age represented over a third (35 per cent). Headteachers over 50 years of age formed the greater percentage. The results
indicated a correlation between headteachers who perceive they have
difficulties and:

- the age of the headteachers who are facing the difficulties;
- sex of the headteacher;
- the qualifications of the headteacher;
- the length of time the headteacher has been in post;
- the size of the school in which the headteacher was employed.

Experience and age were the most significant variables indicating the
existence of career phases.

After analysing questionnaires and interviews it was found that headteachers experienced four different phases which could be classified as
initiation, development, autonomy and disenchantment.

Development phases of headteachers

Years 1–4, initiation phase (idealism, uncertainty, adjustment)

In this phase 36 per cent of the questionnaire respondents were below
45 years of age and all of the interviewees were between 43 and 48 years
of age. Headship was seen as a new opportunity to achieve their ideals.
The initiation phase was identified by the heads as consisting of two key
processes. One of them was learning on the job, which might take any
length of time depending on the problems encountered and the realisation
that, although they had new ideas, new hopes and aspirations about what
they wanted to do for the school, they had to work to accommodate these

within existing frameworks and structures. For example it appeared that younger and less experienced headteachers had great trouble in coping with the previous head's legacy. Newly appointed headteachers did not agree, for example, with their predecessor's allocation of allowances and responsibilities to staff, which created lasting difficulties in promoting change. Understanding the taken-for-granted norms and daily routines were found to be highly significant problems. Similarly the heads perceived greater problems in improving links with the community, and dealing with parental problems.

In order to explore these problems further these items were investigated through interviews. These confirmed, consistent with the questionnaire analysis, that all the headteachers in the 'initiation' phase had difficulties in taking on previous heads' practice with which they did not agree; and that these were increased by a perceived challenge to initiate change immediately, for example in the organisation and structure of management. During the second year of headship they started to realise the gap between their ideals and the limitations imposed by the school context, and so planning for change became more context-specific.

On taking up the post for the first time, then, headteachers faced a greater amount of uncertainty than they had previously experienced. Although their enthusiasms were at their peak, uncertainty about the job led them to spend a lot of time learning about each aspect of their role. One headteacher with eighteen months' experience stated that,

> The first year was very much a learning experience for me. I felt a lot happier when the first year was over . . . When I faced the routine the second time was easier, it felt more relaxing. I think you are more confident, you can cope with most of the things.
>
> (Headteacher W)

Another head with 2.5 years of experience admitted that,

> When I was appointed I felt certain of gaps in my knowledge . . . I have not produced a timetable in any point in my career.
>
> (Headteacher Y)

The variety of new roles created confusion and a vital task in the beginning was to learn about these. This period was described as the hardest time in headteachers' careers. It was clear that this phase included within it three sub-steps. These were: idealism, uncertainty and adjustment.

Development phase

Twenty-four per cent of the questionnaire respondents were 46–50 years of age. In the interviews all of the informants in this phase were 48 to 60 years of age and had four to eight years of experience.

After the third or fourth years headteachers reached an effective period in terms of their own professional development and ability to influence school improvement. There was an increase in the headteachers' confidence and knowledge, enabling them to make decisions based on previous experience. In this new 'development' phase great changes occurred. Headteachers started to address staff needs and provide them with the opportunities and responsibilities for developing major areas within the school. Having become familiar with the daily routine of school and the school culture, they started to make major changes or complete those which were planned within the 'initiation' phase but which had not been achieved. Some head-teachers allowed themselves to feel that the organisation was running the way that they wanted; whilst some reported that they had 'plateaued' most did not, stating that this would be detrimental to school-improvement efforts. They had little difficulty in establishing better standards of discipline, improving channels of information within the school, coping with a weak member of the senior management team, and dealing with the media. Additionally, they had established strong external relationships, for example, developing a better public image of the school, improving liaison with feeder schools, improving links with the local community.

This phase was perceived to be the most active, most satisfactory, most rewarding phase by headteachers. Headteachers had begun to feel at ease and to apply their vision to the development of their schools. Government-imposed changes, which did not always meet with unqualified approval, were implemented, but growing confidence and increased effectiveness of the headteacher's own vision were the principal characteristics.

'Development'-phase headteachers appeared to be more confident about the way to deal with staffing relationships, staff discipline and staff compe-tency. They became more effective in handling staff. They created changes of direction in school and staff development and the perception of enhanced effectiveness of the school and the headteachers themselves. In almost all cases as a result of the retirement of members of the inherited senior management team, headteachers had opportunities to build a new manage-ment team. As time went by, young and enthusiastic staff were appointed and this seemed to be a factor which increased the effectiveness of the school. A participatory approach was preferred by heads during this phase through increased team work and consultative decision-making.

> We've got a community development team. What they do is to work quite closely with primary schools to develop liaison. Our governors go to other schools as well. We've regular meetings with our 'family' of schools. We've got a parent–teacher association, we've also got connections with local community centre.
>
> (Headteacher P)

Ambitions seemed to be fulfilled and a 'comfort' stage was reached. In this phase career ambition persisted. There were two alternatives for further development perceived by heads: either to continue their career in the same school or look for a bigger school and apply acquired experience there. Secondment was also used by heads in this phase as an opportunity to develop and as a 'breathing space' to make up their minds about the future of their careers.

Interestingly, these headteachers exhibited characteristics of 'reflective' professionals. They appeared to engage in constructive self-questioning, having greater confidence in some areas while being aware of the existence of areas about which they were still uncertain.

Autonomy phase

Analysis of the questionnaire responses indicated that although head-teachers of over 50 years of age appeared to be generally competent, they found establishing better standards of discipline, coping with an increasing range and variety of tasks, dealing with the media and LEA restrictions on staff recruitment as a serious or very serious problem. This phase was characterised by a greater resistance to change, increasing nostalgia for their earlier years and for an autocratic management style. Most heads criticised the government's education policy in various respects and resented their less active role in determining curriculum and management policy. They believed that there had been so many initiatives imposed at the same time that the possibility of achieving all of them successfully was difficult. They seemed to have become overwhelmed and struggled to implement multiple change, unable to complete one of them, before moving to another.

> I wish that Government would stop having good ideas in order that we could actually consolidate the ideas they have already had in the last three years.
>
> (Headteacher D)

Heads in this phase doubted their ability to manage their schools in a rapidly changing environment. As a consequence of that the beginnings of disenchantment was identified. There may be a link here with life stage. Peterson and Prick (quoted in Huberman, 1989) reported that teachers of 50–60 years of age begin to become more conservative, tend to complain a lot and find the new generation less disciplined and less motivated. Newman and others (1980) also indicate that with the same age group there is a loss of energy and loss of enthusiasm.

Disenchantment phase

Lack of confidence and enthusiasm and 'fatigue' were seen as characteristic features of this phase, as a sense of mortality increased. Headteachers started either to 'ease off', lost their motivation or their health deteriorated as they approached retirement. Here, the individual reached a plateau, a point where there was no further development, increasing work pressure, stress, ageing and emotional or physical sickness. This was mirrored by perceived deterioration in staff motivation.

A head of an inner-city school with eleven years of headship experience explained his feeling of fatigue as a consequence of the heavy burden of responsibility;

> If there is a reason why I am mentally and emotionally tired, it is an accumulation of carrying those responsibilities which have grown over the last 2–3 years and I think there is a limit to how much longer this can go on.
>
> (Headteacher B)

In this phase many headteachers suffered illness (mental or physical) and on return from absence felt they had 'lost control' over the school. All of the heads who became ill and disillusioned reported that they used to work eighty to ninety hours per week in order to cope with the pressures. This was accompanied by increasing concern about ageing, life expectancy and mortality and led them to spend more time planning for their lives outside school. Concern with school improvement decreased as personal-life considerations increased. They perceived a general deterioration in their effectiveness, confusion of role, a feeling of being insufficiently prepared for the management in new initiatives, and 'frozen' professional expertise. Later research (Ribbins, 1998) has proposed (after Huberman, 1989) that there are heads in this phase who may also remain 'enchanted' with their work.

Weindling (1999) has combined the results of this and other researches (Weindling and Earley, 1987; Gabarro, 1987; Hart, 1993; Ribbins, 1998; and Gronn, 1993, 1999) to produce a useful model mapping out 'stages of transition' through headship:

> Stage 0 – Preparation prior to headship – here the need for a variety of experience is contrasted with the enormous 'gulf' between deputy and headteacher knowledge, qualities and skills.
> Stage 1 – Entry and encounter (first months) – where the new head attempts to make sense of and develop a 'cognitive map' of the school, its communities, culture and problems.
> Stage 2 – Taking hold (three to twelve months) – the 'honeymoon' period, where the new head begins to challenge the 'taken for granted' nature of the school and introduce changes.
> Stage 3 – Reshaping (second year) – a period of major change based upon realistic expectations and assessment of strengths and weaknesses.
> Stage 4 – Refinement (years three to four) – refining the structural changes made in years one and two.
> Stage 5 – Consolidation (years five to seven) – this may be affected by unplanned externally initiated change which causes turbulence.

Stage 6 – Plateau (years eight and onwards) – this is a key phase which may lead to heads seeking to change schools, having achieved their aspirations; or to remain stimulated by their work in the school and looking for further improvements; or to become frustrated/disenchanted by the perceived limitations in themselves and others and their lack of success in finding another job.

(Weindling, 1999: 98–9)

Weindling emphasises that the phases are approximate. For example, difficult social circumstances and personal/professional limitations may mean that some heads may never move beyond Stages 2 or 3. Nevertheless, like Huberman's (1989) mapping of teachers' phases of development, they provide a useful basis for further empirical research and information which may be helpful to those designing training and development programmes.

Three lessons may be drawn from this research into headteachers' career phases: (1) like that of teachers, their development is uneven, discontinuous and unpredictable; (2) the capacity to engage in critical reflection is vital to their growth; and (3) reflection itself, as a learning process, is subject to 'incremental fluctuation'.

In speaking of critical reflection as a learning process, adults often describe a rhythm of learning that might be called incremental fluctuation: put colloquially, it can be understood as two steps forward, one step back, followed by four steps forward, one step back, followed by one step forward, three steps back, and so on in a series of fluctuations marked by overall movement forward. It is a rhythm of learning which is distinguished by evidence of an increased ability to take alternative perspectives on familiar situations, a developing readiness to challenge assumptions, and a growing tolerance for ambiguity, but it is also one which is characterised by fluctuating moments of falling back, of apparent regression. When learners are in the middle of these temporary regressions they report that they experience them as devastatingly final, rather than inconvenient interludes. They are convinced that they will never 'get' critical thinking, that 'it's beyond me', and that they may as well return to tried and trusted ideas and actions on the grounds that even if these didn't account for everything in life at least they were comfortable, known, familiar.

(Brookfield, 2000: 98)

Teachers' work in many countries is increasingly being directed by closely monitored government policy initiatives, suggesting that only 'technical' reflection – a relatively simple form of practice evaluation – is necessary. The research evidence suggests, however, that effective principals are those who move beyond this limited notion and encourage their teachers to do the same. They exercise 'metacompetencies' such as self-management, self-evaluation, learning from experience and 'juggling' (Glatter, 1996). In this study principals saw themselves and their teachers as having a responsibility for the education of students which went beyond the instrumental, encompassing responsibilities to educate for citizenship and to imbue in their students a positive disposition towards lifelong learning.

Leadership and reflection

Recent research has revealed that successful leadership in schools is connected closely to the commitment and capacity of heads to engage in reflective practice (Day *et al.*, 2000). Through such engagement these principals develop and maintain their critical thinking and emotional intelligence, exercise people-centred management, and remain 'one step ahead of the game' in mediating between externally determined initiatives and internal autonomy. Two hundred interviews were conducted with parents, governors (Board Members), teachers, students, ancillaries and principals in twelve schools in different parts of England. Each of the principals (from eight primary, three secondary and one special school) were known by their peers to be effective leaders and each of the schools had been ranked 'good' or 'excellent' by independent external (Ofsted) inspections.

> It is not by chance that some principals are more effective than others, even when all are faced with the same demands and constraints. Effective principals have a better understanding of how the world of schooling and school leadership works . . .
>
> (Sergiovanni, 1995: 29)

It has long been argued that reflection is a necessary condition for teachers' learning (Grimmett and Erickson, 1988; Calderhead and Gates, 1993; Zeichner and Liston, 1996; Day, 1993). One of the forces that help or hinder teachers in this respect is the school culture; and chief among those who are recognised as exerting a powerful influence upon this is the principal. Because principals, like teachers, pass through particular development phases (Day and Bakioglu, 1996; Reeves *et al.*, 1997), as 'leading learners' in the school community (Barth, 1990; Sergiovanni, 1992), they too must engage in reflective practices and revisit and review their own commitments, qualities and skills if they are to encourage others to do so. Whilst there is much lip service given to the value of reflection and reflective practice there remains also a lack of clarity about which purposes and processes might be appropriate to principals who will have different value positions, personal histories and professional growth needs and which will contribute most to improving practice. There are few studies, also, which examine the relationship between reflection, critical thinking and principal effectiveness. Various writers have coined the terms reflection-in-action, reflection-on-action, reflection-about-action and reflection-for-action which involves forward planning. (Schon, 1983; Zeichner, 1993). Recently there have been critiques about the notion of reflection-in-action which, it is claimed, is impossible in practice because there is insufficient time at a conscious level (Eraut, 1995). Reflection-on-action takes place when reviewing the action from outside its setting; reflection-about-action and reflection-for-action take place when reviewing the broader personal, social, economic and political contexts in which the action occurs or is likely to occur. These are often accompanied by a desire to achieve social justice, emancipation or improvement. However, different kinds of reflection are indicative of different views of what behaving as a professional means. They represent different values regarding the purposes and roles of principals.

The data revealed a number of key characteristics by which the stakeholders recognised their principals' effectiveness. Underpinning these, either implicitly or explicitly, was their capacity to be reflective in different ways about (1) their values, beliefs and practices; (2) those of their staff; (3) the position and progress of their schools in relation to others in local and national contexts; (4) current and emerging policy matters which affected management and the curriculum; and (5) conditions of service for teachers in their schools. The capacity to reflect in, on and about a broad range of contexts and through this to form, sustain, review and renew an holistic view of the school, its needs and its direction was central to their leadership. The data suggest further that hierarchical notions of reflective purposes and processes (van Manen 1977; Carr and Kemmis, 1986; Handal, 1990; Hatton and Smith 1995) are less helpful to enhancing understandings and improving practice than those which argue for its application across a range of contexts and practices experienced by all effective professionals.

Evidence from and about each of the twelve principals in this study suggests that all engaged in at least five kinds of reflection:

- the holistic where the emphasis is upon vision and culture-building;
- the pedagogical (on and in action) in which they place emphasis upon staff acquiring, applying and monitoring teaching which achieves results allied to their vision (which includes but is greater than the demands made by policy-implementation imperatives);
- the interpersonal where the focus is upon knowing and nurturing staff, children, parents and governors;
- the strategic where the focus is upon entrepreneurship, intelligence-gathering and networking to secure some control of the future;
- the intrapersonal where the focus is upon self-knowledge and self-development and fulfilment.

Holistic reflection

This kind of reflection meant maintaining an overview of the key purposes for the school.

> Leadership is about getting across to the staff where we are now and where we are going.
>
> (Secondary head)

> I think it's important for a head to have vision, to see the whole game. You have to be ahead of the rest and see the overall picture, otherwise you won't be able to manage effectively.
>
> (Primary head)

> Leadership is about vision, having some idea of what the establishment will look like in the future.
>
> (Primary teacher)

To principals, vision meant 'being clear about the direction in which you are going' and 'translating your beliefs into actions'. It was about, 'keeping the overview, the big picture'. Integrity, always associated with vision, meant 'sticking to core values and beliefs' and having 'a steadiness of purpose' in the face of rapid change. School ancillary staff, especially secretaries, arguably involved most intimately in all the work of the principal, described them variously as forward thinkers who seek 'the best way from experts, and seeks opinions' (schoolkeeper/janitor). Parents and governors also recognised in the principals their 'ability to look ahead', to have their fingers 'on the pulse' and to engage in continuous development:

> He has an overview of everything . . . He gets everyone . . . to work to the common goal of higher standards.

Students spoke of principals' wisdom, and their willingness to listen and seek the best ways forward:

> She likes listening to children . . . There is a 'suggestion box' outside her office for sorting our problems.

And:

> He is a wise, knowledgeable leader – he would know what to do in a crisis.

Teachers recognised that being a good leader was not only about caring for students, staff and the community or about vision, 'having some idea of what the establishment will look like in the future'. The voices of deputy principals, at the heart of the management and leadership of the school and among the most experienced of its teachers, echoed those of other stakeholders. Like them, they highlighted the need for vision, but recognised the elements essential to its maintenance:

> Leadership is about . . . constantly reviewing what you are doing and holding on to things you value. Management is about the functions, procedures and systems by which you realize the vision.
>
> (Primary deputy)

> The Head has to keep an overall view of what is happening in the school. He is always monitoring progress and keeping a check on things. He has to keep his finger on the pulse.
>
> (Secondary deputy)

Pedagogical reflection

This kind of reflection related to the principals' role as standard-bearers for high-quality teaching and learning. The teachers articulated most clearly the key role played by the principals in their maintenance of high standards of teaching and learning as they 'look to the future, recognizing strengths and building on them . . . identifying weaknesses and remedying them'. Principals themselves all spoke of the need to 'be the front person of the organisation', 'motivate, support and appreciate staff and others', 'provide feedback on a daily basis', 'patrol the boundaries [between school and the local and policy communities], making sure that every child gets a fair chance' and 'being true to oneself', indicating their commitment to a range of reflective practice in order 'to be prepared continuously to think how to do the job better'. Standards meant 'good quality of life for all the people in the school, so that the people who work here are contented in what they are doing, feel valued, can meet expectations'.

Interpersonal reflection

Reflection was also about knowing, understanding and interacting empathetically with the staff and students:

> She seems to know all about us and is always there to talk if we need to . . . She pushes staff forward and encourages them to go on to bigger and better things.
>
> (Primary teacher)

It was the values and actions which went alongside such knowledge which really made a difference to teachers:

> She wraps her arms around the school and . . . is someone who knows how the lifeblood of the schools ebbs and flows.
>
> (Infant teacher)

This recognition of and caring for the emotional well-being of staff and students was a key characteristic of the principals:

> To him everyone is valued because he believes that if all have a sense of their own self-worth they will do their best.
>
> (Primary teacher)

> The Head makes staff feel valued and worthwhile and trusted to get on with the job. He knows when to leave people alone and what they need.
>
> (Primary teacher)

> The door is always open. You can come and talk about anything in your life . . . a concern with your family or . . . a problem in the classroom or . . . someone's parent . . . He has time for you.
>
> (Secondary teacher)

> A shoulder to cry on and a sound friend and guide . . . just a good human being . . .
>
> (Secondary teacher)

They were constantly assessing their staff's strengths and weaknesses:

> You can only make the right decisions if you know your staff personally . . . I talk to a lot of pupils individually . . . I walk around the school . . . still try to build up personal knowledge of staff . . .

As a result they recognised the importance to school effectiveness and improvement of educating the staff and maintaining morale:

> Teachers must sparkle, for the good of the children . . .

> They need new knowledge . . . a sense of direction and opportunities to do . . . what they want to do it . . . is important to maintain their own sense of self-worth.

Strategic reflection

All the principals were clear about the need to 'run ahead of the game', to 'look at other schools . . . listen to colleagues from across the county':

> Outwards looking in is often better than sitting in and not looking out.
>
> (Secondary head)

A head has to have the ability to analyse problems and work out solutions . . . To do this he has to be intellectually capable of thinking and
making judgements on his feet.

(Secondary head)

I'm somebody who will look at other schools . . . and listen to colleagues
from across the country . . . There is a cross fertilisation all the time of
ideas . . .

(Primary head)

I enjoy getting the bigger picture . . . you pick up what's going on.

(Primary head)

I think part of the role of a head is . . . to network, network, network.

(Primary head)

You're looking at government papers, you're reading, talking, listening
to other people . . . you're looking back into your own school and thinking, 'will that work?' Or 'Isn't that a good idea?' Or 'Thank God I don't
do it that way.'

(Primary head)

I do all I can in liaison with parents, governors, social and welfare agencies, LEA, HMI, Civic and commercial leaders.

(Primary head)

Deputy Principals, like others, saw the 'networking' role as a means of
reflection on current and future practice and direction:

He uses the local network of headteachers as a source of information
and as a means of filtering out what should be brought into the schools.

(Primary deputy)

They recognised the need for intelligence gathering as a means of monitoring progress:

The Head has to keep an overall view of what is happening in the
school . . . is always monitoring progress and keeping a check on things.
He has to keep his 'finger on the pulse'.

A classroom assistant recognised that the principal was 'good at pushing for
things . . . he's kept the school on the right track'.

A knowledge of macro-, meso- and micro-contexts and an ability to
connect these into an holistic view was, then, clearly perceived as a keystone
of good leadership:

> The Head is very good at seeing the school as a whole rather than as little bits of interaction. She has a good overview of the organisation and knows how to get the most from everyone here.

Students also recognised their strategic capacities. They were, 'like detectives, always on the case, sniffing out trouble and finding out the evidence. . . . Always want to get to the bottom of it'. Critical judgement – having 'the ability to analyse problems and work out solutions . . . to be intellectually capable of thinking and making judgements' and 'knowing what I think is good for the school and being able to discard what I think is not' – was often associated with the ability to be strategic.

Intrapersonal reflection

Here the focus was upon self as lifelong learner. Although they were at different stages of their careers, of different ages and experiences and in very different settings – ranging from small rural primary schools to suburban and large inner-city primary and secondary schools – all the principals associated leading with learning:

> I like the idea of being the leader of learning – children now have a range of opportunities in the world and I have the chance to provide them with more . . . I want them to be excited by the possibilities open to them when they leave.

Some principals had enrolled for a higher degree – 'because I cannot persuade staff to invest in their own professional development unless I invest in mine'. Others were members of informal networks of peers who met regularly to exchange information, whilst others were part of more formal networks which organised their own professional development programmes. Such active involvement in their own development enabled them to maintain their integrity of purpose.

All those interviewed had observed the long hours which all the principals spent in fulfilling the range of roles, responsibilities and commitments of their work, and the inevitable tensions and personal and professional stress which were associated. Almost all the principals had confronted these difficulties and had found ways of maintaining their mental, emotional and physical health. Some were part of peer-support groups – 'We take turns in discussing issues'. Some used stress management strategies learnt from in-service courses; and others had regular support from family and friends.

The principals in this study all belonged to peer partnerships and networks.

The problems in pursuing reflective practice on one's own have been well documented in research on the busyness of classrooms and schools, the pressures caused by increased bureaucracy associated with new forms of accountability, and the difficulties of self-confrontation which challenges beliefs and practices which have become valued routines and may lead to possibilities of potentially uncomfortable, temporarily disruptive change processes (Day, 1993). These, and school cultures which often discourage disclosure, feedback and collaboration, act as potential barriers to the kinds of participation in all forms of reflective practice previously identified. The problem with reflecting alone is that there is a limit to what can be disclosed and what information can be collected and received by an individual with a 'vested' interest in avoiding uncomfortable change processes. Others are necessary at some points in the process. Peer partnerships and networks – discussions and dialogues between practitioners with common purposes – are needed to move from routine to reflective practice in schools. A comment from one of the principals serves to summarise the feelings expressed by all about their work:

> Over the years, enthusiasm seems to grow rather than wane. The pace of life within the school has increased 100%, but you learn to live with the pace. . . . Where we are now is in a position where we are striving to be better than yesterday.

Reflection essentially involves principals in a critique of practice, the values which are implicit in that practice, the personal, social, institutional and broad policy contexts in which practice takes place, and the implications of these for improvement of that practice. It is about the past, in the present and for the future; it is about 'problem-posing' as well as 'problem-solving' (Mezirow, 1991: 105); and it was essential to building and maintaining head-teachers' capacity to provide effective leadership for all in their schools whose work focuses upon the care and development of all children, young people and adults in changing circumstances in order to ensure that they too maintain their effectiveness. Reflective principals are able to distance themselves from the worlds in which they were everyday participants and open themselves to influence by others whilst at the same time being present and proactive in those worlds.

Effective leadership is as much about developing the self as it is about capacity-building in others and such effective leadership requires an intelligent head and an intelligent heart. It requires principals to engage simultaneously in reflection in, on, about and for the action in each context in which they work. Effective principals are, in fact, critical thinkers who have developed an awareness of the assumptions under which they and others think and behave. They are sceptical of quick-fix solutions to problems:

> When we think critically, we . . . refuse to relinquish the responsibility for making the choices that determine our individual and collective futures. . . . We become actively engaged in creating our personal and social worlds . . . We take the reality of democracy seriously.
>
> (Brookfield, 1987: ix and x)

In more recent work, Brookfield (2000: 90) identifies four strands which, he claims, are distinctive about the adult dimension of learning: 'the capacity to think dialectically, the continuous exploration of the interrelationships between general rules and contextual necessities, to move back and forth between objective and subjective frames of reference with the realisation that no fixed patterns of thought or conduct, and no permanent resolutions to intractable problems, are possible'.

The extent to which these constant efforts to resolve contradictions between ideals and actuality in oneself and others meet with success, albeit 'pro tem', is claimed to be a key indicator of 'wisdom' (Sternberg, 1990); and has been found to be a key characteristic of successful 'values-led contingency' leadership in schools (Day *et al.*, 2000). It relates directly to Argyris and Schön's (1974: 91) identification of the need to examine inconsistencies within and between espoused theories and to employ practical logic 'concerned with reasoning within a well defined situation in a way that pays attention to its internal features'.

This is similar to the 'practical knowledge' of Wagner (1992), Clandinin and Connelly (1985), 'situated cognition' (Lave and Wenger, 1991; Wilson, 1993), 'expertise' (Tennant, 1991) and Aristotle's 'practical reasoning'. It represents a recognition of the special knowledge of the complexities of the dynamics of particular contexts by those who work in them. The application of 'practical logic' is, therefore, not based upon externally derived rules of rationality but is, rather, 'experiential and inferential'. Whilst such logic is by no means infallible, it does represent the most common means of teachers operating in classrooms and of headteachers' day-to-day unplanned and spontaneous interactions. The successful application of practical logic, then, is bound up with the capacity to think dialectically and an intimate knowledge of self and others

the capacity to know how we know what we know (learning to learn):

> being self consciously aware of our learning styles and being able to adjust these in different situations . . . when we set out to examine the assumptions and explore the causes (biographical, historical, cultural), the nature (including moral and ethical dimensions), and consequences (individual and interpersonal) of . . . [our] frames of reference to ascertain why . . . [we] are predisposed to learn in a certain way or to appropriate particular goals.
>
> (Mezirow, 1998: 195)

Critical reflection

> the process by which adults become critically reflective regarding their assumptions, beliefs and values (often assimilated during childhood and adolescence) can only occur as they pass through experiences in

their interpersonal, work and political lives which are characterized by breadth, depth, diversity and different degrees of intensity.

(Mezirow, 1998: 95)

Such critical thinking is underpinned by a recognition of the power of the heart as well as the head in influencing beliefs and practices. The ability to recognise emotions in others, handle relationships, manage emotions and know one's own emotions has been defined as 'emotional intelligence' (Goleman, 1995) and is fundamental to effective leadership.

Traditional leadership theory, whilst useful, cannot apply in 'non-linear' conditions in which 'every decision that is made in response to conditions at the base time (time 1) changes these conditions in such a way that successive decisions also made at time 1 no longer fit' (Sergiovanni, 1995: 42). The data from the English study (Day *et al.*, 2000) confirmed that head-teachers' responses to the increasing complexity and intensity of their lives caused by imposed reform had been to use their capacities for reflection in a variety of real and imagined circumstances. We found that these principals were reflective and reflexive in a range of contexts, and that:

- reflection was integral to their success;
- the core informing concepts for reflection were their personal and educative values which were closely linked;
- they reflected simultaneously in, on, about and for their work, that of their staff and students in different contexts interactively;
- reflection was always also for the purpose of self-development (they were, it seemed, lifelong learners) as well as for the good of the school;
- reflection combined the cognitive and emotional.

Principals asserted their own agency and that of their staff through their core values of 'fairness', 'equity' and 'equality of opportunity' for students and staff, the kinds of 'dialectic' reflection associated by some with their broader educative responsibilities:

> If they are not to be mere agents of others, of the state, of the military, of the media, of the experts and bureaucrats, they need to determine their own agency through a critical and continual evaluation of the purposes, the consequences and the social context of their calling.
>
> (Zeichner and Liston, 1996: 11)

Such agency requires both principals and teachers to be 'knowledgeable, experienced, thoughtful, committed and energetic workers' (Devaney and Sykes, 1988: 20). It follows that in order to maintain capacity, they need regular opportunities to exercise discretionary judgement; reflect upon their moral and social purposes; work collaboratively with colleagues in and out-side school; engage in a self-directed search; and struggle for continuous learning related to their own needs for growth of expertise and maintenance of standards of practice as well as those of the school. They need to move beyond experience and intuition:

> In the actual world of schooling, the task of the principal is to make sense of messy situations by increasing understanding and discovering and communicating meanings. Situations of practice are typically characterized by unique events; therefore, uniform answers to problems are not likely to be helpful. . . . Intuition becomes necessary to fill in the gaps of what can be specified as known and what cannot. Yet, ordinary intuition will not do. Intuition must be informed by theoretical knowledge on one hand and adept understandings of the situation on the other.
>
> (Sergiovanni, 1995: 31–2)

Many principals (and teachers) mistakenly still rely mainly upon experience and intuition – with all the limitations to change which these contain – to guide them through their careers.

In this century, heads are not recognised and rewarded solely for their managerial skills. Now they must be 'leaders of curricular change, innovative and diversified instructional strategies, data-driven decision making, and the implementation of accountability models for students and staff'. They must:

- set the tone for their buildings;
- facilitate the teaching and learning process;
- provide leadership and direction to their schools instructional programs and policies;
- spend significantly more time evaluating staff and mentoring new teachers;
- sustain professional development for themselves and their staff members; and
- nurture personalized school environments for all students (Tirozzi, 2001: 438).

There is now a recognition at policy level and in the outcomes of research on school effectiveness and school improvement of the key role which heads play in structuring and culturing their schools for the purpose of raising standards of achievement. This is expressed, in England, in the establishment of a prestigious National College for School Leadership which focuses upon pre- and post-headship and middle-management development programmes and on promoting leadership research. There is also a growing rhetoric that associates successful leadership with change, the continuing professional development of teachers, increased pupil achievement and, through these, school improvement. Indeed, in some quarters it is almost as if those removed from schools have forgotten (so intent are they on urging teachers to do more and better) on the one hand, the highly significant influence of peers, families and socio-economic background on pupils, and, on the other, the need to attend to the emotional and ethical dimensions which are at the heart of teachers' work and purposes. The word often associated with this push for raising standards by government and its agencies is 'empowerment', a word to which some attach a cautionary note:

> It is imperative that we recognise what empowerment is not ... Empowerment is not kidding teachers into thinking pre-planned initiatives were their ideas (that is entrapment).
>
> Empowerment is not holding out rewards emanating from positive power (that is enticement). Empowerment is not insisting that participation is mandated from above (that is enforcement) ...
>
> Empowerment is not just concluding that enlarged job expectations just go with the territory (that is enslavement). Empowerment is, rather, giving teachers and students a share in important organisational decisions, giving them opportunities to shape organisational goals, purposely providing forums for staff input, acting on staff input, and giving real leadership opportunities in school specific situations that really matter.
>
> (Renihan and Renihan, 1992: 11)

Even the most recent training programmes fail to address the key themes that have emerged from research. If the needs of those aspiring, new and experienced heads who wish to become and remain successful in the changing times of the twenty-first century are to be met, then programmes must focus upon:

- analysis of personal and professional values, central to successful leadership;
- critical, reflective thinking;
- promotion of people-centred continuing professional development as a means of maintaining and raising levels of commitment and morale (echoing Roland Barth's wise dictum that heads must be the 'leading learners' in their schools);
- emphasis upon intra- as well as interpersonal skill development;
- recognition of the importance to successful learning and achievement of attending to the emotional as well as the cognitive mind;
- problem-solving and the management of 'competing forces' – key components of leadership training for school improvement if schools are to become the high-achieving learning communities espoused by government.

Commentary

Currently, there is no coherent set of programmes which addresses the development of such key leadership qualities and skills. Yet such training and development cannot be left to chance. Perhaps one of the primary tasks for the National College for School Leadership in England will be to ensure that expertise from appropriate fields of education and business is used to develop programmes that are based upon the real needs of heads attempting to exercise successful leadership in changing times.

Within governments' overall strategic vision for education in all countries, the training, reskilling and certification of heads occupies a central place. The problem is that many of the training models focus upon managerial rather than leadership functions. In doing so they fail to build capacities of heads to reflect upon their own values and those of the whole-school community and do not place sufficient emphasis upon building the range of interpersonal qualities and skills necessary and appropriate to effective leadership. For governments' rhetoric lifelong learning, high teaching standards, pupil achievement and school improvement to become a reality, schools need to be led by headteachers who are not only knowledgeable and skilled in managerial techniques but also people-centred leaders who are able to combine the management of internal and external change with a strong development and achievement orientation. Their practices need to be based upon clear and communicated values to which all in their community subscribe.

References

Argyris, C. and Schön, D.A. (1974) *Theory in Practice: Increasing Professional Effectiveness*, New York, Jossey-Bass.

Bakioglu, A. (1993) 'Headteacher Development: Relationships between Role Effectiveness and Headteachers' Career Phases', unpublished PhD thesis, University of Nottingham School of Education.

Barth, R. (1990) *Improving Schools from Within: Teachers, Parents and Principals Can Make a Difference*, San Francisco, Jossey-Bass.

Beatty, B.R. (2001) 'Emotions Matter in Educational Leadership: An Analysis of Teacher-Recalled Interactions with Administrators', paper presented at the Annual Meeting of the American Educational Research Association, 10–14 April, Seattle.

Biott, C. and Spindler, J. (2001) 'Towards a Contemporary History of School Leadership. Headteacher as witness writing and unwilting testimony', paper presented at the Annual Meeting of the American Educational Research Association, 10–14 April, Seattle.

Blasé, J. and Anderson, G. (1995) *The Micropolitics of Educational Leadership*, London, Cassell.

Bray, D.W., Campbell, R.J. and Grant, D.L. (1974) *Formative Years in Business*, New York, John Wiley.

Brookfield, S. (1987) *Developing Critical Thinkers: Challenging Adults to Explore Alternative Ways of Thinking and Acting*. New York, Teachers College Press.

Brookfield, S.D. (1988) 'Understanding and Facilitating Adult Learning', *School Library Media Quarterly*, 16(2): 99–105.

Brookfield, S. (2000) 'Adult Cognition as a Dimension of Lifelong Learning', in J. Field and M. Leicester (eds), *Lifelong Learning: Education across the Lifespan*, London, RoutledgeFalmer.

Burns, J.M. (1978) *Leadership*, New York, Harper and Row.

Calderhead, J. and Gates, P. (eds), (1993) *Reconceptualising Reflection in Teacher Development*, London, Falmer Press.

Carr, W. and Kemmis, S. (1986) *Becoming Critical: Knowing Through Action Research*, London, Falmer Press.

Clandinin, D.J. (1985) *Classroom Practice: Teacher Images in Action*, Lewes, Falmer Press.

Clandinin, D.J. and Connelly, F.M. (1985) 'Teachers' Personal Practical Knowledge: Calendars, Cycles, Habits and Rhythms and the Aesthetics of the Classroom', paper presented at the University of Calgary – OISE Conference on Teachers' Personal Practical Knowledge, Toronto.

Clark, C.M. and Yinger, R. (1987) 'Teacher Planning', in J. Calderhead (ed.), *Exploring Teachers Thinking*, London, Cassell.

Conners, B. (1991) 'Teacher Development and the Teacher', in P. Hughes (ed), *Teachers' Professional Development*, Hawthorn, ACER.

Cooper, C. and Kelly, M. (1993) 'Occupational Stress in Headteachers: A National UK Study', *British Journal of Educational Psychology*, 63: 130–43.

Day, C. (1993) 'Reflection: A Necessary but not Sufficient Condition for Professional Development', *British Educational Research Journal*, 19(1): 83–93.

D'Andrea, A.L. (1986) 'Teachers and Reflection? A Description and Analysis of the Reflective Processes which Teachers Use in their Experiential Learning', unpublished doctoral dissertation, Ontario Institute for Studies in Education, Toronto, Canada.

Daresh, J.C. (1987) 'The Highest Hurdles for the First Year Principal', paper presented at the Annual Meeting of the American Research Association, 20–4 April, Washington, DC.

Day, C. and Bakioglu, A. (1993) 'Developments in the Thinking and Practice of Headteachers', paper presented at the annual meeting of the ISATT, Gothenburg, Sweden.

Day, C. and Bakioglu, A. (1996) 'Development and disenchantment in the professional lives of headteachers', in I.F. Goodson and A. Hargreaves (eds), *Teachers' Professional Lives*, London, Falmer Press.

Day, C., Harris, A., Hadfield, M., Tolley, H. and Beresford, J. (2000) *Leading Schools in Times of Change*, Buckingham, Open University Press.

Devaney, K. and Sykes, G. (1988) 'Making the Case for Professionalism', in A. Lieberman (ed.), *Building a Professional Culture In Schools*, New York, Teachers College Press.

Eraut, M. (1995) 'Schön Shock: a case for reforming reflection-in-action?' *Teachers and Teaching: Theory and Practice* 1(1): 9–22.

Erikson, E.H. (1963) *Childhood and Society*, New York, Norton.

Gabbarro, J. (1987) *The Dynamics of Taking Charge*, Boston, Harvard Business School Press.

Glatter, R. (1996) 'The NPQH: Where is Juggling?' *Management in Education*, 10(5): 27–8.

Goleman, D. (1995) *Emotional Intelligence*, New York, Bantam Books.

Grimmett, P.P. and Erickson, G.L. (1988) *Reflection in Teacher Education Columbia University*, New York, Teachers College Press.

Gronn, P. (1993) 'Psychobiography on the Couch: Character, Biography and the Comparative Study of Leaders', *Journal of Applied Behavioural Science*, 29: 3.

Handal, G. (1990) 'Promoting the Articulation of Tacit Knowledge through the Counselling of Practitioners', keynote paper at Amsterdam Pedalogisch Centrum Conference, Amsterdam, The Netherlands, 6–8 April 1990.

Hargreaves, A. (2002) 'Teaching in a Box: Emotional Geographies of Teaching', in C. Sugrue and C. Day (eds), *Developing Teachers and Teaching Practice*, London, RoutledgeFalmer, pp. 3–25.

Hargreaves, A. (2002) 'Teaching in a Box: Emotional Geographies of Teaching', in C. Sugrue and C. Day (eds), *Developing Teachers and Teaching Practice: International Research Perspectives*, London, RoutledgeFalmer.

Hargreaves, A. (1998) 'The Emotional Politics of Teaching and Teacher Development: With Implications for Educational Leadership', *Leadership in Education*, 1(4): 315–36.

Hart, A.W. (1993) *Principal Succession: Establishing Leadership in Schools*, New York, SUNY Press.

Hatton, N. and Smith, D. (1995) 'Facilitating Reflection: Issues and Research', *Forum of Education*, 50(1): 49–65.

Hay Group (2000) 'Emotional Intelligence: A "Soft" Skill with a Hard Edge', http://ei.haygroup.com/about_ei

Hochschild, A.R. (1993) *The Managed Heart: Commercialization of Human Feeling*, Berkeley, University of California Press.

Hodgkinson, C. (1991) *Educational Leadership: The Moral Art*, Albany State, University of New York Press.

Huberman, M. (1988) 'Teacher Careers and School Improvement', *Journal of Curriculum Studies*, 20(2): 119–32.

Huberman, M. (1989) 'The Professional Life Cycle of Teachers', *Teachers College Record*, 91(1): 31–57.

Huberman, M. (1995) *The Lives of Teachers*, London, Cassell.

Jaques, E. (1965) 'Death and Mid-life Crisis', *International Journal of Psycho-Analysis*, 46(4).

Jarvis, P. (1983) *Adult and Continuing Education: Theory and Practice*, London, Croom Helm.

Jung, C.G. (1933) *Modern Man in Search of a Soul*, New York, Harcourt Brace.

Lave, J. and Wenger, E. (1991) *Situated Learning: Legitimate Peripheral Participation*, Cambridge, Cambridge University Press.

Leithwood, K. and Jantzi, D. (1990) 'Transformational Leadership: How Principals Can Help Reform School Cultures', *School Effectiveness and School Improvement*, 1(4): 249–80.

Leithwood, K., Jantzi, D. and Steinbach, R. (1999) *Changing Leadership for Changing Times*, Buckingham, Open University Press.

McGregor, D. (1960) *The Human Side of Enterprise*, New York, McGraw-Hill.

Mezirow, J. (1991) *Transformative Dimensions of Adult Learning*, San Francisco, Jossey-Bass.

Mezirow, J. (1998) 'On Critical Reflection', *Adult Education Quarterly*, 48(3): 185–98.

Möller, J. (2001) 'Norwegian Head-Teachers' Leadership Identity – Making Sense of Mission and Mandates', paper presented at the Annual Meeting of the American Educational Research Association, 10–14 April, Seattle.

Moos, L. (2001) 'Danish School Leaders Constructing their Identities in Turbulent Times', paper presented at the Annual Meeting of the American Educational Research Association, 10–14 April, Seattle.

Mortimore, P., Sammons, P., Stoll, L., Lewis, D. and Ecob, R. (1988) *School Matters*, Wells, Open Books.

Newman, K.K., Burden, P.R. and Applegate, J.H. (1980) 'Helping Teachers Examine Their Long Range Development', paper presented at the Annual Conference of the Association of Teacher Educators, Washington, DC, February 1980. (ERIC No: Ed204321).

Palmer, B. Walls, M., Burgess, Z. and Stough, C. (2001) 'Emotional Intelligence and Effective Leadership', *Leadership and Organisation Development Journal*, 22(1): 5–10.

Parkay F.W., Currie, G. and Rhodes, J.W. (1992) *Professional Socialisation: A Longitudinal Study of Twelve High School Principals*, Educational Administration.

Reeves, J., Mahoney, P. and Moos, L. (1997) 'Headship: Issues of Career', *Teacher Development* 1(1): 43–56.

Renihan, F. and Renihan, P. (1992) 'Educational Leadership: A Renaissance Metaphor', *Education*, Canada, Spring, p. 11.

Ribbins, P. (1998) 'On Ladders and Greasy Poles; Developing School Leaders' Careers', paper presented at the third ESRC seminar, Milton Keynes, June.

Schein, E.H. (1971) 'The Individual, the Organisation and the Career: A Conceptual Scheme', *Journal of Applied Science*, 7: 401–26.

Schon, D.A. (1983) *The Reflective Practitioner: How Professionals think in Action*, New York, Basic Books.

Sergiovanni, T.J. (1992) *Moral Leadership: Getting to the Heart of School Improvement*, San Francisco, Jossey-Bass.

Sergiovanni, T. (1995) *The Principalship: A Reflective Practice Perspective,* Boston, Allyn and Bacon.

Sternberg, R.J. (1990) *Wisdom: Its Nature, Origins and Development*, New York, Cambridge University Press.

Stoll, L. and Fink, D. (1996) *Changing our School*, London, Open University Press.

Sugrue, C. (1996) 'The Policy Reader in Social Theory (1994)', in *Complexities of Teaching Child-centred Perspectives*, London, Falmer Press, p. 349.

Sugrue, C. and Furlong, C. (2001) 'The Cosmologies of Irish Primary School Princiapls' Identities: Between the Modern and the Postmodern?', paper presented at the Annual Meeting of the American Educational Research Association, 10–14 April, Seattle.

Super, D.E. (1957) *The Psychology of Careers*, New York, Harper and Row.

Tampoe, M. (1998) *Liberating Leadership*, London, The Industrial Society.

Teacher Training Agency (1998) *Leadership Programme for Serving Headteachers*, London, Teacher Training Agency.

Tennant, M. (1991) 'Expertise as a Dimension of Adult Development: Implications for Adult Education', *New Education*, 13(1): 49–55.

Tennant, M. (1991) 'The Psychology of Adult Teaching and Learning', in J.M. Peters, P. Jarvis and Associates (eds), *Adult Education*, San Francisco, Jossey-Bass.

Tirozzi, G.N. (2001) 'The Artistry of Leadership: The Evolving Role of the Secondary School Principal', *Phi Delta Kappan*, February: 434–9.

Van Manen, M. (1977) Linking Ways of Knowing to Ways of Being Practical, *Curriculum Inquiry*, 6(3): 205–28.

Wagner, R.K. (1992) 'Practical Intelligence', in A. Tuijnman and M. van der Kamp (eds), *Learning across the Lifespan: Theories, Research, Policies*, New York, Pergamon.

Watts, A.G. (1981) 'Career Patterns', in A.G. Watts, D.E. Super and J.M. Kidd (eds), *Career Development in Britain*, Cambridge, Crac.

Weindling, D. (1999) 'Stages of Headship', in T. Bush, L. Bell, R. Bolam, R. Glatter and P. Ribbins (eds), *Educational Management: Redefining Theory, Policy and Practice*, London, Paul Chapman Publishing Ltd, pp. 90–100.

Weindling, D. and Earley, P. (1987) *Secondary Headship: The First Years*, Slough: NFER-Nelson.

Wilson, A.L. (1993) 'The Promise of Situated Cognition', in S.B. Merriam (ed.), *An Update on Adult Learning Theory*, San Francisco, Jossey-Bass.

Zeichner, K.M. (1993) 'Action Research: Personal Renewal and Social Reconstruction', *Educational Action Research*, 1(2): 199–220.

Zeichner, K.M. and Liston, D.P. (1996) *Reflective Teaching: An Introduction*, New Jersey, Lawrence Erlbaum Associates.

Part II

Contemporary views of leadership

Chapter 3

Instructional leadership and school improvement[1]

David Hopkins

Introduction

It is now more than twenty years since leadership was identified as one of the key components of 'good schools' by HMI who stated that, without exception, the most important single factor in the success of these schools is the quality of the leadership of the head (DES, 1977: 36). Since that time the changes imposed upon the UK education system and indeed most other 'developed' educational systems have radically altered the role and responsibilities of the headteacher or principal. In particular, the devolution of responsibility for local management of schools in many systems has resulted in the headteacher or principal becoming a manager of systems and budgets as well as a leader of colleagues. Also, the increasingly competitive environment in which schools operate has placed a much greater emphasis upon the need to raise standards and to improve the outcomes of schooling.

Contemporary educational reform therefore places a great premium on the effective leadership and management of schools. The logic of this position is that an orderly school environment that is efficient and well managed provides the preconditions for enhanced student learning. Empirical backing for a relationship between leadership and higher levels of student outcomes is often claimed, and the school-effects research is usually cited in support. At one level this contention is self-evidently true. However, the correlational nature of the research evidence that is often cited in support inevitably masks the exact relationship between leadership and enhanced student learning. Consequently, policy initiatives that focus solely on leadership and management have difficulty in achieving more than a generalised impact on student learning.

The purpose of this chapter is to sketch out more precisely the relationship between leadership and learning. The theme pursued here is that although leadership is essential for successful school improvement, the leadership function does not necessarily rest exclusively with the head or principal. It will also be argued that the prime function of leadership for authentic school improvement is to enhance the quality of teaching and learning. 'Instructional leadership', as this approach has been termed, is about creating learning opportunities for both students and teachers. More specifically in this chapter, I will:

1   Contrast transactional, transformational and instructional views of leadership.
2   Review the three domains of instructional leadership; *viz*
    • defining the values and purposes of the school
    • managing the programme of teaching and curriculum
    • establishing the school as a professional learning community.
3   Briefly discuss how instructional leadership supports both school improvement and transformation.

Transactional, transformational and instructional views of leadership

During the past decade the debate about educational leadership has been dominated by a contrast between the (so-called) 'transactional' and 'transformation' approaches. As we have noted elsewhere, there seems to be a presumption for 'transactional' models in systems where strong central control has been retained, while in those systems where decentralisation has been most evident convertible interest in 'transformational' models has emerged (West *et al.*, 2000). It is worth briefly contrasting these two 'stereotypes' of the leadership role.

In the more stable system where maintenance has a higher priority than development, and the headteacher is seen as playing a major role in protecting and promoting the interests of the system, a transactional approach is frequently found. In such an approach, the emphasis will tend to be on the management of the school's systems and structures. It may be an effective method for bringing about a certain kind of organisational change – those kinds where parameters are very clearly identified, where conformity rather than creativity is valued, where it is hoped to retain organisational structures and relationships despite changing (say) education content or method. Transactional models of leadership therefore seem best suited to static school systems and communities.

It has been widely argued that complex and dynamic changes, such as the 'cultural' changes that are required for sustained school improvement, are less likely to occur as a result of transactional leadership (Stoll and Fink, 1996). A model of leadership more congruent with the requirement of cultural change is that of transformational leadership (Leithwood and Jantzi, 1990). This style of leadership focuses on the people involved, their relationships, and requires an approach that seeks to transform feelings, attitudes and beliefs. Transformational leaders not only manage structure, they also purposefully seek to impact upon the culture of the school in order to change it. Consequently, transformational leadership would appear to be consistent with a desire to bring about school improvement, rather than simply 'change' the school.

Unfortunately there is a problem when reviewing the literature on educational leadership. It is that most commentators, certainly those writing during the past ten or twenty years, tend to conflate their own views about what leadership should be with their descriptions of what leadership actually is and fail to discipline either position by reference to empirical research. This can lead us towards a somewhat mythical view of leadership that is often embellished by rhetoric. Consequently transformational leadership is, as with many concepts in education, a somewhat plastic term. For the purposes of this chapter I have selected from our more comprehensive review a few sources that capture the range of conventional wisdom on transformational leadership and that have adequate empirical support (Hopkins, 2001).

So for example:

- On the issue of change Cheng (1997) claims that transformational leadership is critical to meeting educational challenges in a changing environment, and Turan and Sny (1996) argue that strategic planning, like transformational leadership, is vision-driven planning for the future.
- Innovation, inclusion and conflict management have all been linked to transformational leadership behaviours. Berg and Sleegers (1996) found that transformational school leadership plays a 'particularly crucial' role in the development of the innovative capacities of schools.
- According to research by Leithwood (1997), principal leadership exercised its strongest independent influence on planning, structure, and organisation, as well as on school mission and school culture.

These studies support the contention that the main outcome of transformational leadership is the 'increased capacity of an organisation to continuously improve' (Leithwood et al., 1999: 17). It is for this reason that I consider the approach a necessary but not sufficient condition for school improvement for the simple reason that it lacks a specific orientation towards student learning. In line with many other educational reforms transformational leadership simply focuses on the wrong variables.

There is now an increasingly strong research base that suggests that initiatives such as local management of schools, external inspection, organisation development, or teacher appraisal only indirectly affect student performance. These 'distal variables' as Wang and her colleagues (1993) point out are too far removed from the daily learning experiences of most students. The three key 'proximal variables', according to their meta-analysis, that do correlate with higher levels of student achievement are psychological, instructional and home environments. The clear implications for policy are that any strategy to promote student learning needs to give attention to engaging students and parents as active participants, and expanding the teaching and learning repertoires of teachers and students respectively.

Yet a sole focus on teaching and learning is also not a sufficient condition for school improvement. A leading American commentator on school reform explains it this way (Elmore, 1995: 366):

> Principles of [best] practice [related to teaching and learning] . . . have difficulty taking root in schools for essentially two reasons: (a) they require content knowledge and pedagogical skill that few teachers presently have, and (b) they challenge certain basic patterns in the organisation of schooling. Neither problem can be solved independently of the other, nor is teaching practice likely to change in the absence of solutions that operate simultaneously on both fronts.

What Elmore is arguing for is an approach to educational change that at the same time focuses on the organisational conditions of the school, in particular the approach taken to staff development and planning, as well as the way teaching and learning are conducted. For these reasons I am attracted to the construct of 'instructional leadership'. Leithwood and his colleagues (1999: 8) define it as an approach to leadership that emphasises 'the behaviours of teachers as they engage in activities directly affecting the growth of students'.

Once again the term is subject to conceptual pluralism by the many commentators who are attracted to the notion (see, for example, Duke, 1987; Geltner and Shelton, 1991; Sheppard, 1996). However the most fully tested approach to instructional leadership is that of Hallinger and his colleagues (see for example Hallinger and Murphy, 1985). They propose a model of instructional leadership that consists of twenty specific functions within three broad categories: defining the school mission; managing the instructional programme; and promoting school climate. There is considerable empirical support for this model particularly as it relates to student outcomes (Hallinger, 1992; Sheppard, 1996).

The focus on instructional leadership is, however, not exclusive of a range of other leadership skills. It implies a general orientation towards leadership rather than an exclusive approach. There are three key skill clusters that consistently inform school leadership. The following is indicative only of these skills.

Organisational leadership involves the coordination of the work of the school through direction-setting, allocating roles and establishing structures, and maintaining an effective human resource and school support strategy. Organisational leadership is enthusiastic about innovation but strategic in predicting, interpreting and applying change.

Instructional leadership is actively and visibly involved in the planning and implementation of change, but encourages collaboration and working in teams. It emphasises the quality of teaching and learning with high expectations of all staff and all pupils, whilst recognising that support and encouragement are needed for everyone to give of their best.

Personal/interpersonal leadership inspires commitment to the school's mission which gives direction and purpose to its work. It cares passionately for the school, its members and reputation but with the ability objectively to appraise strengths and weaknesses in order to preserve and build upon the best of current practice and to remedy deficiencies. There is skilled communication, and a commitment to knowing oneself as a precursor to leading others.

The focus of this chapter, however, is explicitly on instructional leadership. Our own work in supporting a variety of school improvement initiatives suggests that in line with the work of Hallinger the focus of instructional leadership needs to be on three domains in particular (Hopkins, 2001, ch. 7):

- defining the values and purposes of the school;
- managing the programme of teaching and curriculum;
- establishing the school as a professional learning community.

As contemporary policy and practice exhibits a lack of precision in operationalising these domains, the rest of the chapter is devoted to a discussion of each of them individually.

The first domain of instructional leadership – defining the values and purposes of the school

I have argued recently that instructional leadership needs to be purposeful, inclusive and values-driven (National College for School Leadership, 2001). Purposeful insofar as there is clarity as to the goals of education and schooling; inclusive to ensure that these aims are widely owned within and outside the school community; and values-driven because it is only an unrelenting focus on learning and empowerment that will ensure success in the knowledge society. Although clarity of purpose and ownership are necessary conditions for effective leadership, it is the underpinning values and beliefs that give leadership its power. It is these values and beliefs that also inform the moral purpose of education and leadership style.

The values and beliefs that infuse successful leadership focus on learning and empowerment. This implies a broader and deeper view of learning. It is broader because within the instructional perspective learning refers not just to the progress of students, but also to the learning of teachers and leaders, and organisational learning on the part of the school. It is deeper because learning reflects not just induction into knowledge but the acquisition of a range of learning skills that allow the learner be they student or teacher to take more control of their world. Becoming more skilful and more competent is the basis of empowerment. Without such a holistic view of learning for leadership the rhetoric of school improvement will remain just that.

Across the range of public and private organisational settings, it is clear that effective leadership is infused by a commitment to clearly articulated values and beliefs. In all of these settings this also has profound implications for style of leadership and the predisposition's of leaders. It implies a personal style that is congruent, intuitive and unafraid to selectively show weakness; and a leadership style that provides focus, engenders trust and is unafraid to practice 'tough empathy'.

Above all school leadership should be infused with a moral purpose. The reason for this is the vital importance of closing the gap between our highest and lowest achieving students and to raise standards of learning and achievement for all. This is the contemporary moral purpose of leadership that informs its values and beliefs and provides the impetus for transforming the school as a learning community for students and staff, adequate to the expectations of a knowledge society and economy.

Although some indication of the types of values that infuse instructional leadership have been given, it is inappropriate to be too prescriptive about what they should be. The important point is that each school and school system should articulate their own values position appropriate to the context within which they operate, and the broad focus on student learning and achievement. Simply discussing values in some abstract way, however, is also insufficient. Values need to be translated into criteria and principles that inform the way in which teachers and students behave, and the way in which the school organises itself. In particular, the dialogue about values, besides providing the school with a clear sense of direction and purpose, also has clear implications for the other two domains of instructional leadership. It is to a discussion of the second domain, 'managing the teaching and curriculum programme' that we now turn.

The second domain of instructional leadership – managing the teaching and curriculum programme

The research evidence on effective patterns of teaching that result in higher levels of student learning is burgeoning (e.g. Brophy and Good, 1986; Creemers, 1994; Joyce and Weil, 1996, Joyce et al., 2002). One can summarise the evidence from the research on teaching and curriculum and their impact on student learning as follows:

- There are a number of well-developed models of teaching and curriculum that generate substantially higher levels of student learning than does normative practice.
- The most effective curricular and teaching patterns induce students to construct knowledge – to inquire into subject areas intensively. The result is to increase student capacity to learn and work.
- Models of teaching are really models of learning. As students acquire information, ideas, skills, values, ways of thinking, and means of expressing themselves, they are also learning how to learn.
- To ensure maximum impact on learning any specific teaching strategy needs to be fully integrated within a curriculum. Too often 'thinking skills' or 'study strategies' are presented in isolation, with the consequence, (a) that it is left to the student to transfer the strategy to real settings, and (b) that teachers have no 'curriculum vehicle' in which to share good practice.

This analysis supports the view that teaching is more than just presenting material, it is about infusing curriculum content with appropriate instructional strategies that are selected in order to achieve the learning goals the teacher has for her or his students. Successful teachers are not simply charismatic, persuasive and expert presenters; rather, they create powerful cognitive and social tasks to their students and teach the students how to make productive use of them. The purpose of instructional leadership is to facilitate and support this approach to teaching and learning within a curriculum context.

A key problem in achieving this is the lack, in England at least, of a sufficiently robust and sophisticated language for teaching. Despite the contemporary emphasis on the importance of classroom practice, the language of discourse about teaching remains in general at a restricted level. Even in those instances where more precision of language is achieved, say in the debate on whole-class teaching, there are few operational definitions against which teachers can assess their own practice and thereby develop and expand their range of classroom practices. It is not just the words that are lacking, but also the frameworks and specifications necessary to inform action and reflection. The vocabulary of teaching needs to be expanded, and expanded in a systematic and intelligent way. Creating a discourse around teaching and learning is a key task for the instructional leader (Gray et al., 1999).

In our own school-improvement work we have found the framework for teaching proposed below helpful in enabling instructional leaders to organise their thinking around the teaching and learning process. The framework revolves around three aspects of teaching that are often regarded as being contradictory rather than complementary (see Hopkins and Harris, 2000; Hopkins, 2001):

- teaching skills
- teaching relationships
- teaching models.

Teaching skills

There is an extensive research literature on teaching effects. Consistently high correlations are achieved between student achievement scores and classroom processes (see, for example, Creemers, 1994). One general conclusion stands out: 'The most consistently replicated findings link achievement to the quantity and pacing of instruction' (Brophy and Good, 1986: 360). The amount learned is as Good (1989, cited in Hopkins, 2001) subsequently noted, determined in part by opportunity to learn, which is determined by four broad teacher behaviours:

- First, the extent to which teachers are businesslike and task-oriented, emphasise instruction as basic to their role, expect students to master the curriculum, and allocate most classroom time to those activities that have relevant academic objectives.
- Second, teachers whose students make reasonable academic progress frequently use classroom organisation and management strategies that maximise the time students spend engaged in academic activities.
- Third, effective teachers allow students to move through the curriculum briskly but also relatively successfully.
- Fourth, these teachers were found to spend most of their time actively instructing their students in group lessons or supervising their work on assignments rather than allowing students to spend inordinate time on individual seatwork practice without supervision or feedback.

From this perspective, a teacher promotes student learning by being active in planning and organising his or her teaching, explaining to students what they are to learn, arranging occasions for guided practice, monitoring progress, providing feedback, and otherwise helping students understand and accomplish work. Despite the impressive gains associated in the research literature with the range of teaching skills described above, they should be regarded as a necessary but not sufficient condition for effective teaching.

Teaching relationships

There is another set of factors that characterise quality teaching; they are less technical and are more related to the teacher's 'artistry'. Here there is a recognition that teaching involves creativity and is carried out in a highly personalised way. While this need not deny the potential value of considering particular models of teaching or examining the impact of specific skills, it draws attention to the fact that once in the classroom each teacher has the sole responsibility for creating the conditions within which each student can expect some success.

It is much more difficult to report research evidence that arises from this frame of reference. The evidence does not lend itself readily to specifications or lists of features. Yet this perspective on teachers' work is one that is immediately recognised by practitioners and, indeed, others in the wider community. It is not uncommon for teachers to be told by friends from outside the profession of the 'teacher who made a difference'. The personality and flair of the individual teacher is increasingly receiving belated attention.

The 'artistry' of teaching lies in the teacher's ability to generate and sustain high-quality relationships with her students. For example, one of John Gray's (1990) three performance indicators of an 'effective' school is the proportion of pupils who 'have a good or "vital" relationship with one or more teachers'. An essential aspect of this is for the teacher to have high expectations of the students. A supportive, rigorous and optimistic learning environment is fundamental for high levels of student achievement.

This is what is we have referred to previously as the need to establish *authentic relationships* within the classroom (Hopkins *et al.*, 1998). It implies establishing the classroom as a safe and secure learning environment in which pupils can expect acceptance, respect and even warmth from their teachers, without having to earn these – they are intrinsic rights that are extended to pupils because they are there.

Teaching models

There is a further and equally strong body of research and practice that suggests that student achievement can be additionally enhanced by the consistent and strategic use of specific teaching models (Joyce and Weil, 1996; Hopkins and Harris, 2000; Joyce *et al.*, 2002). There are many powerful models of teaching – each with their own 'syntax', phases and guidelines – that are designed to bring about particular kinds of learning and to help students become more effective learners.

These models of teaching (actually models for learning) simultaneously define the nature of the content, the learning strategies, and the arrangements for social interaction that create the learning environments of students. All of the models are research-based insofar as they have been developed and refined through cycles of development and evaluation and have proven effectiveness. It is important to be clear about what is meant by a 'model of teaching'. One can regard the research on teaching effects or teaching skills as providing the teacher with (say) tactical knowledge. The research on 'models of teaching' on the other hand gives teachers more strategic knowledge about how to create whole-classroom settings to facilitate learning.

The crucial point is that models of teaching are also models of learning. How teaching is conducted has a large impact on students' abilities to educate themselves. As students acquire information, ideas, skills, values, ways of thinking and means of expressing themselves, they are also learning how to learn. In fact, the most important long-term outcome of teaching may be the students' increased capabilities to learn more easily and effectively in the future both because of the knowledge and skill they have acquired, and because they have mastered learning processes.

The relationship between some commonly used models of teaching and learning are seen in Table 3.1. In terms of managing the process of teaching and learning within the school, the models of teaching are simply tools that teachers can use to create more powerful learning experiences. Instructional leaders will of course not be expert in the complete range of teaching and learning strategies. It is their task, however, to be familiar with them and to create the conditions for staff in the school to expand their individual and collective repertoires of teaching skills, relationships and models. It is the nature of professional learning communities within schools that provides the focus for the next section of the chapter.

The third domain of instructional leadership – establishing the school as a professional learning community

It is axiomatic that if teachers are to become more versatile in their creation of learning experiences for their students then a major focus for the work of instructional leaders is the establishing of effective staff development processes. This is for the obvious reason that many of the curricular and teaching patterns alluded to above are new for most teachers – they represent

Table 3.1 Relationship between models of teaching and learning skills

Model of teaching	Learning skill
Advanced organiser	• extracting information and ideas from lectures and presentations
Group work	• working effectively with others to initiate and carry out cooperative tasks
Inductive teaching (classification)	• building hypotheses and theories
Mnemonics	• memorising information
Concept attainment	• attaining concepts and how to invent them
Synectics	• using metaphors to think creatively

additions to their repertoire that require substantial study and hard work if implementation in the classroom is to take place.

The approach to staff development developed by Joyce and Showers (1995) is specifically directed at assisting teachers to expand their range of teaching strategies. On the basis of their research they have identified a number of key training components that need to be used in combination. They are:

- presentation of theory or description of skill or strategy;
- modelling or demonstration of skills or models of teaching;
- practice in simulated and classroom settings;
- structured and open-ended feedback (provision of information about performance);
- coaching for application (hands-on, in-classroom assistance with the transfer of skills and strategies to the classroom).

Joyce (1992) has also distinguished between the locations these various forms of staff development are best located – either in the 'workshop' or the 'workplace'. The workshop, which is equivalent to the best practice on the traditional INSET course, is where teachers gain *understanding*, see *demonstrations* of the teaching strategy, and have the opportunity to *practice* in a non-threatening environment. If, however, we wish to transfer those skills back into the workplace – the classroom and school – then merely attending the workshop is insufficient. The research evidence is very clear that skill acquisition and the ability to transfer vertically to a range of situations requires 'on-the-job-support'. This implies changes to the way in which staff development is organised in schools (Joyce and Showers, 1995). In particular this means providing the opportunity for *immediate and sustained practice, collaboration and peer coaching,* and *studying development and implementation.*

Instructional leaders realise that one cannot 'ad hoc' staff development – time has to be found for it. The range of staff development activities required for successful school improvement are considerable. For example, time is required for:

- whole-staff in-service days on teaching and learning and school-improvement planning as well as 'curriculum tours' to share the work done in departments or working groups;
- inter-departmental meetings to discuss teaching strategies;
- workshops run inside the school on teaching;
- partnership teaching and peer coaching.

These activities constitute a staff development infrastructure or, in other words, a professional learning community. We have described the key elements elsewhere as having the following components and logic (Joyce *et al.*, 1999, ch. 1):

- build in time for collective inquiry;
- collective inquiry creates the structural conditions for school improvement;
- studying classroom practice increases the focus on student learning;
- use the research on teaching and learning to improve school-improvement efforts;
- by working in small groups the whole-school staff can become a nurturing unit;
- staff development as inquiry provides synergy and enhanced student effects.

There are two other aspects of developing a professional learning community that we have found to be important in supporting our improvement work with schools (Hopkins, 2001, ch. 7). They are the creation of a school-improvement group within the school and the establishing of 'peer coaching' triads.

School-improvement groups are in our experience an essential feature of sustained school improvement (Hopkins, 2002). We sometimes refer to these 'internal change agents' as the cadre group, a term borrowed from Schmuck and Runkel's (1985) organisational development cadres in Oregon who fulfilled a similar role in those schools. They are responsible for the day-to-day running of the project in their own schools, and for creating links between the principles and ideas of school improvement and practical action. Typically, the cadre group is a cross-hierarchical team of between four and six members of staff. Though one of these is likely to be the head-teacher, it is important to establish groups that are genuinely representative of the range of perspectives and ideas available in the school. Cadre group members should also not come together in any existing group within the school, such as the senior management team or a heads of department group, so that the problem of pooled rationalisations is minimised.

In our work, the school-improvement group is supported through a core training programme, through networking with cadre groups from other schools, and by external support from the university and other support agencies. In terms of their school-improvement work, cadre group members are involved in:

- out-of-school training sessions on capacity-building and teaching and learning;
- planning meetings in school;
- consultancy to school working groups;
- observation and in-classroom support.

The cadre or school-improvement group is essentially a temporary membership system focused specifically upon inquiry and development. This temporary membership system brings together teachers (and support staff) from across the school, with a range of ages or experience and from a cross-section of roles to work together in a status-free collaborative learning context. One teacher has described it as the educational equivalent of a research and development group, and the traditional school as analogous to a company in which everyone works on the production line, without any research and development function. The result is stagnation, and that is how schools have been. The establishment of a school-improvement group creates the research and development capacity, whilst retaining the existing structures required also for organisational stability and efficiency. It also unlocks staff potential often stifled within formal structures, and opens up new collaborations.

The professional learning communities described in this section of the chapter represent a wide range of staff development activity and a fairly sophisticated infrastructure for sustained professional development. A further key element in all of this is the provision of in-classroom support or in Joyce and Showers term 'peer coaching'. It is the facilitation of peer coaching that enables teachers to extend their repertoire of teaching skills and to transfer them from different classroom settings to others.

In particular, peer coaching is helpful when:

- curriculum and teaching are the content of staff development;
- the focus of the staff development represents a new practice for the teacher;
- workshops are designed to develop understanding and skill;
- school-based groups support each other to attain 'transfer of training' (Joyce et al. 1999: 127).

During the implementation of this approach during our IQEA school-improvement projects we have made refinements in the use of peer coaching to support student learning. We have found that when the refinements noted below are incorporated into a school-improvement design, peer coaching can virtually assure 'transfer of training' for everyone:

- Peer-coaching teams of two or three are much more effective than larger groups.
- These groups are more effective when the entire staff is engaged in school improvement.
- Peer coaching works better when heads and deputies participate in training and practice.
- The effects are greater when formative study of student learning is embedded in the process.

In discussing an approach to leadership that is committed to school improvement the creation of professional learning communities is vital. Such a staff development infrastructure unites the focus on teaching and learning and the schools values and purpose. The links between cadre-group working and the constellation of staff-development activities just described makes the structural link between the work of teachers and enhanced levels of student achievement clear and achievable. In highly effective schools it is this that provides the essential infrastructure for school improvement. That is why the third domain of instructional leadership is establishing the school as a professional learning community.

Commentary

In this chapter I have been arguing for a style of leadership that is consistent with raising levels of student achievement. From this perspective instructional leaders are able to create, within a context of values, synergy between a focus on teaching and learning on the one hand, and building professional learning communities on the other. If we are serious about raising the levels of student achievement and learning in our schools then we need styles of leadership that promote, celebrate and enhance the importance of teaching and learning and staff development, and that contribute directly to school improvement.

In the sense that I have been using the term in this chapter, school improvement is a distinct approach to educational change that enhances student outcomes *as well as* strengthening the school's capacity for managing change. School improvement is about raising student achievement through focusing on the teaching–learning process and the conditions that support it. It is about strategies for improving the school's capacity for providing quality education in times of change (Hopkins, 2001). It is within this context, and in the confluence between expanding the teaching and learning repertoires of teachers and the creation of a staff development infrastructure, that instructional leadership defines itself.

The argument for linking instructional leadership and school improvement goes far beyond simply an instrumental approach to educational reform, and leads towards transformation. The emphasis on transformation is both deliberate and necessary. Reform strategies and leadership programmes can no longer take only an incremental approach to change. Such policies and strategies have to date not resulted in substantial changes to student learning and attainment. Leadership now needs to be seen within a whole-school or systems context and to impact both on classroom practice and the work culture of the school. Hence the emphasis on transformation. This implies an expansion in the capacity of the school to manage change in the pursuit of student learning and achievement, and the creation of professional learning communities within the school to support the work of teachers. The implications of this perspective for school leadership are as obvious as they are profound.

In reflecting on this theme, it is fitting to conclude this chapter by briefly referring to the approach taken to school leadership by colleagues and myself as part of our work as members of the National College for School Leadership's Think Tank. Our brief was to advise the National College on best practice and futures thinking concerning leadership from across a range of public and private settings. The evidence and experience considered by the Think Tank was diverse in context, inspiring in aspiration, yet presented remarkably consistent images of leadership.

The challenge was to render this richness in a form that is both accessible and challenging as well as being faithful to the ideas and practice from which it emanated. On further reflection it became clear that what had been learned from this inquiry could be expressed economically as a set of propositions. The following ten propositions are grouped into three sections reflecting the values, nature and context of school leadership. The propositions should be regarded as a set, they build on and amplify each other as the argument develops (National College for School Leadership, 2001).

The values of school leadership

- Proposition one – school leadership must be purposeful, inclusive and values-driven.
- Proposition two – school leadership must embrace the distinctive and inclusive context of the school.
- Proposition three – school leadership must promote an active view of learning.

The nature of school leadership

- Proposition four – school leadership must be instructionally focused.
- Proposition five – school leadership is a function that needs to be dispersed throughout the school community.
- Proposition six – school leadership must build capacity by developing the school as a learning community.
- Proposition seven – school leadership must be futures-orientated and strategically driven.

Developing and supporting school leadership

- Proposition eight – school leadership must be developed through experiential and innovative methodologies.
- Proposition nine – school leadership must be served by a support and policy context that is coherent, systemic and implementation-driven.

- Proposition ten – school leadership must be supported by a National College that leads the discourse around leadership for learning.

Taken together the propositions comprise a manifesto for the future of school leadership that is systemic, genuinely transformational and firmly grounded in learning.

Note

1 Previous rehearsals of this argument can be found in papers commissioned by the National College for School Leadership and in ch. 7 of *School Improvement for Real* (Hopkins, 2001).

References

Berg, R. and Sleegers, P. (1996) 'The Innovative Capacity of Secondary Schools: A Qualitative Study', *International Journal of Qualitative Studies in Education*, 9(2): 201–23.

Brophy, J. and Good, T. (1986) 'Teacher Behaviour and Student Achievement', in H. Wittrock (ed.), *Handbook of Research on Teaching*, 3rd edn, New York, Macmillan.

Cheng, Yin Cheong (1997) 'The Transformational Leadership for School Effectiveness and Development in the New Century', paper read at International Symposium of Quality Training of Primary and Secondary Principals toward the 21st Century, 20–24 January, Nanjing, China.

Creemers, B. (1994) *The Effective Classroom*, London, Cassell.

DES (1977) *Ten Good Schools: A Secondary School Enquiry*, London, Department of Education and Science.

Duke, D. (1987) *School Leadership and Instructional Improvement*, New York, Random House.

Elmore, R. (1995) 'Teaching, Learning, and School Organisation: Principles of Practice and the Regularities of Schooling', *Educational Administration Quarterly*, 31(3): 355–74.

Geltner, B. and Shelton, M. (1991) 'Expanded Notions of Strategic Instructional Leadership', *The Journal of School Leadership*, 1(43): 38–50.

Gray, J. (1990) 'The Quality of Schooling: Frameworks for Judgement', *British Journal of Educational Studies*, 38: 203–33.

Gray, J., Hopkins, D., Reynolds, D., Wilcox, B., Farrell, S. and Wilcox, B. (1999) *Improving Schools: Performance and Potential*, Buckingham, Open University Press.

Hallinger, P. (1992) 'The Evolving Role of American Principals: From Managerial to Instructional to Transformational Leaders', *Journal of Educational Administration*, 30(3): 35–48.

Hallinger, P. and Murphy, J. (1985) 'Assessing the Instructional Management Behaviour of Principals', *Elementary School Journal* 86(2): 217–47.

Hopkins, D. (2001) *School Improvement for Real*, London, RoutledgeFalmer.

Hopkins, D. (2002) *Improving Quality of Education for All*, 2nd edn, London, David Fulton.

Hopkins, D. and Harris, A. (2000) *Creating the Conditions for Teaching and Learning*, London, David Fulton.

Hopkins, D., West, M. and Beresford, J. (1998) 'Creating the Conditions for Classroom and Teacher Development', *Teachers and Teaching: Theory and Practice*, 4(1): 115–41.

Joyce, B. (1992) 'Cooperative Learning and Staff Development: Teaching the Method with the Method', *Cooperative Learning*, 12(2), 10–13.

Joyce, B. and Showers, B. (1995) *Student Achievement through Staff Development*, 2nd edn, White Plains, NY, Longman.

Joyce, B. and Weil, M. (1996) *Models of Teaching*, 5th edn, Englewood Cliffs, NJ, Prentice-Hall.

Joyce, B., Calhoun, E. and Hopkins, D. (1999) 'The New Structure of School Improvement, Buckingham, Open University Press.

Joyce, B., Calhoun, E. and Hopkins, D. (2002) *Models of Learning – Tools for Teaching*, 2nd edn, Buckingham, Open University Press.

Leithwood, K. (1997) 'Distributed Leadership in Secondary Schools', paper read at Annual Meeting of the American Educational Research Association, 24–28 March, Chicago, IL.

Leithwood, K. and Jantzi, D. (1990) 'Transformational Leadership: How Principals Can Help Reform School Cultures', *School Effectiveness and School Improvement* 1(4): 249–80.

Leithwood, K., Jantzi, D. and Steinbach, R. (1999) *Changing Leadership for Changing Times*, Buckingham, Philadelphia, Open University Press.

National College for School Leadership (2001) *Leadership for Transforming Learning* (Think Tank Report – Chair Professor David Hopkins), Nottingham, NCSL.

Schmuck, R. and Runkel, P. (1985) *The Handbook of Organisation Development in Schools*, 3rd edn, Palo Alto, CA, Mayfield.

Sheppard, B. (1996) 'Exploring the Transformational Nature of Instructional Leadership', *Alberta Journal of Educational Research* 42(4): 325–44.

Stoll, L. and Fink, D. (1996) *Changing our Schools*, Buckingham, Open University Press.

Turan, S. and Sny, C. (1996) 'An Exploration of Transformational Leadership and its Role in Strategic Planning: A Conceptual Framework', paper read at Annual Meeting of the International Society for Educational Planning, 19–21 September, New Orleans, LA.

Wang, M., Haertel, G. and Walberg, H. (1993) 'Towards a Knowledge Base for School Learning', *Review of Educational Research*, 63(3): 249–94.

West, M., Jackson, D., Harris, A. and Hopkins, D. (2000) 'Learning through Leadership, Leadership through Learning', in K. Riley and K. Seashore Louis (eds), *Leadership for Learning*, San Francisco, Jossey-Bass.

Chapter 4

Teacher leadership and school improvement

Alma Harris

Introduction

The issue of leadership for school improvement is now high on the research and policy agendas of many countries. With some inevitability, thinking about leadership has tended to focus on headteachers and how they exercise leadership. There remains a prominent belief in the leadership of the headteacher as the single source and direction of leadership in the school. This reinforces the 'heroic view' of leadership where the skills and abilities to turn things around in a school are located in certain individuals. Sergiovanni (2001: 55) notes:

> It remains that the superhero images of leadership do not work. And it remains that mandates and incentives are not powerful enough to function as engines that will drive our efforts to improve schools. In tomorrow's world success will depend upon the ability of leaders to harness the capacity of locals, to enhance sense and meaning and to build communities of responsibility.

However, research has shown that the commonly held view concerning the effects of headteacher leadership on school outcomes is not warranted. Hallinger and Heck (1996) found that the headteacher effect is small and that most effects on students were indirect. This led to the recommendation 'that more attention should be given to school conditions through which such leadership flowed' (Leithwood and Jantzi, 2000: 50).

Interestingly, school leaders' own conceptions of leadership tend to be shaped by rather conventional views of the leadership task. In a study of effective leadership in changing times MacBeath *et al.* (1998) describes leaders were asked to depict themselves in a drawing. The subsequent illustrations revealed that most leaders saw themselves at the apex of things, at the top of the hill, at the centre of a complex web of activity. However, while it cannot be denied that leaders are inevitably in the midst of the action, effective leadership is not always derived from the top. Fullan (2001) suggests that leaders lead from the centre of a complex myriad of human relationships. Their leadership is dependent upon others and the relationships they have with others. Senge (1990: 352) suggests that:

> In a learning organisation leaders may start by pursuing their own vision, but as they listen carefully to others' vision they begin to see that their own personal vision is part of something larger. This does not diminish any leader's sense of responsibility for the vision – if anything, it deepens it.

Research evidence concerning school improvement underlines the importance of devolved leadership at different levels within the organisation. (Hopkins *et al.*, 1994; Hopkins *et al.*, 1997). The importance of school level, department level and classroom level change has been shown to be essential in successful school-improvement programmes (e.g. Hopkins *et al.*, 1996; Hopkins and Harris, 1997). Research has shown that a substantial proportion of the variation in effectiveness among schools is due to variation within schools. This work has emphasised the importance of exploring differential effectiveness particularly at the level of the department (Creemers, 1992; Scheerens, 1992; Sammons *et al.*, 1997; Harris *et al.*, 1996; Harris, 1998). In particular, the leadership role at the departmental level has been shown to be an important 'missing link' in secondary school improvement (Harris, 2001).

While the research evidence concerning school improvement and school effectiveness has highlighted the importance of the leadership of the headteacher, for the most part neither field has concentrated intensively on issues of leadership. There has been a consistent view emerging from the research base on effective schools that professional leadership is an important factor. Yet the ways in which this form of leadership is developed and practised is a underdeveloped area.

Leadership for school improvement

Studies of school change have paid generally little attention to the ways in which leadership is nurtured and developed. The literature propagates a view of leadership that is centred upon strong headteachers with a singular and clear vision for the school. These leaders have dynamic and outgoing personalities with high levels of commitment to their role. In terms of school improvement, the model of leadership that dominates much of the writing is transformational leadership. This style of leadership is people rather than organisation-orientated and requires a leadership approach that transforms the feelings, attitudes and beliefs of others. In other words, it transforms 'school culture'.

West *et al.* (2000) suggest that there are two particular problems with transformational leadership. The first problem concerns the sustainability of transformational leadership approaches over time. They suggest that 'transformational characteristics are . . . unsustainable over the long haul' (West *et al.*, 2000: 39). The second problem relates to the availability of high-quality headteachers who are transformational in their leadership approaches. The simple fact is that there are not enough headteachers to go around. This inevitably points towards developing and securing leadership at other levels within the organisation, to provide leadership that can continuously improve the school.

This suggests that if school improvement is to be achieved, the emphasis should be upon transformational rather than transactional leadership. Consequently, there are increasing calls for and acceptance of a leadership role for teachers in achieving goals in the context of their own areas of direct responsibility. Although schools need to be led by individuals (who do make a difference) that overarching leadership has to be replicated right through the organisation and found in every aspect of school life.

Recent assessments of the leadership role within school improvement implies that giving others real responsibility and developing others is the best possible way of the organisation moving forward. One of the most consistent findings from recent studies of effective leadership is that authority to lead need not be located in the person of the leader but can be dispersed within the school in between and among people (Elmore and MacDonald, 2000; Day *et al.*, 2000). Evidence would suggest that where this is in place leadership is a much stronger internal driver and is mutually reinforcing. In practice, dispersed leadership means giving authority to others and helping others to use authority wisely. This means relinquishing the idea of structure as control and viewing structure as the vehicle for empowering others. For this approach to work requires a high degree of trust as trust is essential to support the leadership climate. As Evans (1998: 183) notes:

> Trust is the essential link between leader and led, vital to people's job, status functions and loyalty, vital to fellowship. It is doubly important when organisations are reaching rapid improvement, which requires exceptional effort and competence, and doubly so again in organisations like schools that offer few motivators.

In the absence of trust, disagreement and conflict are more difficult to control. Conversely, where there is mutual respect and moral authority, it is much easier to accept the differences or conflicts that might emerge. MacBeath (1980) suggests that in an improving school differences are not simply respected but engaged with in a genuine search for meaning.

In this sense leadership is reconceptualised as a set of behaviours and practices that are undertaken collectively. It is suggested that leadership for school improvement is not as a role or function assigned to those only with leadership responsibilities but as a dynamic between individuals within an organisation. In this sense, leadership encompasses a broad group of people that contribute to the school's distinctive culture and community. This view of leadership focuses on the relationships and the connections among individuals within a school. It is separated from person, role and status but reflects the dynamic created out of shared purpose and being part of a school community.

Distributed leadership

The work of Linda Lambert (1998) and Peter Gronn (2000) inevitably informs much of this chapter as its focuses upon distributed properties of leadership and teacher leadership. A key element in the model of leadership proposed is that the nature and purpose of leadership is 'the ability of those within a school to work together, constructing meaning and knowledge collectively and collaboratively' (Lambert, 1998: 5). Effective schools tend to be marked by a constant interchange of professional information at both a formal and informal level. Similarly, schools that are improving have ways of working that encourage teachers to work together towards shared goals. There is a body of evidence that demonstrates that teachers work most effectively when they are supported by other teachers and work together collegially. Hopkins *et al.* (1996: 177) note that 'successful schools create collaborative environments which encourage involvement, professional development, mutual support and assistance in problem solving'.

Building leadership capacity therefore involves teachers working together and learning together to bring about effective change. It is derived from the explicit and shared values of a community. These are not necessarily 'professional values' but those which hold a community together and which, of themselves, guide actions and accountability. What people do is driven not by what is rewarded, or what works, nor by self-interest. Instead, it is led by a sense of what is right and in the interests of the whole school.

This implies a model of leadership 'where leadership and leader are not the same' (Lambert, 1998: 8). Leadership is a shared and collective endeavour that engages all members of the organisation. It means the context in which people work together and learn together, where they construct and refine meaning leading to a shared purpose or set of goals. This model of leadership implies a redistribution of power and a realignment of authority within the organisation.

A major assumption made by those endeavouring to bring about change is that schools operate rationally and are goal-directed organisations. As

Van Den Berg and Sleegers (2000: 671) note 'the development of policy is construed as a systematic and methodic method for leading a school'. However, in Weick's (1995: 85) view the notion of an organisation is far from rational but is seen rather as an 'assemblage of individuals' or as 'congeries of persons in more or less autonomous arrays' (Burns, 1996: 1). This interpretation of the organisation is one that is evolving rather than static, comprising of subcultures and complex interrelationships.

Gronn's (2000: 323) view of organisational development promotes a view of leadership that is distributed and is premised upon the interactions and collective understandings of individuals. This view suggests that leadership is best conceived as a group quality, as a set of functions which must be carried out by the group. The categorisation of leaders and followers therefore becomes redundant as leadership is distributed throughout the organisation. The central idea is that leaders and followers are collaborators in accomplishing group tasks and frequently exchange leadership roles.

Taking this stance, leadership is seen as 'fluid and emergent rather than as a fixed phenomenon' (Gronn, 2000: 324). It is related to collective problem-solving and to collaborative ways of working within the organisation. Gronn (2000) notes that some version of distributed leadership has always been in evidence, through the existence of collaborative decision-making bodies within educational organisations such as teams or committees. At different times, individuals within teams or committees take on a range of leadership tasks and responsibilities. At various points therefore, individuals exert influence and exhibit leadership behaviour within the group. This implies that leadership as a phenomenon is distributed within the group and is not embodied in just one individual. Distributed leadership is generated from the interactions and dynamics within the group or team.

There are also less obvious instances of distributed leadership within organisations. In most working relationships individuals are part of informal teams and their effectiveness is dependent upon their relationship with others. In this sense, leadership may be distributed in the daily interactions between individuals and in their interpersonal relationships. The way in which tasks, roles and responsibilities are shared require some form of negotiation and collective decision-making that involve some form of distributed leadership practice.

Gronn (2000: 333) has suggested that 'distributed leadership is an idea whose time has come'. Part of the reason for this resides in the fact that traditional leadership approaches have had little, if any, direct or sustained impact on organisational effectiveness. The notion of the leader as a visionary champion who is able to drive through change and improvement is one that has been shown to be fundamentally flawed. In England, this has been demonstrated very clearly in the superheads' experience where the 'heroic' notion of leadership proved insufficient to improve schools designated as failing.

A distributed model of leadership will inevitably mean some redefinition of roles and internal boundaries within the school. Firstly, it implies a different power relationship within the school where the distinctions between followers and leaders tend to blur. Secondly, it has implications for the division of labour within a school, particularly when the tasks facing the organisation are shared more widely. Thirdly, it opens up the possibility of all teachers becoming leaders at various times. It is this last dimension that has most potency and potential for school improvement because it is premised upon collaborative forms of working among teachers.

Teacher leadership

Teacher leadership is premised upon a power redistribution within the school, moving from hierarchical control to peer control. In this leadership model the power base is diffuse and the authority dispersed within the teaching community. An important dimension of this leadership approach is the emphasis upon collegial ways of working. For teacher leadership to be most effective it has to encompass mutual trust and support. In the last decade, many claims have been made about the contribution of strong collegial relationships between teachers to school improvement. Little (1990) suggested that collegial interaction at least lays the groundwork for developing shared ideas and for generating forms of leadership. Rosenholtz (1989) argued even more forcibly for teacher collegiality and collaboration as a means of generating positive change in schools. Collaboration is at the heart of teacher leadership, as it is premised upon change that is enacted collectively.

There is shared understanding and shared purpose at the core of teacher leadership. It engages all those within the organisation in a reciprocal learning process that leads to collective action and meaningful change. Teacher leadership is premised upon the belief that leadership potential is widely spread amongst organisational members. As West *et al.* (2000: 39) point out:

> If this leadership potential is to be realised, then it will have to be grounded in in a commitment to learn and develop that inhabits the structures of schools as well as the classroom − it is likely that the school will conceive and act differently from the traditional explanations of leadership and structure. This view of leadership, then is not hierarchical, but federal. It is a view which is both tight and loose; tight on values, but loose on the freedom to act, opportunity to experiment and authority to question historical assumptions.

For teacher leadership to be maximised there has to be shared values and goals along with the ability to take action. This can only be achieved as part of a democratic process where individual ideas and actions can be freely expressed. When schools operate democratically, then teachers will be more likely to contribute to their development in a positive way.

Teacher leadership in action

In the 1970s, Ron Edmonds stated that 'all children can learn'. More than thirty years later Roland Barth (2000) has suggested that this statement should be supplemented by the equally revolutionary idea that 'all teachers can lead'. He proposes that if schools are going to become places in which all children are learning, all teachers must be leaders. The fact of the matter is that all teachers harbour leadership capabilities waiting to be unlocked and engaged for the good of the school. All teachers have leadership potential that can benefit the school and themselves; the question is, how to unleash that potential? In order to create communities of teacher leaders it is important to link professional development and leading. Teachers who are engaged in learning with their peers are most likely to embrace new initiatives and to innovate. Within the most successful school improvement projects internationally there is evidence to demonstrate how teacher leadership leads to improvements at school and classroom level (Harris, 2000, 2002a).

Successful school improvement projects focus specifically upon the teaching and learning processes and the 'conditions' at school and classroom level that support and sustain school improvement. Such conditions are viewed as the internal features of the school that build capacity for change and development. One of the most important conditions at the school level is teacher collaboration. This is premised upon generating collegial and collaborative ways of working that provide teachers with the freedom to innovate and take collective action.

Evidence from highly successful improvement projects suggests that teacher leaders have a number of key functions that support school-level change. One important function is the ability to communicate with other teachers and to outline the purposes of the change. A key leadership task is the clarification of goals and purposes and sharing them more widely within the school. If the relationship between the goals set and the organisational aspirations match, subsequent implementation of change is more likely to be successful. This is because teachers understand what the broader purposes are and what will be expected of them.

Another important function of teacher leaders is obtaining the resources necessary to instigate change successfully. These resources may be technical, emotional, temporal or physical in nature. Huberman and Miles (1984) suggest that an important part of programme implementation is creating the learning opportunities for staff to engage in the activities expected of them. Teacher leaders are important role models. Their behaviour and responses will provide important cues to others about acceptable patterns of behaviour during innovation and change.

Providing encouragement and recognition is another function of teacher leadership. Change inevitably causes stress and anxiety in others, hence social support is needed. Harris and Chapman (2001) found evidence that informal encouragement in schools was an important dimension of success-ful school improvement. It was significant that the encouragement came from a variety of sources, particularly teachers. Directly linked to the pro-vision of support is the monitoring of the change effort. Teachers are best placed to observe the impact of changes upon teaching and learning processes. They will be able to gauge the extent to which the proposed change is being implemented.

Although further research concerning the role of teacher leadership within school improvement is needed, there are some tentative conclusions that can be made. There are four discernable and discrete dimensions of the teacher leadership role within school improvement. The first dimension concerns the way in which teachers translate the principles of school improvement into the practices of individual classrooms. This brokering role remains a central responsibility for the teacher leader. It ensures that links within schools are secure and that opportunities for meaningful development among teachers are maximised.

A second dimension of the teacher leader role focuses upon empowering teachers and giving them some ownership of a particular change or devel-opment. An emphasis is placed upon participative leadership where all teachers feel part of the change or development. Teacher leaders assist other teachers to cohere around a particular development and to foster a more collaborative way of working. They work with colleagues to shape school improvement efforts and take some lead in guiding teachers towards a collective goal.

A third dimension of the teacher leadership role in school improvement is a mediating role. Teacher leaders are important sources of expertise and information. They are able to draw upon additional resources and expertise if required and to seek external assistance. Finally, a forth and possibly most important dimension of the teacher leadership role is forging close relationships with individual teachers where mutual learning takes place. The way in which teachers learn together is an important determinant of school improvement. Wohlstetter's (1995) research found that professional development and learning were distinguishing characteristics of schools that were improving. Wohlstetter (1995: 274) noted that:

> Intense interest in professional development was viewed as an ongoing success for every teacher in the school, as well as for the principal . . . such schools worked to build the capacity of the entire staff to help

manage the school . . . and to develop a common knowledge base among all members.

At a macro-level this might involve monitoring attainment, assessing performance and setting clear targets. At the micro-level it suggests an important coaching or mentoring role for teacher leaders as they work with others on issues of improving teaching and learning.

Commentary

Research on school leadership remains heavily orientated towards headship. The reviews conducted by Hallinger and Heck (1996) illustrate how narrowly school leadership is conceived and the relatively limited empirical base from which it is derived. If, as Hallinger and Heck (1996) claim, there are approximately forty empirical studies of headteacher leadership, that are acceptable, over a fifteen-year time-span, the evidential base is narrow. This inevitably raises some questions about the relationship between leadership and school outcomes consistently identified in literature. Interestingly, there are no studies that consider the relative influence on the school of those in different leadership roles.

Recently, research has examined how school and teacher leadership affect levels of student engagement This work explored the effects of school and teacher leadership on students' engagement with school (Leithwood and Jantzi, 2000). The study considered principal and teacher leadership separately, as well as the relative effects of these two sources of leadership. One of the main findings from this study was that the 'effects on student engagement of both sources of leadership are substantially moderated by family educational culture' (Leithwood and Jantzi, 2000: 59). However, the research also found that 'the relationships between principal and teacher leadership are moderately strong explaining 66% of the variation in school conditions, a proportion that does not change by adding family educational culture to the analyses' (Leithwood and Jantzi, 2000: 59).

The research study concluded that 'teacher leadership far outweighs principal leadership effects before taking into account the moderating effects of family educational culture' (Leithwood and Jantzi, 2000: 60). Evidence from this study suggests that principal leadership does not stand out as a critical part of the change process but that teacher leadership demonstrates a significant effect on student engagement. While the study does not support widely distributed forms of leadership, it does 'support the distribution of a larger proportion of current leadership development resources to the development of teacher leadership' (Leithwood and Jantzi, 2000: 61).

Teacher leadership is premised upon the ability to empower others to lead. It is a shared commodity owned by those who work within the school and by those who work on behalf of the school. To cope with the unprecedented rate of change in schools in the twenty-first century requires alternative approaches to school improvement and school leadership. If schools are to be learning communities this cannot be achieved by operating with models of change and improvement dependent upon individual leadership. Consequently, a new paradigm is emerging, one that is premised upon the leadership capability of the many, rather than the few.

References

Barth, R. (1990) *Improving Schools From Within: Teachers, Parent and Principals Can Make a Difference*, San Francisco, Jossey-Bass.

Barth, R. (2000) *Learning by Heart*, San Francisco, Jossey-Bass.

Creemers, B.P.M. (1992) *The Effective Classroom*, London, Cassell.

Day, C., Harris, A., Hadfield, M., Tolley, H. and Beresford, J. (2000) *Leading Schools in Times of Change*, Milton Keynes, Open University Press.

Evans, L. (1988) *Managing to Motivate*, London, David Fulton.

Fullan, M. (2001) *Leading in a Culture of Change*, San Francisco, Jossey-Bass.

Goddard, T. (1998) 'Of Daffodils and Dog Teams: Reflections on Leadership', paper presented to Annual Meeting of the British Educational Management and Administration Society, Warwick, England.

Gronn, P. (2000) 'Distributed Properties: A New Architechure for Leadership', *Educational Management and Administration*, 28(3): 317–38.

Hallinger, P. and Heck, R.H. (1996) 'The Principal's Role in School Effectiveness: An Assessment of Substantive Findings, 1980–1995', paper presented at AERA Annual Conference, New York.

Hargreaves, A. (1994) *Changing Teachers: Changing Times*, London, Cassell.

Harris, A. (1998) 'Improving the Effective Department: Strategies for Growth and Development', *Education Management and Administration*, 26(3): 269–78.

Harris, A. (1999a) *Teaching and Learning in the Effective School*, London, Arena Press.

Harris, A. (1999b) *Effective Subject Leadership: A Handbook of Staff Development Activities*, London, David Fulton.

Harris, A. (2000) 'Effective Leadership and Departmental Improvement', *Westminster Studies in Education*, 23: 81–90.

Harris, A. (2001) 'Department Improvement and School Improvement: A Missing Link?', *British Educational Research Journal*, 27(4): 477–87.

Harris, A. (2002a) *School Improvement: What's in it for Schools?*, London, Routledge.

Harris, A. (2002b) *Leading the Improving Department*, London, David Fulton.

Harris, A. and Chapman, C. (2001) 'Democratic Leadership for School Improvement in Challenging Contexts', paper presented at the International Congress on School Effectiveness and Improvement, Copenhagen.

Harris, A., Day, C. and Hadfield, M. (2001) 'Headteachers' Views of Effective School Leadership', *International Studies in Educational Administration*, 29(1): 29–39.

Harris, A., Jamieson, I.M. and Russ, J. (1996) *School Improvement and School Effectiveness: A Practical Guide*, London, Pitman Press.

Hopkins, D. (2000) *School Improvement for Real*, London, Falmer.

Hopkins, D. and Harris, A. (1997) 'Improving the Quality of Education for All', *Support for Learning*, 12(4): 147–51.

Hopkins, D. and Harris, A. (2000) 'Differential Strategies for School Development', in D. Van Veen and C. Day (eds), *Professional Development and School Improvement: Strategies for Growth*, Mahwah, NJ, Erlbaum.

Hopkins, D., Ainscow, M. and West, M. (1994) *School Improvement in an Era of Change*, London, Cassell.

Hopkins, D., West, M. and Ainscow, M. (1996) *Improving the Quality of Education for All*, London, David Fulton.

Hopkins, D., Harris, A., West, M., Ainscow, M. and Beresford, J. (1997) *Creating the Conditions for Classroom Improvement*, London, David Fulton.

Huberman, M. and Miles, M. (1989) *Innovation Up Close*, London, Falmer Press.

Lambert, L. (1998) *Building Leadership Capacity in Schools*, Association for Supervision and Curriculum Development Alexandria, Virginia, USA.

Leithwood, K. and Jantzi, D. (2000) 'The Effects of Transformational Leadership on Organisational Conditions and Student Engagement', *Journal of Educational Administration* 38(2): 112–29.

Leithwood, K., Jantzi, D. and Steinback, R. (1999) *Changing Leadership for Changing Times*, Buckingham, Open University Press.

Little, J.W. (1990) 'The Persistence of Privacy: Autonomy and Initiative in Teachers' Professional Relations', *Teachers College Record*, 91: 500–36.

Little, J.W. (1993) 'Teachers Professional Development in a Climate of Educational Reform', *Educational Evaluation and Policy Analysis*, 15(2): 129–51.

Louis, K. *et al.* (1996) 'Teachers' Professional Community in Restructuring Schools', *American Educational Research Journal*, 33(4): 757–89.

MacBeath, J. (ed.) (1998) *Effective School Leadership: Responding to Change*, London, Paul Chapman.

Mitchell, C. and Sackney, L. (2001) *Profound Improvement: Building Capacity for a Learning Community*, Lisse, Swets and Zeitlinger.

Mortimore, P. (2000) *The Road to School Improvement*, Lisse, Swets and Zeitlinger.

Rosenholtz, S. (1989) *Teachers Workplace*, New York, Longman.

Sammons, P. (1999) *School Effectiveness: Coming of Age in the Twenty-First Century*, Lisse, Swets and Zeitlinger.

Sammons, P., Thomas, S. and Mortimore, P. (1997) *Forging Links: Effective Schools and Effective Departments*, London, Paul Chapman.

Scheerens, J. (1992) *Effective Schooling: Research, Theory and Practice*, London, Cassell.

Senge, P. (1990) *The Fifth Discipline*, New York, Doubleday.

Sergiovanni, T. (2001) *Leadership: What's in it for Schools?*, London, RoutledgeFalmer.

Silns, H. and Mulford, B. (2002) 'Leadership and School Results', *Second International Handbook of Educational Leadership and Administration* (in press).

Southworth, G. (1995) *Talking Heads: Voices of Experience*, Cambridge, University of Cambridge Institute of Education.

Van Velzen, W., Miles, M., Elholm, M., Hameyer, U. and Robin, D. (1985) *Making School Improvement Work*, Leuven, Belgium ACCO.

Wenger, E. (1998) *Communities of Practice: Learning, Meaning and Identity*, Cambridge, Cambridge University Press.

West, M., Jackson, D., Harris, A. and Hopkins, D. (2000). 'Leadership for School Improvement', in K. Riley and K. Seashore Louis (eds), *Leadership for Change*, London, RoutledgeFalmer.

Wohlstetter, P. (1995) 'Getting School-Based Management Right: What Works and What Doesn't', *Phi Delta Kappan* 77(1): 22–4, 26.

Chapter 5

Building the capacity for leading and learning

David Hopkins and David Jackson

[The] . . . differences between schools in outcome were systematically related to their characteristics as social institutions . . . All of these factors were open to modification by the staff, rather than fixed by external constraints . . . The implication is that the individual actions or measures may combine to create a particular ethos, or set of values, attitudes and behaviours which will become characteristic of the school as a whole.

(Rutter *et al.*, 1979)

School capacity can be defined as the collective competency of the school as an entity to bring about effective change. . . . It is now clear that for school improvement, leadership needs to focus on two dimensions – the teaching and learning focus on the one hand and capacity on the other.

(NCSL, 2001)

Introduction

The quotation from Michael Rutter and colleagues above, taken from *Fifteen Thousand Hours*, is one of the most optimistic statements on schooling that we know. It emphasises that it is the quality of the school as a social system that is the key contributor to the effectiveness of the school and that this can be modified and enhanced by the actions and aspirations of its members. It was this belief that gave impetus to the first wave of school-improvement efforts and which laid the basis for the emphasis during the last two decades on issues relating to school culture and climate as concepts which lie at the heart of school-improvement endeavours.

However, other factors have moved those of us who work in the school-improvement and leadership-development fields to look beyond these concepts to something deeper. Culture and climate remain comparatively static concepts, yet the world in which schools find themselves is turbulent and uncertain – containing forces that act in dynamic interplay with the climate of the school. The list of such forces is well known: the ubiquitous-ness of change; the pressures from succeeding waves of standards-based reforms; the imperative to respond to the impact of digital technologies; new understandings about the nature of learning from brain research; school-level autonomies; workload issues; public accountability pressures; the expansion of paraprofessional roles. All these factors (and others) have led to a focus worldwide upon progressive school restructuring, redesign or re-engineering.

In simple terms, the requirement to handle continuous multiple change has changed our emphasis. Modern complexity means change, but above all it means rapidly occurring, unpredictable, non-linear change (Fullan 2001). The management of change has thus itself become an inadequate or outmoded concept. Similarly, the establishment of an appropriate culture or climate is still a necessary but nonetheless an insufficient foundation for success. Contemporary discussions are focusing far more on the concept of 'school capacity' – as mentioned in the second of the two opening quotations from the NCSL's Think Tank report (2001). In this chapter we will argue that 'capacity' is the key construct in creating the conditions within the school to enhance both leading and learning. In developing the argument we will:

- trace the evolution of the concept of capacity within the school-improvement tradition;
- explore different conceptualisations of capacity;
- develop a model for capacity and identify strategies to develop it;
- suggest that networking is the most appropriate way of developing and enhancing capacity;
- conclude by identifying the key implications of the analysis for leading and learning.

The OECD International School Improvement Project

A major impetus to the development of school improvement as a strategic response to the challenge of educational change was given by the OECD through its Centre for Educational Research and Development (CERI), which between 1982 and 1986 sponsored an International School Improvement Project (ISIP). ISIP built on previous OECD/CERI initiatives such as The Creativity of the School (Nisbet, 1973) and the INSET (Hopkins, 1986) projects. Although school self-evaluation was regarded as an important strategy for school improvement, the ISIP took a more holistic and systemic view of educational change. At a time when the educational system as a whole faced not only retrenchment but also pressure for change, a project that focused on school improvement – at change at the meso-level, at strategies for strengthening the school's capacity for problem-solving, at making the school more reflexive to change, as well

as enhancing the teaching and learning process – was seen as both important and necessary. More detail of the knowledge that emanated from ISIP is
found elsewhere (van Velzen *et al.*, 1985; Hopkins, 1987, 1990).

ISIP proposed a very different way of thinking about change than the
ubiquitous 'top-down' or 'outside-in' approaches. When the school is
regarded as the 'centre' of change, then strategies for change need to take
this new perspective into account, focusing upon expanding the capacity
of the school to take control of its own development. School Improvement,
for example, was defined in the ISIP as:

> A systematic, sustained effort aimed at change in learning conditions
> and other related internal conditions . . . with the ultimate aim of
> accomplishing educational goals more effectively.
>
> (van Velzen *et al.*, 1985: 48)

School improvement as an approach to educational change, according to
ISIP, therefore rested on a number of assumptions, among which is a key
focus on the 'internal conditions' of schools. These include not only the
teaching and learning activities of the school, but also its organisational
norms, professional learning systems, knowledge-transfer processes,
leadership arrangements and its receptiveness to external learning (Hopkins
et al., 1994: 69). This conception is very close, as we shall see later, to current
views on school capacity.

The ISIP occurred at a fruitful time for the evolution of school improvement more generally. During this period some large-scale studies of
school improvement projects were also conducted. The 'Study of Dis-
semination Efforts Supporting School Improvement' (see the ten-volume
report, *People, Policies and Practices: Examining the Chain of School Improvement* by David Crandall, 1982) was particularly important. This mammoth
study was responsible for the fine-grained analysis of 'Innovation Up
Close' (Huberman and Miles, 1984), and an analysis of policy implications
(Crandall *et al.*, 1986). Much was consequently learned about the dynamics
of the change process during this period. In particular, there was an increasing interest in the internal organisational characteristics of the school – what
we are now referring to as 'capacity.'

This has led to a widely accepted notion of school improvement – that it is
a strategy for achieving positive educational change that focuses on student
achievement by modifying classroom practice whilst simultaneously adapting the management arrangements within the school to support teaching
and learning (Hopkins, 2001).

Increasing understanding about the nature of school improvement,
though, has in itself proved insufficient. Understandings about the component parts from the ISIP analysis have led to a need for clarity about how to
put them together in practice. The early emphasis upon 'know what' has

moved to a need for 'know how'. The shift to school ownership of change inevitably leads to a requirement for greater understanding about how to create 'capacity.' It is to a definition of capacity that we turn in the following section.

Capacity – an exploration

As has been mentioned above, the idea of capacity occurs in the writings of a range of theorists and practitioners involved in school improvement over the last two decades. During this period it has been linked with a wide range of overarching constructs and concepts. These range from Meyer's (1992) general notion of 'readiness', or a staff's preparedness to deal with change, through to Senge's (1990) institution-related image of the 'learning organisation'. Mitchell and Sackney's (2000) concept of a 'learning community' seeks to embrace both of these, and is a way of viewing capacity that we will return to at the end of this section.

The phrase, 'the school's capacity for development' is, then, now widely used. Without a clear focus on 'capacity', a school will be unable to sustain continuous improvement efforts or to manage change effectively. That we know. It is therefore critical to be able to explore, explain and illustrate the concept of 'capacity' in operational terms – and this is more complex and elusive than it might seem.

What follows is an attempt to do this from a number of perspectives. We are seeking to avoid simplistic attempts to 'define' capacity, but rather to reflect its complexity and multidimensionality by taking a number of 'cuts' at it from different aspects of our work and that of others in the field. Finally, we present a conceptual model arising from recent research undertaken at the National College for School Leadership which we have found to be helpful as an organising construct or 'tool' in our work with schools and school leaders.

Our IQEA work has demonstrated that without an equal focus on the internal conditions of the school, innovative work quickly becomes marginalised. These supporting 'conditions' have to be worked on at the same time as the curriculum or other priorities the school has set itself. Conditions are the internal features of the school, the 'arrangements' that enable it to get work done. In terms of the IQEA project, it is these 'conditions' that have provided a working definition of the *development capacity* of the school over the last decade or more (Hopkins, 2001, 2002).

The work of Newman, King and Young (2000) provides another perspective on building learning capacity that complements that of the IQEA work. They argue that professional development is more likely to advance achievement for all students in a school if it addresses not only the learning of individual teachers, but also other dimensions of the organisational capacity of the school. They define *school capacity* as the collective competency of the school as an entity to bring about effective change. They suggest that there are four core components of capacity:

- knowledge, skills and dispositions of individual staff members;
- a professional learning community in which staff work collaboratively to set clear goals for student learning, assess how well students are doing, develop action plans to increase student achievement, whilst being engaged in inquiry and problem-solving;
- programme coherence –'the extent to which the school's programmes for student and staff learning are co-ordinated, focused on clear learning goals and sustained over a period of time' (2000: 5);
- technical resources – high-quality curriculum, instructional material, assessment instruments, technology, workspace, physical environment, etc.

Fullan (2000) comments that this four-part definition of school capacity includes 'human capital' within the first bullet, the knowledge and skills of individuals, but he concludes that no amount of professional development of *individuals* will have an impact if certain *organisational* features are not in place to support and to connect the work.

He maintains that there are two key organisational features in this conceptualisation. The first is the concept of 'professional learning communities'. This provides the 'social capital' aspect of capacity. In other words, the skills of individuals can only be realised if the *relationships* within the schools are continually developing. The other key component of organisational capacity for Fullan is what he calls programme coherence. Since complex social systems have a tendency to produce overload and fragmentation in a non-linear evolving fashion, schools are constantly being bombarded by overwhelming and unconnected innovations (Fullan, 1999). In this sense, the most effective schools are not those that take on the most innovations, but those that are able to integrate, align and coordinate innovations into their own focused programmes.

A third perspective on capacity is provided by Corcoran and Goertz (1995: 27). They point out that the term also relates to 'the maximum or optimum amount of production' and in so doing relates to issues of efficiency – the 'optimal amount of production that can be obtained from a given set of resources and organisational arrangements'. In other words, this perspective includes not only the capacity to manage more, but also to perform optimally in whatever we have to do. It relates to enhancement of process (efficiency) and outcomes (effectiveness). This in turn leads to questions about how the product of the school, which is viewed as being high-quality teaching and learning, can be enhanced, within 'a given set of resources', and how the 'organisational arrangements' can be so designed as to generate synergies, interdependencies and efficiencies much as in Fullan's concept of programme coherence.

A fourth and intriguingly compatible analysis of capacity components is provided in the work of David Hargreaves, through which he explores the notion of 'capital'. Like Corcoran and Goertz, he works backwards from the imperative of 'outcomes' (however defined), seeing three dimensions as critically linked in a causal chain. In order to improve outcomes, schools need to increase 'leverage'- the ability (or capacity) of teachers to enhance student learning. In order to expand leverage a school needs to be able to increase its intellectual capital (what teachers know and can do – the knowledge, skills and dispositions of Newmann, King and Young's definition), which it does especially by developing its ability (or capacity) to create and to transfer knowledge. Critical to effective knowledge creation and transfer, though, is social capital – especially a school's capacity to generate trust and to sustain both internal and external networks (Hargreaves, 2001).

There are some unifying concepts across these four sources and perspectives that can lead us towards an operational model – a conceptual tool for use in school-development work. One is the importance of the people, the leaders, educational professionals and students, and the expansion of their contributions. A second relates to the alignment and synergies created when internal arrangements, connections and teams are working optimally. A third corresponds to the organisational arrangements (the 'programme coherence' and the 'internal networks') which support personal and interpersonal capacity development. The fourth is more subtle, but crucially important. It is the intangible or 'higher order' domain – the territory of shared values, social cohesion, trust, well-being, moral purpose, involvement, care, valuing and being valued – which is the operational field of 4-'leadership'.

This last dimension of capacity returns us to the opening discussion of 'climate' and 'culture' (and takes it further), but it also sets it within a coherent whole that is not independent of people, the interpersonal and the organisational components of schools. It further gives us tools to begin to construct a model. The two key components of such a model will be the concept of the *professional learning community* (the people, interpersonal and organisational arrangements working in developmental or learning synergy) and the idea of *leadership capacity* as the route to generating the moral purpose, shared values, social cohesion and trust to make this happen and to create impetus and alignment.

NCSL's research – developing a model

Shortly after its launch in November 2000, the National College for School Leadership in England initiated a research programme entitled 'Building

Capacity for School Improvement'. The intention was to draw from theory (on the one hand) and from successful schools' practice (on the other) in order to develop a model for capacity that could have practical and applied utility for schools. We are committed to a view that, in defining capacity as a variable in schools, we need to go beyond passive descriptions of school conditions to analysing the processes that build such conditions, and, beyond that, to the ways in which those conditions are mobilised and released in the creative and dynamic enactment of change. Ultimately, all capacity-building notions need to be related to process of change. Whilst maintenance is important in school improvement, it is in the creative operationalisation of change that capacity is most powerfully expressed (Hadfield, 2002).

This is not the place to enlarge upon the National College's research orientation, nor the methodological details of this particular study. It is important, though, to emphasise the College's preoccupation with the application of knowledge – with the translation of theory and research into active tools and models able to support school leaders with the process of improvement and raising student achievement. The discussion of the capacity model needs to be seen in this light. It is derived from deep theoretical underpinnings, but is not an attempt to provide an advanced theoretical model – quite the reverse. The model is an attempt to offer a tool within which operational images of successful practice arising from the research can be located, and which can be used as an analytical and planning tool by schools and school leaders.

The model is built from a framework, which contains five elements which, taken together contribute to what we understand by *capacity*:

1 foundation conditions;
2 the personal;
3 the interpersonal;
4 the organisational;
5 external opportunities.

The synergies, interconnections and the emotional and spiritual glue that arise from and surround these components is the heartland of 'capacity'.

The foundation conditions represent the infrastructural stability without which capacity-building has no foothold. Without them, there is little or no security, respite, time or space to move forward. Managing complex change, and juxtaposing internal and external forces, is inconceivable with-out stable systems, a safe and secure working environment, an appropriate level of orderliness, managed pupil-learning behaviours and a clear sense of purpose and direction. This is not in itself 'capacity' – it is the starting point! In our research we have found, too, that it may need to be addressed both as a separate component (tackling the volatile or the unacceptable) and *simultaneously* , as a part of the personal, interpersonal and organisational development.

The three interconnected elements – personal, interpersonal and organisational – are, as has been argued earlier, at the heart of capacity at the operational (rather than the emotional and spiritual) level. They are the key elements of the Professional Learning Community concept, which has little meaning unless grounded in the reality of these interdependent dimensions. As Mitchell and Sackney (2000) argue: 'Scholars often speak about building capacity without explicating what capacity actually means, what kind of capacity, or capacity for what. That is, there has been insufficient attention to what we might call a curriculum of capacity' – a curriculum built around three pivotal components: personal, interpersonal *and* organisational.

In Mitchell and Sackney's terms, building *personal capacity* relates not only to knowledge and skills, but also to the active and reflective construction of knowledge – a personal and potentially transforming phenomenon. *Interpersonal capacity* involves working together on shared purposes – and taking collective responsibility for each other's learning and well-being. *Organisational capacity* is concerned with building, developing and redesigning structures that create and maintain sustainable organisational processes. Organisational capacity entails creating a flexible system that is open to all sorts of new ideas. It is about honouring diversity and about opening doors and breaking down walls. Organisational capacity is about building a system that invests heavily in professional learning and relationship building.

When a school resolves to build its *personal, interpersonal* and *organisational* dimensions, it is not about simply sharpening the edges of what it already does. It is about doing completely different things – and about doing the same things completely differently. One cannot build a professional learning community by developing in one area and expecting that to suffice. Rather, there needs to be direct, sustained and focused attention on building strength in all three areas so that the synergies can develop. NCSL's work, and that of Mitchell and Sackney, suggests that the element requiring first attention is probably context specific. That is, whether a school starts to build personal, interpersonal or organisational growth will depend on the needs of the individual location – and indicators as to where the most leverage will be obtained.

Finally, schools operate within a context of outside forces, which we have called *external opportunities* in order to emphasise their positive potential to contribute towards improvement. They are the change forces and reform directives so often paralysing, destabilising or debilitating. However, as capacity develops within the organisation, a school develops greater confidence to work in creative and resourceful ways with external agencies and initiatives. It becomes entrepreneurial about opportunities to use external change for internal purposes. External factors can then be used, within the existing framework of organisational imperatives, in order to enhance (rather than to divert or fragment) current ways of working. It is relevant here to pick up on Firestone's (1989) notion of 'capacity to use reform', as this fits well with the notion of internal capacity aiding the utilisation of 'external opportunities'. Firestone states that 'if *will* refers to the commitment to a decision, *capacity* refers to the wherewithal to actually implement it. The capacity to use reform is the extent to which the [school] has the knowledge, skills, personnel, and other resources necessary' (our italics). It relates to Fullan's (1991) idea of schools that are 'entrepreneurial', who exploit external change for internal purposes, or Jackson's complementary (2000) concept of 'intrapreneurialism', as applied to schools that are connected and creative about opportunities for development, both internally and externally – and for finding synergies between the two. In addition, capacity growth within the school increases the likelihood of consultants and external facilitators being used; it strengthens linkages within networks or with universities and other partners and opens the school up to learning from and with others.

As school leaders are well aware, these components are interrelated elements of complex change, rather than separable ingredients as 'ultimately, building a professional learning community involves ongoing attention to the interdependent elements of a model of capacity-building' (Mitchell and Sackney, 2000).

What we have called *the heart of capacity* – and we are uncomfortable about the terminology – is, as discussed earlier, an outcome of the integration of the above three. (The stronger and more interconnected the elements of professional learning community, the greater the school's capacity.) It involves values, moral purpose, social cohesion and includes also leadership of the capacity-building process itself. It includes the depth and breadth of leadership. It arises from the synergies, interdependencies and 'connectedness' between the other core elements. Its four core components are:

1   distributed leadership;
2   social capital and cohesion (and trust);
3   values coherence and moral agency;
4   intellectual capital – knowledge creation, transfer and utilisation.

From our work, the critical dependent variable amongst the four is *leadership*.

The components can be formulated into an interconnected model. The model does not seek to be definitive. It is, though, helpful to us in our work. It is both a representation of a complex reality and a tool to help schools with analysis, understanding, collaborative planning, alignment and purposeful action. In this way the model becomes an active agent for school leaders and external facilitators to make sense of the world of the school and the capacity-creating process.

For this reason, within NCSL's applied research project we have differentiated between capacity itself, a static concept ('the school's potential to give form to strategic possibilities') and the process of capacity-building, an active one ('those strategies that allow the school to harness the abilities, skills and knowledge acquired during one process of change to facilitate subsequent changes'). It is this latter process that leads to capacity (Hadfield, 2002). Such a concept of capacity-building is not new. It is closely related to Senge's (1990) notion of the school becoming a 'self-developing force'. NCSL is keen also to extend this beyond the school, to take in the notion of networks and external relationships and partnerships, a broader sense of 'self' – and this is consistent with the College's other research and development programmes, which include a focus upon networks, and upon the particularities of context (Jackson and Southworth, 2001).

This strategic and active view of capacity also raises an issue (hinted at earlier) that is only rarely addressed, both in the research literature and in policy initiatives. Much school improvement work assumes in practice that all schools are the same, and that any strategy will work as well in one school as another. Yet evidence of the research on school effectiveness is unequivocal – schools are differentially effective (see, for example, Teddlie and Reynolds, 2000). This leads to the conclusion that schools at different levels of effectiveness, or in different contextual environments, require different school improvement strategies. When circumstances exist that are less supportive of change, it is necessary to concentrate much more in the initial stages of development work on creating those foundation conditions within the school that facilitate development. Work on the priorities of deeper capacity creation may be limited until these conditions are in place.

This is not well trodden territory. Nor is their space here for a full consideration of what is complex terrain. However, the model is specifically framed in such a way that it can recognise both the developmental 'growth state' of a school and the contextual factors that impact upon its developmental capacity. It is perhaps sufficient to say here that we know that different kinds of school require different kinds of intervention (Hopkins et al., 1997). We also know that for professional learning community growth and external support (two elements of the model) schools require both internal and external networking – a theme that we have also written about elsewhere (Hopkins, 2001).

The role of networks in supporting school improvement and building capacity

There has recently been much international interest in the role of networks in supporting school improvement (e.g. OECD, 1999). There are, however, various interpretations of the network concept. Although networks bring together those with like-minded interests, they are more than just opportunities to share 'good practice'. The following definition of networks emerged from an analysis of effective networks identified by the OECD (quotation and discussion in this section based on Hopkins, 2001, ch. 10):

> Networks are purposeful social entities characterised by a commitment to quality, rigour, and a focus on outcomes. They are also an effective means of supporting innovation in times of change. In education, networks promote the dissemination of good practice, enhance the professional development of teachers, support capacity building in schools, mediate between centralised and decentralised structures, and assist in the process of re-structuring and re-culturing educational organisations and systems.

The qualities exhibited by such networks are, however, not easily acquired. A number of key conditions need to be in place if networks are to realise their potential as agents of educational innovation. In line with the argument advanced so far in this chapter, networks in education also have a key role to play in supporting innovation and school improvement and in building both school and system capacity. Accordingly, networks need to be regarded as support structures for innovative schools, not only in disseminating 'good practice', but also in helping schools to share and understand 'good process' – the capacity-creating processes that lead to 'best practice'. They are also important in overcoming the traditional isolation of schools, and to a certain extent even challenging traditional hierarchical system structures. In the past most school systems have operated almost exclusively through individual units; be they teachers, departments, schools or local agencies. Such isolation may have been appropriate during times of stability, but during times of change there is a need to 'tighten the loose coupling', to increase collaboration and to establish more fluid and responsive structures.

It is important to realise, however, that networks do not just facilitate innovation. By offering the possibility of new ways of working, networks can also be an innovation in themselves. This is particularly important in contemporary educational systems, as there is currently a tendency to reduce 'meso-level' support for schools. It may well be that these support structures – the role that local education authorities or school districts, local universities, and other agencies have traditionally played – are also more effective at buttressing the status quo, rather than supporting change. They may serve both schools and the system better by adapting to a facilitation mode that is respectful to and adds value to the efforts of school-to-school networks.

What is needed are not outmoded institutions, but more creative and responsive structures for working with and between schools. Networks can provide a means of facilitating innovation and change as well as contributing to large-scale reform. They offer the potential for 'reinventing' the meso-level by promoting different forms of collaboration, linkages, and multifunctional partnerships. These are sometimes referred to as 'crossover structures' (Fullan, 2000). In this respect the network enables stakeholders to make connections and to synergise activities around common priorities.

One key reason why national reforms have not yet had the desired impact is because government policy on education has not always been adequately informed by what is known about how schools improve. This provides a strong argument for government to embrace networks, not only as a strategy to assist in the implementation of its reform agenda, but also as a capacity-building innovation in its own right. Without some form of networking, it is highly unlikely that the aspirations for governmental programmes of educational reform, particularly in decentralised systems, will be realised. If one issue is certain it is that the future of schooling requires a systemic perspective, which implies a high degree of consistency across the policy spectrum and an unrelenting focus on student achievement and learning. Networks, as a natural infrastructure for both innovation and the informing of government policy, provide a means for doing just that, which is highly consistent with the capacity-creating theme of this chapter.

Implications for leadership – distributed leadership as capacity building

In our research with school leaders, they have favoured the concept of capacity 'growth' rather than 'building', preferring ecological rather than construction metaphors (Hadfield, 2002). Although the model that we have developed appears to some extent to be 'constructed', this attitude fits with our own evolving thinking. The core elements (the personal, interpersonal and organisational) together create the elements for professional learning communities – which are grown, not made. Equally, the components at the core of capacity as we have described it (distributed leadership, social cohesion and trust, shared values, moral purpose and intellectual capital) are all organic and authentic organisational and communal qualities.

As we have described it, capacity is fundamentally a metaphorical concept. In this it has much in common with notions of 'leadership'. Such an analysis clearly has profound implications for the headteacher's role, and in particular the central importance of the notion of distributed leadership. Above all, we have been arguing for a concept of capacity that demonstrates flexibility, adaptability, responsiveness and adroitness in processing continuous change in a volatile and unpredictable environment. It is a notion of capacity that is synonymous with concepts of distributed or – perhaps even more compatible with the metaphor – 'dispersed' leadership.

This concluding section of the chapter explores issues relating to this core capacity component – dispersed leadership – and its interrelationship with the organisational, interpersonal and personal components of school. Distributed or dispersed leadership is central to capacity creation – we have hopefully established that. However, we would also contend that distributed leadership cannot happen if schools stay as they are. This section explores this paradox and its implications for capacity growth.

Despite more than two decades of writing about organisational learning (Argyris, 1976; Senge, 1990), community leadership (Sergiovanni, 1994) and servant leadership (Greenleaf, 1970; Spears, 1995) we are still in a position of needing to develop understandings about what leadership really involves when it is distributed, how schools might function and act differently and what operational images of distributed leadership in action might look like.

There are some basic questions we need to ask in order to clarify thinking and to offer a basis for debate. To us the key questions would seem to be the following, and, having set them down, we will go on to discuss each of them in turn:

- What do we mean by *leadership* when we are talking about distributed manifestations?
- What are the organisational implications?
- How might distributed leadership operate in practice?
- What is the role of the designated 'leader' – the headteacher?

What do we mean by distributed leadership?

Leading is an enacted activity. It is a doing word. It exists only through its manifestations. It is profoundly interpersonal (can you lead without others?) and exists via direct impact upon or exchange with others or through their perceptions of leadership actions. When we talk with teachers about their headteachers, for example, they describe what he or she does, how he or she relates with them or others. They are as preoccupied with what leaders do as with the rhetoric of what they say. They want to see the talk walked!

Leader*ship* is more complex than leading. It is as much akin to potential energy as it is to kinetic. Leadership is about the latent as well as the lived and enacted expressions of leading. As metaphor, it has much in common with the notion of intellectual capital – the potentially banked and available capacity to be drawn, and the interest that can be added! As such it potentially exists very widely within an organisation.

Leadership, as we have come to understand it, does not exist in a literal sense. If it did, independent of context, then effective leaders would be equally successful whatever the context. (The history of football management tells us that this is not the case.) If, then, leadership does not reside in one person and is not independent of context, what is it?

Leadership, from this perspective, resides in the potential available to be released within an organisation. In essence, it is the intellectual capital of the organisation residing (sometimes dormant or unexpressed) within its members. The role of the leader is to harness, focus, liberate, empower and align that leadership towards common purposes and, by so doing, build and release capacity.

The logic of this argument takes us to another aspect of the question. If leadership is a shared function, and if it only expresses itself with and through others, how is it denoted? Who 'allocates' it? How is it 'distributed'? Intriguingly, when analysed in this light, the growth metaphor mentioned earlier becomes important – and the organisational implications are profound.

Firstly, its increase in capacity terms is not about key, hierarchically highly placed leaders getting better – it is not about training the few. It is about creating the spaces, the contexts and the opportunities for expansion, enhancement and growth.

Secondly – and this is a crucially important concept – it cannot be imposed. Leadership has to be bestowed, given wilfully by those who are to be led. We *allow* ourselves to be led, just as we allow ourselves to be coached. It is a reciprocal relationship.

As such, and thirdly, it cannot be delegated. Growth in leadership is about empowerment – opportunity, space, support, and capacity growth. Jobs and tasks are 'delegated' (passed down a managerial structure) but roles and the scope they offer provide the invitations for leadership.

As so far described, leadership capacity can be seen as being an amorphous concept. Its purposefulness (and its accountabilities) comes from the other elements of *capacity*, the tightness around values and the moral purpose (the shared beliefs and the urgency to act and to achieve together for higher-order purposes), the intellectual capital (the combined and shared and expanding knowledge base) and the social capital (relationships and trust). As Sergiovanni writes (2001), schools need to be 'culturally tight and managerially loose. Teachers and other school workers respond much more to their values and beliefs, to how they are socialised and the norms of their work group than they do to managerial controls'. It is tough love, leadership!

So, values make leadership tight. There are, though, other critical concepts to the capacity dimension of leadership. One is synergy, allowing fluidity and flexibility between people – variable leadership patterns and flexible teams. Another is alignment, moving this distributed function in a common direction utilising new organisational metaphors, too. Such leadership patterns not only liberate leadership, they are emancipatory for the person in the professional. Those who work in schools give of who they are as well as what they do. The release and expression of potential through leadership creates the context for personal as well as professional realisation. Leading the growth of leadership capacity is an intensely human and social process – deeply emotionally and spiritually intelligent. Tending to leadership capacity is a caring and authentic business.

What are the organisational implications?

Leadership is multi-directional. It can function down an organisation, can grow up an organisation or can operate across an organisation. Problems occur both vertically and horizontally.

Paradoxically, the most complex and difficult form of leadership for dispersed and capacity-building models is that which operates down through management systems, because it then becomes entwined with power relationships and role responsibilities. It is not that leadership and power are incompatible, but, having noted earlier that leadership has to be bestowed, power (or authority) does not necessarily facilitate this – the right to lead has to be earned, granted by the followers. So, as leadership cannot be imposed, the conflation of power (managerial relationships) and empowerment (leadership relationships) proves problematic. The more hierarchical the management structure, the more the liberation of leadership capacity is likely to be stifled. This has huge implications for the organisational arrangements of schools. The more the status and worth systems of schools relate to position in hierarchy, the harder it is for dispersed leadership to operate. Peter Senge (1990) argues that in learning organisations leaders have to leave their status at the door. Even more problematic, though, is for others to leave the leader's status at the door.

Lateral leadership is equally problematic. For leadership to operate across an organisation, opportunities for collaboration between adults of different role and status levels need naturally to occur across and between what might otherwise be organisationally separate and balkanised cells or units (departments, faculties, phase teams etc). Organisationally, schools find this hard. So, if leadership cannot readily be delegated down the system (because people have to be empowered), and if opportunities to lead across the system are problematic (because of organisational barriers) then, for leadership to grow, the argument is that 'school as organisation' must adapt and reshape its practices in order to generate natural contexts for people to take responsibility in working with and through others. What is needed is the development of internal networks (Demos, 2001) – a theme explored earlier.

How does distributed leadership function or operate in practice?

There is a relationship between leadership and learning. Linda Lambert (1998: 00) argues the interdependence of the two. She views opportunities for collaborative learning as being the core activity for the expansion of leadership capacity. For her, the key element in the development of leadership 'is the notion of learning together, and the construction of meaning and knowledge collectively and collaboratively. Such leadership allows opportunities to surface and it mediates perceptions, values, beliefs, information and assumptions through continuous conversations'. Similarly, Michael Fullan (1998) offers an insight into the organisational conditions that can give rise to multiple forms of leadership when he writes that:

> All change is a hypothesis – a process of action, enquiry and experimentation to create a cumulative and collective knowledge about what works and how it works from within. Engaging staff in this process is a means of reculturing. This change to the ways of working – the norms, values and relationships – is a process of restructuring. . . . There are no clear solutions. Life is a path you beat while you walk it. It is the walking that beats the path. It is not the path that makes the walk.
>
> (Fullan, 1998: 00)

Leadership opportunities such as inquiry partnerships, action learning sets and study groups generate a dialectic within schools. This model of capacity creation – knowledge-driven, socially cohesive, purposeful – encourages the study of practice and the collaborative generation of ideas. It involves collective meaning-making in the light of emerging knowledge and understandings from inquiry. It is where leadership and organisational growth collide; where knowledge creation and the implementation of change connect, because 'such leadership also creates action that grows out of these new and shared understandings. This transformative dimension (positive and purposeful change) is the core of leadership – and, by definition, it is dispersed or distributed' (Lambert, 1998: 00).

Lambert and Fullan are not alone in drawing this relationship between collaborative activity, leadership and capacity. Silins and Mulford (2001) in a major study involving Australian schools concluded that dispersed forms of leadership are characterised by 'shared learning through teams of staff working together to augment the range of knowledge and skills available for the organisation to change and anticipate future developments'. They further discovered a positive relationship between such forms of leadership learning and student achievement.

It follows, then, that groups of teachers, working together on collaborative inquiry or planning activity, led by someone whose leadership is not entwined with role status, provide opportunities for the expression and growth of leadership capacity. It also provides the lateral learning impetus required to break down organisational barriers and to foster cultural norms hospitable to internal networks. Knowledge creation and knowledge-sharing are processes at the heart of leadership of collaborative enquiry. Capacity generation is the outcome – of both the process and the products.

What is the role of the designated leader?

Leadership is not trait theory – leadership and leader are not the same thing. Leadership is about collaborative learning that leads to purposeful change. This learning has direction towards higher aspirations and shared purposes. Organisational redesign is required to develop contexts in which such leadership and learning happen naturally. Such design change can facilitate professional engagement.

Everyone has both the potential and the entitlement to contribute towards leadership. The designated leader's role in the scenario described here is to facilitate this entitlement – to create the organisational conditions, the climate and the support for all members to be able to contribute their latent leadership – to release both the kinetic and the potential energy of leadership. Leading is a skilled and complicated undertaking, but one that every member of the school community can learn in a supportive context. Leadership, after all, is democracy in action. It involves the valuing of the multiple voices that make up the lived experience of school – and in this way will inevitably begin to embrace pupil voices, too.

Expressed as such, leadership is a collective endeavour. School change is a shared undertaking. The improvement journey requires the capacity that shared, inclusive and collaborative activity can bring. Leadership of this order requires the redistribution of power and authority. It follows that in organisations seeking to learn together, school leaders give away power, distribute leadership and support others to be successful.

Consistent with the changed forms of leadership action outlined in the above discussion, all of the images in Joseph Murphy's (Murphy *et al.*, 1993, adapted) metaphors for modern school leaders have resonance:

- Headteacher as Leader
- School Leader as Moral Agent
- School Leader as Organisational Architect
- School Leader as Social Architect
- School Leader as Educator
- School Leader as Servant

- School Leader as Member of a Community
- School Leadership as Capacity-Building

In organisations where leadership is liberated, available to all, related to collaborative processes and learning, the role of the symbolic leader (the headteacher) is, as Murphy suggests, pivotal, but not superordinate. In moving towards distributed leadership models, the leader is the critical change agent – the guardian and facilitator of transitions. Transition management is the new focus for transformation.

Such leaders, then, will create the social capital that facilitates distributive leadership and collaboration – a social capital built on trust. Trust relationships allow open engagement and knowledge-sharing. Such leaders will unite the school around shared values and higher-order purposes. They will be articulate in mobilising values identification and alignment and in articulating and reaffirming beliefs. They will 'disseminate eloquence' (Weick, 1976) and will hold people accountable to shared value commitments.

They will have the moral courage progressively to restructure the school around twin strands of higher-order purpose – distributive leadership and the values of the school.

Commentary

Schools are not currently well designed for either capacity creation or distributed leadership. Some are weak on the foundation conditions – turbulent, under strain, riven by conflicting pressures. Others are rendered incoherent by the forces of external change, the reform agenda and the expectations of multiple accountabilities. Some schools are inarticulate about shared values, unclear about the beliefs that unite them. Most (secondary in particular) have structures designed when stability, efficiency and the management of stasis were the expectations. They are unsuited to a context of multiple change and creativity. Distributed leadership, the unifying component of *capacity*, requires flexible organisations, metabolisms rather than structures, purposeful permutations of teams and collaborations – and widely available opportunities for leadership. Few schools currently function comfortably in that kind of way.

Schools are not currently structured in ways that facilitate either the growth of leadership or lateral leadership. Predominantly, leadership is currently locked into management structures. If we are to achieve distributive leadership models, we must therefore redesign the internal social architecture of schools. Such redesign should normalise collaborative learning in which leadership can be widely available and unrelated to role status. It should involve a separation of management (maintenance) and leadership (learning and development). Organisational routines and processes should also be redesigned to facilitate widespread leadership and knowledge-sharing.

Through the liberation of leadership in this way, a premium will also be placed upon alignment and common purpose. Highest-order alignment comes from shared values, beliefs and purposes. Designated leaders (head-teachers) in such schools will enact and live out the values, both as leader and follower. They will take seriously their own learning – educational, pedagogical and interpersonal. They will be coach and facilitator, social architect and community builder.

Distributed leadership occupies the spaces between the pebbles in the jar. It is the cohesion that surrounds the management structures, the coherence, and it grows within and works across schools. It requires spaces. Leaders in such schools will orchestrate and nurture these spaces – create the 'shelter conditions' for the leadership of collaborative learning. Whilst management structures provide the organisational stability, distributed leadership forma-tions provide the lubricant for community and social cohesion. It requires schools that place a premium upon social capital and emotionally intelligent internal relationships. It requires spiritual alignment, too – schools in which people work together for higher-order moral purposes. Distributed leader-ship requires social capital and trust relationships. We need to like one another and respect one another.

Distributed leadership also requires shelter from external pressures and accountabilities – and leaders who will deflect, interpret and energise a school by being opportunistic, optimistic and aspirational in the interpreta-tion of public expectations. Not only is distributed leadership as set out in this chapter crucial to stronger learning and educational communities for children, it is also the means to mobilise, to grow and to expand the capacity of schools to manage multiple change.

References

Argyris, C. (1976) *Increasing Leadership Effectiveness*, New York, Wiley-Interscience.

Corcoran, T. and Goertz, M. (1995), 'Instrumental Strategies and High Performance Schools', *Educational Researcher*, 24(9): 27–31.

Crandall, D. (ed.) (1982) *People, Policies and Practices: Examining the Chain of School Improvement* (volumes 1–10), Andover, MA, The Network.

Crandall, D., Eiseman, J. and Louis, K.S. (1986) 'Strategic Planning Issues that Bear on the Success of School Improvement Efforts', *Educational Administration Quarterly*, 22(2): 21–53.

Demos (2001) 'Cracking Good Ideas: Understanding Innovation in Public Policy', paper arising from New Opportunities Fund sponsored seminars, January 2001.

Firestone, W.A. (1989) 'Using reform: Conceptualizing District Initiative', *Educational Evaluation and Policy Analysis*, 11(2): 151–64.

Fullan, M. (1991) *The New Meaning of Educational Change*, New York, Teachers College Press.

Fullan, M. (1998) 'Leadership for the 21st Century: Breaking the Bonds of Dependency', *Educational Leadership*, 55(7).

Fullan, M. (1999) *Change Forces: The Sequel*, London, Falmer.

Fullan, M. (2000) 'The Return of Large-Scale Reform', *Journal of Educational Change*, 2(1): 5–28.

Fullan, M. (2001) *Leadership in a Culture of Change*, San Francisco, Jossey-Bass.

Greenleaf, R.K. (1970) *Servant as Leader*, London, John Wiley.

Hadfield, M. (2002) 'Growing Capacity for School Development', NCSL Research Report, forthcoming.

Hargreaves, D. (2001) 'A Capital Theory of School Effectiveness & Improvement', *British Educational Research Journal*, 27(4): 487–503.

Hopkins, D. (ed.) (1986) *In-service Training and Educational Development*, London, Croom Helm.

Hopkins, D. (ed.) (1987) *Improving the Quality of Schooling*, Lewes, Falmer.

Hopkins, D. (1987) *Knowledge Information Skills and the Curriculum*, London, British Library.

Hopkins, D. (1990) 'The International School Improvement Project (ISIP) and Effective Schooling: Towards a Synthesis', *School Organisation*, 10(83): 129–94.

Hopkins, D. (2001) *School Improvement for Real*, London, RoutledgeFalmer.

Hopkins, D. (2002) *Improving the Quality of Education for All*, 2nd edn, London, David Fulton.

Hopkins, D., Ainscow, M. and West, M. (1994) *School Improvement in an Era of Change*, London, Cassell.

Hopkins, D., Harris, A. and Jackson, D. (1997) 'Understanding the School's Capacity for Development: Growth States and Strategies', *School Leadership and Management*, 17(3): 401–11.

Huberman, M. and Miles, M.B. (1984) *Innovation up Close*, New York, Plenum.

Jackson, D. (2000) 'School Improvement and the Planned Growth of Leadership Capacity', paper presented at BERA Conference, Cardiff, September 2000.

Jackson, D. and Southworth, G. (2001) 'Braiding Knowledge for Impact: Metaphor and Reality in NCSL's Research Strategy', paper presented at the UCEA Conference, Cincinnati, November 2001.

Lambert, L. (1998) *Building Leadership Capacity in Schools*, Alexandria, VA, ASCD.

Meyer, J.W. (1992) 'Conclusion: Institutionalization and the Rationality of Formal Organizational Structure', in J.W. Meyer and W.R. Scott (eds), *Organizational Environments: Ritual and Rationality*, Newbury Park, London, New Delhi, Sage.

Mitchell, C. and Sackney, L. (2000) *Profound Improvement: Building Capacity for a Learning Community*, Lisse, NL, Swets and Zeitlinger.

Murphy, J., Beck, X. and Lynn, G. (1993) *Understanding the Principalship: Metaphorical Themes 1920s–1990s*, New York, Teachers College Press.

NCSL (2001) 'Leadership for Transforming Learning' (Think Tank Report chaired by Professor David Hopkins), Nottingham, National College for School Leadership.

Newmann, F., King, B. and Young, S.P. (2000) 'Professional Development that Addresses School Capacity: Lessons from Urban Elementary Schools', paper presented to Annual Meeting of the American Educational Research Association, 3 April, New Orleans.

Nisbet, J. (ed.) (1973) *Creativity of the School*, Paris, OECD.

OECD (1999) *Innovating Schools*, Paris, OECD/CERI.

Rutter, M., Maughan, B., Mortimore, P. and Ouston, J., with Smith, A. (1979) *Fifteen Thousand Hours*, London, Open Books.

Senge, P. (1990) *The Fifth Discipline*, New York, Doubleday.

Sergiovanni, T.J. (1994) *Building Community in Schools*, San Francisco, Jossey-Bass.

Sergiovanni, T.J. (2001) *Leadership: What's in it for Schools?*, London, Routledge-Falmer.

Silins, H. and Mulford, B. (2001) 'Reframing Schools: The Case for System, Teacher and Student Learning', paper presented at the Eighth International Literacy and Education Research Network Conference on Learning, Spetses, Greece, 4–8 July 2001.

Spears, L. (1995) *Reflections on Leadership*, London, John Wiley.

Teddlie, C. and Reynolds, D. (2000) *The International Handbook of School Effectiveness Research*, London, Falmer.

van Velzen, W., Miles, M., Ekholm, M., Hameyer, U. and Robin, D. (1985) *Making School Improvement Work – A Conceptual Guide to Practice*, Leuven, Belgium, ACCO.

Weick, K. (1976) 'Educational Organisations as Loosely Coupled Systems', *Administrative Science Quarterly*, 21(1): 1–19.

Part III

Building leadership capacity

Chapter 6

Building capacity versus growing schools

Mark Hadfield

Introduction

Soon after you start reading about the idea of capacity two observations strike you. First the concept of 'capacity' has been applied to so many different aspects of individuals and schools in the last twenty years. Policy makers, theorists and practitioners have used it to account for the failure of school reform programmes (Spillane and Thompson, 1997; Leithwood and Jantzi, 2000). It has been used to connect key theoretical areas together, such as leadership and organisational change. For example, Dibbon (1999) employs the idea of organisational learning capacity to link transformational leadership with the idea of organisational learning. It has also been used to justify new working relationships and leadership styles within schools (Jackson, 2000). Second as a concept it appears to have gone in and out of fashion over the last twenty years, with various writers charting its rise and fall (O'Day *et al.*, 1995; Seller, 2001). These shifts in popularity reflect changes in its relevance to the dominant management and organisational theories of the time. Putting these two observations together one begins to wonder whether the hybridity and longevity of capacity is based on its unique conceptual power or whether it has become a convenient catchall term for any issues related to school development.

The idea of schools having a certain 'capacity', or capacities, for dealing with change, for improvement or for leadership is now increasingly being discussed amongst theorists in the UK and elsewhere (Hopkins and Reynolds, 2001) in reference to what some call 'Third Age' school-improvement projects. In the UK there could even be said to be an 'official' definition in that the national inspection authority, Ofsted, uses the term when assessing poorly performing schools' ability to maintain their improvement out of 'special measures' by asking whether they have developed 'the capacity (that is the commitment, strategy and systems in place) to secure further improvement' (Ofsted, 1997: 3).

In this chapter I do not want to focus on the question, 'What is capacity?', or chart its various incarnations. Rather I want to look at its relevance to current school leaders and the issues they face. The practical and theoretical utility of the idea of capacity, and the notion of building capacity, has to be judged not just by its ability to help school leaders meet pressing pragmatic demands but also by the way it helps them construct the problems they face. Does it support them in clearly defining the challenges they face? How they prioritise them? How they respond? If not, then the current popularisation of capacity becomes in the words of one headteacher I recently interviewed, 'just another new idea to keep school-improvement researchers in business'.

To explore its utility I want to move between the current literature on capacity and my own research with school leaders (Day *et al.*, 2000), particularly a recent project in which I had the opportunity to interview some fifty headteachers from schools identified as having undergone recent high levels of improvement or having sustained a high level of effectiveness. During the project I explored with the headteachers what 'capacity' meant to them, the development of leadership capacity within their schools and to what extent capacity-building featured within their school-improvement agendas. A number of health warnings have to be applied to any analysis based on a series of group interviews with only fifty headteachers. Their comments, though, provide not only an interesting snap shot of their initial reactions but also reveal how closely current theoretical frameworks match with the practices and beliefs of successful headteachers.

In this chapter I want to concentrate on the reflective potential of the idea of capacity, particularly its ability to support school leaders to reflect critically on the nature of school leadership and improvement. In Chapter 7 I discuss the practical issues of focusing on 'capacity' and how it fits into the wider debates around accountability and the measurement of improvement.

Does the concept of capacity encourage leaders to reflect critically?

There is an old cliché, 'There is nothing as practical as a good theory', so why should we be concerned about whether the ideas of capacity and capacity-building can engender critical reflection? Surely if the writings in the area can provide leaders with effective new ways of acting and help them put some of their existing ideas into practice, then why should we be concerned with whether it makes them critically reflect?

In part the answer to this question is another cliché: 'We don't encounter problems we construct them'. Schon (1993) argues that in dealing with many social problems, such as how to improve schools and pupil achievement, a great deal of effort is wasted and ineffective because we operate with the wrong kind of stories or 'generative metaphor' which leads us to set the wrong problems and hence develop the wrong solutions:

Problem settings are mediated, I believe, by the 'stories' people tell about troublesome situations – stories in which they describe what is wrong and what needs fixing. When we examine the problem-setting stories told by the analysts and practitioners of social policy, it becomes apparent that the framing of problems often depends upon metaphors underlying the stories that generate problem setting and set the direction of problem solving . . . The notion of generative metaphor then becomes an interpretive tool for the critical analysis of social policy. My point here is not that we *ought* to think metaphorically about social policy problems, but that we *do* already think about them in terms of certain pervasive, tacit generative metaphors; and that we ought to become critically aware of these generative metaphors, to increase the rigor and precision of our analysis of social policy problems.

(Schon, 1993: 138)

Defining the issues and problems we face in improving schools, thinking about schools as organisations and the nature of leadership, all involve us in using some form of generative metaphor. If we take Schon's warning seriously then in part the increased use of capacity reflects a possible failure in the way in which school improvement has been conceptualised to date. If our current metaphors are 'incorrect' then the problems we have constructed and the solutions we are adopting are likely to result in failure. The key question is whether the generative metaphors on which the notions of capacity and capacity-building are based support school leaders in constructing the 'right' problems and help them to articulate the issues they face in improving schools.

Generative metaphors about capacity

When I first started to reflect on 'capacity' it brought to mind a series of metaphors based around energy, with notions of batteries storing capacity, and questions about how it was created and released. Lambert (1998) uses a slightly more complex 'energy' metaphor to stress the dynamic and interconnected nature of capacity when discussing the growth of leadership capacity.

This concept [leadership capacity] is broader than the total sum of its 'leaders', for it also involves an energy flow or synergy generated by those who choose to lead. Sometimes we think of our reactions in an energized environment as being caught up in the excitement and stimulation of an idea or a movement. It is this wave of energy and purpose that engages and pulls others into the work of leadership.

(Lambert, 1998: 5)

Current leadership and school-improvement theorists have drawn on much broader sets of generative metaphors, with slightly more complex theories of energy than batteries and circuits:

> The current model of schools is based on 17th century scientific theory of simple cause and effect relationships. The new sciences, for example quantum theory, chaos theory and complexity theory, provide a new world conception underpinned by webs of relationships and inter-connectedness created by energy (Capra, 1991). This means that any one action has a rippling effect on its environment. In line with these ideas, internal capacity needs to be viewed as a more generic and holistic concept.
>
> (Stoll, 1999: 506)

Notions of holism, reactivity and interconnectedness lie at the heart of many of the current generative metaphors of capacity. Theorists want to stress the links between different elements of a school, the types of capacities they potentially house and how these can be developed and connected. It is through these connections and linkages that capacity can build:

> Individuals feel confident in their own capacity, in the capacity of their colleagues and in the capacity of the school.
>
> (Mitchell and Sackney, 2000: 78)

In the search for more holistic and interconnected metaphors a wide range of theoretical frameworks have been drawn upon, from the biological to chaos theory. Hannay *et al.* (2001) in their discussion of the links between chaos theory and school restructuring and reculturing used the metaphors of beating butterfly wings and hurricanes to depict the fragility and inter-connectedness of school reform. A little less prosaically Stoll (1999) used an organic metaphor, the amoeba, to depict how key influences on a school's internal capacity interact and affect its development.

> An amoeba-like shape depicts the school. This emphasises the dynamic and adaptive nature of school; in many ways they could be seen as organisms.
>
> (Stoll, 1999: 506)

Mitchell and Sackney (2000) used a rather mixed metaphor, bringing together organic growth and the flow of a river, as they discussed capacity and capacity-building across and between the different aspects of a school.

> We propose a recursive model in which the three categories (individual, interpersonal and organisational) mutually influence one another, and

growth in each category is built upon prior growth in itself and other categories, and builds a formation for subsequent growth. . . . Growth (and limits) will occur simultaneously in all three. Capacity builds not in a smooth, linear flow but in eddies and swells as well as in dips and depressions when no learning appears to be going on. . . . Growing seasons can yield the capacity to illuminate the mysteries of life and learning; non-growing seasons can yield the capacity to consolidate prior learning.

(Mitchell and Sackney, 2000: 12)

If these theorists were getting excited by different metaphors of capacity what were the reactions from the headteachers I interviewed about how they developed the capacity of their schools? Many of whom were being introduced for the first time, if not to new ideas, then certainly to new terminology.

It's complex, capacity, you need to grasp what you really mean by it in simple terms. It isn't a terminology one really uses, it's that sort of alien feeling.

(Primary headteacher)

Practitioners' views of capacity

There are no agreed criteria for judging the reflective potential of a 'new' concept. I want therefore to focus on two aspects: first, the barriers that stopped capacity being used as a reflective tool, those aspects or connotations that either caused it to be too quickly disregarded, made it unappealing, or led to its being applied incorrectly; second, and more important on whether it actually helped the headteachers clarify what they saw as their problems, whether it supported them in evaluating their current practice and helped them clarify what they should do next.

Within the context of school improvement and capacity-building it is this ability of a new theory or concept to aid communication by making the tacit aspects of professional knowledge explicit which ultimately defines its utility. This is because the ability to articulate these aspects of their professional knowledge base is, as Fullan (1999) stresses, one of the key tools leaders have to create what he terms 'living companies', or what others have called learning organisations

The secret to living companies . . . learning communities or whatever we wish to use, is that they consist of intricate embedded interaction . . . which converts tacit knowledge to explicit knowledge on an on-going basis.

(Fullan, 1999: 15)

The difficulty of making such knowledge explicit, and developing these intricate interactions, is not to be underestimated, as one headteacher related:

> One of my governors asked me What's the secret of your success? I was nonplussed, I couldn't articulate it. I realised that much of what I was doing and still am doing is very instinctive. It's all sorts of competencies and skills I have assimilated.
>
> (Secondary headteacher)

The importance of new concepts being embedded within actions and wider personal frameworks of values and theories also needs to be stressed. Just because a term or issue becomes popular and enters the discourse of leadership and school improvement doesn't necessarily mean that it is actually being used for the purposes it was intended for. Head teachers in the UK over the last ten years have become skilled at subverting new ideas and policies to their own agendas:

> I think you have a double reaction when you come across a word like this [capacity]. The first one is to feel alienated. This is something I don't know. What is this about? Are we keeping researchers in work? Then I think the more seasoned British educational headteacher approach is to say, 'How can I subvert this to do what I want to do in my school?' That is a very human thing. I can see all sorts of ways that one can use this concept usefully.
>
> (Secondary headteacher)

Barriers

Headteachers have not only been bombarded by a great many new ideas and policies, but at times have felt manipulated and undermined by the way they have been used. Not unsurprisingly, then, the first barrier encountered was the fear that this was just another buzzword that would be used 'on them' rather than a useful idea 'for them'.

> I felt very de-skilled by the term, this is another term I don't understand or know about.
>
> (Secondary headteacher)

> I don't like the word capacity I think it's just another buzzword. I don't really see the need for another set of terminology. I put the word ability in. Improve the school's abilities.
>
> (Primary headteacher)

The above headteachers were not alone in wanting initially to replace 'capacity' with more familiar and, for them, meaningful terms such as 'potential'.

Initially the term capacity, at least for these headteachers, was difficult to apply because its novelty was outweighed by its seeming similarity with more familiar constructs, especially those current within the literature on school improvement and change management.

> Is it a linguistic issue or a conceptual issue? If you use capacity as a stand-alone word it needs other things to go with it. If it's conceptual we need to tease in what way capacity is different to some of the conceptual frameworks that have existed in the past in relation to change and the management of change.
>
> (Secondary headteacher)

These, though, were initial barriers which most teachers persevered through. The next barrier was rather more challenging. The term capacity itself seemed to have the very mechanistic connotations that its current popularisers wanted to avoid. The discussion of these connotations, and their rejection, began to create clear water between the notion of capacity and other metaphors of improvement and development.

Helping articulate the tacit

Probably one of the major ways in which we start to clarify and articulate our own views and approaches is to reject the views of others, however we might interpret them. This was the case when we started to unpack the issue of capacity and particularly the nature of its growth. The initial reactions from the headteachers were that the term 'capacity' seemed to hint at there being a limit to the development of a school:

> It seems to have a very sort of limiting effect as if the capacity of something is how much it can hold and it more or less seems to be saying the school can develop to a certain limit and there is this finite ability to change and I don't think that is true of schools.
>
> (Primary headteacher)

The discussion of whether capacity was finite or infinite arose because the term suggested the measurement of a fixed phenomena or static entity, the amount of liquid held by a bottle, the size of an engine or the number of people that could be accommodated by a stadium.

I also feel it's a rather mechanistic term, it's redolent of either a finite body of potential change or whatever, capacity seems to be finite and perhaps it ought to be infinite.

(Headteacher, Manchester)

The term 'capacity' was being linked by the headteachers to the very mechanistic or static notions of schools as organisations that current theorists were arguing against. The problem here being that since this term was first applied to schools our image of them has changed dramatically. It now appeared to be a rather mechanistic 'bolt-on' to the more organic or dynamic theories of schools that practitioners as well as theorists have adopted.

The point at which these school leaders' more organic and interconnected images of schools were most clearly articulated was when they talked about how schools 'grew'. This was no accident and arose not just because of the recent emphasis on school improvement. Here the headteachers once more started the discussions by rejecting some existing notions of improvement. Particularly current policies and targets that appeared naïve because of their belief in the possibility of continuous linear, and sometimes exponential improvement. They believed that the current pace of improvement desired by the government could not be achieved without severe costs and possible damage to their schools:

If you were on a continuous upward slant you would crack in the end. Everybody has got to get to [the] stage where they have got used to an area of learning and then start again. If you are continuously striving you would end up sliding down. It's not always a case of building on but sometimes replacing what is already there.

(Primary headteacher)

I don't see sustainability as just flat or nationally as peaks and troughs.

(Secondary headteacher)

These were not people who felt such levels of improvement were not possible. Many of them had achieved much higher than national average improvements, some in very difficult circumstances. Rather they were arguing about the desirability of such growth in terms of the long-term health of their schools, and even of their own well-being and that of their staff:

You have to take people's health and emotion into account too. Because often people have phases in their lives where they are on a plateau or a cliff edge and [it's] supporting them through their minor or major crises which is quite difficult. You can't let them fall by the wayside because that's when things start to go wrong in the whole institution.

(Primary headteacher)

The headteachers were articulating their beliefs about the differences between short-term improvement and longer-term sustained growth. Improvement could be achieved by 'tightening the screws', 'releasing' potential, 'maximising' effort, 'focusing' energies. There was, though, a limit to how many times this could be done before the school and individuals became stressed. Sustained improvement required capacity to be developed rather than just being more effectively harnessed. For these practitioners capacity was unlimited because it could be 'grown'.

For these headteachers the reality of building capacity and how their schools grew over time, was too complex and episodic to be encapsulated by smooth lines on graphs or simple comparisons between schools. How then to describe this 'growing process'? One of the strongest metaphors used was the 'plateau' to describe a time of rest and consolidation between periods of growth:

I find it very helpful to conceptualise sustainability with the idea of a plateau. I arrived at my present school and it was on a particular plateau and it needed to get on to a much higher plateau. Once you're on that plateau you need to get on to another plateau and you are able to actually identify what you need to do to get on to the next plateau. It [capacity] may help future headteacher[s] know some of the ladders to get on to the next plateau and if it can't do that it may not be worthwhile.

(Secondary headteacher)

The movement between these plateaus was discussed variously as a quantum leap, a growing season followed by fallow periods, or a resting point on a long climb.

The uncertainty of the way up to the next plateau, or the timing of the next growing season, demanded flexibility about both where their schools grew and how. An image of development that sits uneasily with a great deal of the existing language of strategic development and visionary leadership:

Many of our best people take us to different plateaus we can't ourselves conceive of. It's not in the machine, its more geographical: we are going to go up that track to that one, and it's right because we are being led that way but for reasons that are not always susceptible to articulation. It's the helicopter thing, the Grand Canyon thing, what we ultimately want to be is on the top looking down but we need the right guide to take us to different levels and somebody knows that area better than that area and different paths up.

(Secondary headteacher)

These notions of risk, adapting to opportunities that present themselves, uncertainty about where other leaders are taking the school, the need to rest and consolidate – are all images of growth and development that are far from mechanistic. The responses of these headteachers reflected the realities they faced, in that the main 'capacity' they have to had work with, and which needed to be 'built' and connected, was the staff, pupils and parents that filled their schools. A capacity as variable and dynamic as the people it consisted of.

'Building', or 'growing' capacity required a certain type of leadership – leadership that could only rely partially on the knowledge gained in previous phases of development and therefore required risk taking:

> My nephew plays computer games with levels. After a certain amount of time he knows how to get from level 1 to level 2; he knows what is going to happen to him and what will appear when he gets to level 2. Then he goes from 2 to 3: he's got an idea of what's going to happen. From 3 to 4 he doesn't know and that's like us: we get to a particular plateau and then it's a pioneering jump, it's a risk.
>
> (Secondary headteacher)

Their recognition of the risk and uncertainty involved in growing a school emphasised key aspects of their leadership (Leithwood *et al.*, 1999; Day *et al.*, 2000; Hopkins and Reynolds, 2001). They stressed the importance of drawing together the different elements of the school, to help feed its development, issues of connectivity, participation, shifts in relationships and therefore ultimately the culture of the school:

> It's how you gather it all together and take it forward without dropping anything. It's a juggling act with the head standing at the bottom holding it all together. You see different illustrations of headship, sometimes people say it is at the top of the pile. I always see it the other way around completely. Somebody pulling it all together and pushing it up rather than somebody standing there and spreading downwards.
>
> (Primary headteacher)

They managed the culture not only in terms of making connections but also in order to create the kinds of psychological spaces in which people were able to learn from others:

It seems to me that the oil-can model of the head as you get further into headship, where you are making connections, is very important. It's like an old-fashioned telephone operator: you are making all these links which take people out of their normal context, which frees them up psychologically to be open to what other people are doing in different areas. We are the only people as heads who have this overview; it's quite unique. You need that kind of overview to make those connections.

(Secondary headteacher)

The connections these leaders saw as their particular responsibility tended to focus around the professional development of their staff, reflecting their recognition of the centrality of building this level of capacity:

One of the roles of leadership of the head is making connections between different people in the school who are doing different things and if they are connected it would be mutually beneficial. So if you've got someone who is weak in a particular area and someone who is strong in a particular area there's a good coaching and mentoring opportunity.

(Secondary headteacher)

How did they make these connections happen, how do you engender 'connectivity'? Here one headteacher discusses how he/she encouraged staff to make these connections and take on leadership roles:

One of the key roles as a head is to be around talking to your staff all the time. The whole basis of effective leadership is the quality of your relationships. I like the notion of the emotional bank account. Where you can only draw from your account in relation to what you have put in with each member of your staff. If you focus in that way it's a real investment in your most precious resource, your time. That is the way you are going to help that teacher improve in that classroom. You call back, you can only get a pay-back if you if actually have put that emotion in the first place.

(Secondary headteacher)

This approach, and many others they discussed were based on headteachers using the relationships they had with staff to change the patterns and nature of interactions between staff. In terms of leadership styles these approaches sat uneasily between the idea of there being an emotional transaction, payback, between headteacher and staff, and the much more transformational agenda of working through relationships, emotions and values to change people's views of their roles and potentials. Carried out in the wrong ways these kind of approaches could have been seen as manipulative and even coercive. Here, though, were headteachers who had to mix pragmatism with moral leadership. What would work in the particular contexts they faced with what they felt was right:

> So it's using strategies in tune with those kinds of situations and there may be a variety of them. It's using strategies that you feel comfortable with. There is no one way of solving anything.
>
> (Primary headteacher)

Commentary

The question I set out to answer was whether the generative metaphors associated with a capacity and building capacity helped school leaders articulate the issues they faced in improving their schools. The idea of school having a particular 'level' of capacity was limited in its usefulness by its technical connotations and the availability of similar but more meaningful terms. Capacity's links with the idea of measurement tended to strongly colour people's reactions and blocked their desire to use it as a reflective metaphor.

> There is an element of the auditor's model, we are faced increasingly from the DFES with a kind of auditing approach, everything has to be measured, evaluated and moderated. One of my concerns [is]: if we are not careful and pursue the auditors' model down the line, we miss opportunities and the enjoyment will be missed. I [have] some alarms about the word capacity because it's a measurement thing, an accountancy thing; it can in some ways miss out the wider factors.
>
> (Secondary headteacher)

In contrast, when the idea of capacity-building was connected with more organic and interactive notions of how school's 'grow' it not only led to criticisms of dominant views of improvement, it also induced some rather challenging and unsettling images.

These were images that encapsulated the dynamic and patterned nature of growth and highlighted the almost arbitrary nature of change and shifts in schools' capacity.

> These were not comforting ideas. I just feel as a concept we are looking at an extremely complex concept, at times almost random concept of change, of potential and so forth.
>
> (Secondary headteacher)

It was in raising these uncomfortable images that the idea of growing capacity showed its reflective potential. It supported these headteachers in moving out of the comfort zone of more acceptable notions of leadership and the extent of their individual agency in influencing the long-term development of their school. Here were accounts from practitioners that not only echoed the theoretical discussions of academics but also showed their acute awareness of key issues, such as the importance of diversified leadership and the need for highly contextualised responses, which have struggled to become an established part of current professional discourses.

Part of the power of the idea of capacity-building was that it seemed to contradict much of the official rhetoric of improvement; it challenged current government policies concerning the possibilities for growth. The headteachers' accounts also challenge many theoreticians. Not only did they reveal that the actual metaphors and images they worked with were far from mechanistic, but that they had also developed images of growth and development which in many ways were better than those being discussed by academics. How are these academics going to encapsulate the complexities of change and sustainability within a coherent account of how leaders 'grow' their schools? What kinds of accounts can they produce which avoid being so simplistic as to be almost impossible to relate meaningfully to the specifics of their individual schools, without at the same time falling into the trap of lionising personalities?

> One of the problems we have is to replicate outstanding headteachers. People because of their personalities, what we tend to do is celebrate them, which is marvellous. The hard thing though is to move from this anecdotal what they have done, and it cannot be replicated nationally. This [the idea of capacity-building] is helpful, it provides ways of focusing on the issues away from personalities and on to things like the skills and requirements for future heads. These are the ingredients for school improvement. We can call it anything. The important thing here is that conceptually we have a paradigm to consider and weigh against the reality of the job itself. Because it is something fresh, 'capacity', people will explore it if they don't think it is simply school improvement. They would think, 'Not another school-improvement programme, put it in the bin'. I thought the definitions were helpful. It led me into internal thought processes about what I am actually doing.
>
> (Secondary headteachers)

In Chapter 7 I turn to the 'ingredients' for growing capacity discussed by these headteachers, and how they fit within current models of capacity-building.

References

Dibbon, D.C. (1999) 'Stages of Growth in the Organizational Learning Capacity of Schools', Doctoral Dissertation, University of Toronto, September.

Fullan, M. (1999) *Change Forces: The Sequel*, London, Falmer Press.

Hannay, M., Smeltzer Erb, C. and Ross, J. (2001) 'Building Change Capacity within Secondary Schools through Goal-driven and Living Organisations', *School Leadership and Management*, 21(3): 271–87.

Hopkins, D. and Reynolds, D. (2001) *Improving Schools in Challenging Circumstances: A Review of the Literature*, London, DFES.

Hopkins, D. *et al.* (2001) *Creating the Conditions for Teaching and Learning*, London, Fulton Press.

Jackson, D. (2000) 'School Improvement and the Planned Growth of Leadership Capacity', paper presented at British Educational Research Association Annula Conference, Cardiff, September 2000.

Lambert, L. (1998) *Building Leadership Capacity in Schools*, Association for Supervision and Curriculum Development, Virginia.

Leithwood, K. and Jantzi, D. (2000) 'The Effects of Transformational Leadership on Organizational Conditions and Student Engagement with School', *Journal of Educational Administration*, 38(2): 112–29.

Mitchell, C. and Sackney, L. (2000) *Profound Improvement: Building Capacity for a Learning Community*, Lisse, Swets and Zeitlinger.

O'Day, J., Goertz, M.E. and Floden, R.E. (1995) 'Building Capacity for Education Reform Consortium for Policy Research in Education', Policy Briefs, December, CPRE, New Brunswick.

Ofsted (1997) *School Inspections: Removal from Special Measures*, London, Ofsted.

Schon, D. (1993) *Generative Metaphors and Social Policy*, in A. Ortony (ed.), *Metaphor and Thought*, 2nd edn, Cambridge, Cambridge University Press.

Seller, W. (2001) 'Reforming School: Building the Capacity for Change', *School Leadership and Management*, 21(3): 255–9.

Senge, P. (1990) *The Fifth Discipline: The Art and Practice of the Learning Organisation*, New York, Doubleday.

Spillane, J.P. and Thompson, C.L. (1997) 'Reconstructing Conceptions of Local Capacity: The Local Education Agency's Capacity for Ambitious Instructional Reform', *Educational Evaluation and Policy Analysis*, 2: 185–203.

Stoll, L. (1999) 'Realising Our Potential: Understanding and Developing Capacity for Lasting Improvement', *School Effectiveness and School Improvement*, 10(4): 503–32.

Chapter 7

Capacity-building, school improvement and school leaders

Mark Hadfield

Introduction

This chapter focuses on the idea of capacity-building, rather than capacity per se. In it I want to discuss the leadership challenges, both theoretical and practical, of 'building' internal capacity. To do this in the space available here I look at building one particular sort of capacity, the capacity for whole-school improvement. In the first section I look at what is possibly the defining characteristic of whole-school capacity-building and therefore the key challenge for school leaders, the process of drawing together the different developments within a school. Striving for greater 'connectedness' (Stoll, 1999) between different developments and drawing them into some kind of 'generative' relationships, in which the whole becomes more than the sum of the parts, is the basis of generating whole-school capacity. In the second section I pose the question of whether at the personal, interpersonal or team level capacity-building is asking school leaders to do anything that is substantially different from what other theories have already recommended. In answering this question I suggest that there are differences, but of emphasis and scope rather than any fundamental shifts, in the leadership required to build capacity rather than improve school improvement.

Whole-school capacity-building and school improvement

From a school-improvement perspective building capacity is a difficult and complex task, as Gray *et al.* (1999) observed in their research on twelve improving schools:

> In only one of the two schools, however did the schools' practices seem sufficiently well embedded for us to be confident in talking about its capacity to improve. It would seem unwise to rely too heavily on approaches to change which assume that such a capacity is widely in place.
>
> (Gray *et al.*, 1999: 18)

Gray *et al.* (1999), in common with other school-improvement theorists, tend to treat capacity-building as an activity that schools can only undertake after they have gone quite a distance along their 'journey' of school improvement. If not exactly the pinnacle of this journey capacity-building is certainly one of its final stages, as it requires schools not only to have already institutionalised a wide range of developmental processes and approaches but also to have brought these together. As Hopkins *et al.* (2001) point out,

> School capacity can be described as the collective competency of the school as an entity to bring about effective change. This implies four core components: knowledge, skills and dispositions of individual staff; a professional learning community in which staff work collaboratively; program coherence; technical resources.
>
> (Hopkins *et al.*, 2001: 3)

Building capacity for whole-school improvement involves bringing together these four core components: resources, structures, culture and the skills of staff, not only focusing on improvement but doing so in ways which are synergistic. The reason why building capacity at the whole-school level is so difficult to achieve is that all these different elements develop, and decline, unevenly. Or as one of the headteachers we interviewed put it:

> Individuals have this capacity to learn and grow in spurts and the organisation is like that except it's like a lot of interlocking three-dimensional Venn diagrams with lots of interacting factors. Your overall organisation might move from plateau to plateau but elements within it are already forging ahead, one of your departments is pushing through the next barrier.
>
> (Secondary headteacher)

Using a metaphor of the Venn diagram this headteacher stresses the sporadic, uneven and interconnected nature of school development. Although whole-school development is the aim of school improvement, unfortunately schools do not 'naturally' grow in a constant fashion. Not only do different areas of the school start from different points, they also grow at different rates. This requires school leaders to continually intervene to identify and manage the 'growth trajectories' of individuals, teams and departments so that growth in one area can support and sustain growth in another. School leaders use a range of tactics and strategies to enable this to happen, including the movement of staff around a school, mentoring between experts' and novices' procedures, and the creation of flexible and temporary management structures.

This bringing-together of developments at all levels of the school, from the individual to the whole school, into generative relationships has been described as a 'higher-order' capacity-building skill and termed 'connectedness' by Stoll (1999).

> Seek connectedness. For any individual school, understanding the balance of the various influences on internal capacity and how they work together is central. This means not seeing any one activity or intervention as discrete, but considering how it fits within the whole dynamic of the school.
>
> (Stoll, 1999)

Capacity-building requires leaders not only to look holistically at each area of their school but to develop an understanding of how to bring each of these areas together in a way which generates further capacity. This requires leaders to develop a deep understanding of what types of connections work best between certain areas, to create a strategy that guides which, when and how these connections are to be made, and when certain connections need to be broken and replaced by others. The headteachers we talked to found it hard to explain how they managed this process, because they felt so much of it was intuitive and highly contextualised:

> It's rather like trying to describe the weather to someone who is blind. If you have been out in the weather you can say it's doing different things and you know what you are referring to. Other heads would know what you were describing but the outside world couldn't really quantify it. Capacity is another version of that, trying to put descriptors and parameters on a process which some people have intuitively understood and accumulated the information about in their careers whilst other people who have had the same sets of experiences have apparently not, for reasons unknown. What the word is trying to describe is 'How do you create the ability or develop a corporate growing view of the world within a group of people, who have this very disparate range of things they have to think about?'
>
> (Secondary headteacher)

The task of leading capacity-building within a school encompasses not simply shifting cultures, changing structures or developing certain skills but managing the complex ebbs and flows of these developments. It requires leaders to develop the capacity for what Brooks (2000) terms 'metis', from the Greek for a particular kind of 'nous' for dealing with complex interdependencies within social situations. Metis is defined as 'a wide array of practical skills and acquired intelligence in responding to a constantly changing natural and human environment' (Brooks, 2000). Or we could call it a little bit of 'alchemy', making gold from combining base metals with other ingredients:

> It's that alchemy, it's that little bit of being sensitive to exactly what's going on and interacting with those. It is possible to go into enormous depth into each of those little interactions that take place. It though is almost something you instinctively run with but it's based on experience, an understanding of the context you're in, and the learning processes you have gone through.
>
> (Special-school headteacher)

Echoing the observations made by the headteachers in our interviews, Brooks observes that this kind of 'nous'

> cannot be taught or memorized. It can only be imparted and acquired ... Metis is acquired as a series of random acquisitions that only gradually form a whole picture. People sharing metis do not lecture they converse. They work side by side. To acquire metis, a person must not only see but see with comprehension. He or she must observe minutely to absorb the practical consequences of things. He or she must develop a feel for the process, for the interrelationships of things.
>
> (Brooks, 2000: 131)

Understanding the interrelationships between elements of the school may seem a rather prosaic aim in that many headteachers would claim that they already do this in practice:

> It seems to me that the oil-can model of the head makes more sense as you get further into headship, where you are making connections, is very important. It's like an old-fashioned telephone operator: you are making all these links which take people out of their normal context which free them up psychologically to be open to what other people are doing in different areas. We are the only people as heads who have this overview; it's quite unique. You need that kind of overview to make those connections.
>
> (Secondary headteacher)

The challenge is that this type of overview cannot be the prerogative of just the headteacher; it requires leaders at all levels to make these connections. This is necessary because at the whole-school level capacity theorists are arguing for the need to create a 'critical mass' of capacity. This requires the bringing together of developments at all levels, which even from their privileged viewpoint headteachers cannot be totally aware of. Getting schools to this critical mass and keeping them there, sustaining individual and team improvement so that they bind together and feed further development at a whole-school level requires leadership and the development of 'nous' about how to make these connections. It is this form of knowledge that provides individuals with a much broader sense of the 'levers' that can be use to effect change, or prevent it, and conversely an awareness of the way these are used by others. The key challenge for school leaders is how to get other members of the school community to understand how to harness and link different areas of growth and develop a critical awareness of how these can help, and hinder, improvement:

> One of the main problems is people who don't look at things holistically, who have a single pathway approach to how things happen. But schools don't work like that at all on any level. You have twenty-five things going on in the forefront and then there is another thirty behind the scenes and all the plates have got to spin at once. So people keep saying to me 'Can't we finish one thing at a time?' I keep saying that isn't what life is like.
>
> (Primary headteacher)

So what does capacity-building look like in practice?

What does this kind of connection-making look like in practice? To help illustrate this I have used a quotation from a headteacher describing his approach to building one facet of capacity in the school (Figure 7.1). In it he discusses how he has developed a project-based approach to dealing with improvement in the school – an approach which has gradually improved his ability to cope with, and learn from, the numerous initiatives and changes the school has gone through in recent years. To help unpick the nature of the connections he is making I have used Mitchell and Sackney's model of building capacity.

Mitchell and Sackney (2000) view capacity-building as needing to take place within and between three interconnected areas, or spheres: the personal, interpersonal, and organisational.

> One cannot build capacity in one area and expect that to suffice. Rather there needs to be direct, sustained, focused attention on building capacity in all three areas. That will allow for synergy to develop as each capacity builds from and extends the other. That is, increased capacity in one category can exert pressure for improvemnts in the other categories of capacity.
>
> (Mitchell and Sackney, 2000: 00)

Within the personal sphere building capacity is based around making connections between individual teachers' practices, values and knowledge. The making of these connections is based on using different reflective techniques and strategies to help them articulate their personal knowledge and prompt understanding of its links and discontinuities. Within the interpersonal sphere building capacity is based on making links between groups, sharing knowledge about how to build effective teams and sharing good practice. Making these connections requires not only opportunities for collective learning and reflection within teams but also structures and procedures that link different teams, allowing for the exchange of expertise. In the organisational sphere building capacity is based on developing shared leadership, establishing school-wide collaborative processes and supportive structural arrangements that make it possible to connect the activities of the various teams and individuals that make up the school.

So let's look at the way in which one headteacher has tried to pull together these different elements in one area of the school (Figure 7.1). This provides just one example of a particular process and structure that works at a number of levels and it has come about through a mixture of luck, experience and the application of 'nous'.

What does capacity-building at the level of individuals and teams require of school leaders?

Besides stressing the need to make the right sort of connections between different areas within and outside of schools, do theories of capacity-building set any other challenges for school leaders? Are they anything more than just an amalgamation of theories of individual growth, team-building and whole-school change? If they do set new challenges, and the answer very much depends from where you enter the debate, it is generally a case of asking leaders to think about using a greater range of techniques, or shifting the emphasis of their work, in order to make the connections necessary to build capacity. Below I discuss two examples of the sort of shifts in emphasis required. At the level of the individual a good example of this is the balance leaders strike between putting energy into creating supportive relationships between staff, generally by developing trust, and the extent to which they support and harness the individualism of their staff. The second example is at the interpersonal level where I discuss the need for leaders to think about how to break down and rebuild teams as least as much as how to create them in the first place.

Emotions: relationships and individualism

The importance of emotional contact between staff is now an area of considerable research within professional development, but has tended to be

Organisational sphere

Flexible structural arrangements allowing temporary membership of SMT to help build shared leadership.

Interpersonal sphere

They have learnt that team-building needs to be based around establishing trust early via inviting people to take part. The overall team process is clearly defined early to help sustain the group.

Personal sphere

A professionally novel experience for the project leader and others in the team provides a stimulus for reflection. Constructing their own knowledge via research, whose worth is challenged by having to be put into action by them, requires further reflection and links beliefs and actions.

We actually identified a project leader and they were seconded on to the senior management team for a nine-month period so they were cognizant of other issues in the school in terms of that change. We seconded someone on to the SMT right outside of the management structure, which ruffled a few feathers. The key ingredients we look at are the qualities of your project leader, the constitution of the team, making sure your end date is clear, publicising the end date. Then they went out and recruited their project team, rather than asking for volunteers. The group exists to actually do something not just to research something. If research is part of the group's work it is in order to do something. The research in itself isn't the end.

So whenever a change has been managed successfully we analyse that success – what are the key ingredients? – and use that for coaching the next project leader. The way we do [this] is that the team always has an end-of-project review, so we sit down for a couple hours talking to the person who led the project. What went well? How did we help you? How did we get in your way? We do that every time we have a project. The other [thing] we have is a sponsor of the project who isn't the project leader. Basically this means you have someone on the senior team who is the moral backing behind the project, and the project leader goes and says, 'How would you solve this one?' This sponsor goes to every meeting, so she/he becomes the coach of the project [with] a responsibility for keeping an eye on that project, but they may not be directly involved in running the project.

Organisational sphere

Creating this structural arrangement allows for the exchange of knowledge between groups and which identifies how one group has supported or hindered the work of another.

Interpersonal sphere

Provide opportunities for professional conversations to allow for collective reflection that helps to articulate how they see the change process evolving.

Personal sphere

An opportunity for the sponsor to both mentor and observe the way in which others manage change. This helps them articulate their own approach to change while not being directly responsible for the day-to-day management.

Figure 7.1

treated very narrowly in most discussions of school improvement. As Hargeaves (1998) observed, until recently emotions were

> Virtually absent from the advocacy of, and the mainstream literature specifically concerned with, educational change and reform. Strategic planning, cognitive leadership, problem-solving, teacher reflection, higher-order thinking, and standards-based reform have virtually nothing to say about them. Even the idea of organizational learning which is on the very cutting edge of change theory, is almost exclusively cerebral in its emphasis.
>
> (Hargreaves, 1998: 116)

Even when emotions have been discussed they tend to be normative in that they are conceptualised as either 'positive' or 'gentle sedatives' to the upheaval of the change process. Hence, the pre-eminence of emotions such as trust and honesty is stressed and the focus is on the motivational force of relationships between staff that are based on reciprocal acts of support:

> Trust is recognized as a vital element in well functioning organizations. Trust is necessary for effective cooperation and communication, the foundation for cohesive and productive relationships in organizations. Trust functions as a 'lubricant' greasing the way for efficient operations when people have confidence in other people's words and deeds. Trust reduces the complexities of transactions and exchanges far more quickly and economically than other means of managing organizational life.
>
> (Tschannen-Moran and Hoy, 2000)

Capacity theorists recognise the importance of such 'positives'. For example, trust helps build the social capital needed to support many forms of organisational learning (Hargreaves, 2001; Sergiovanni, 2001). But capacity theorists also acknowledge the generative power of what could be seen as less altruistic, and more individualistic, emotions. Hence, you are much more likely in capacity theories to come across discussion of emotions associated with risk, creativity and individual self-fulfilment. Although establishing trusting relationships between staff can help make connections, by providing the right kind of context for open and honest dialogues, practitioners as well as capacity theorists recognise that individuals change and share their practice for complex sets of reasons – as so many of the headteachers we interviewed stressed.

The importance of providing a challenge to overly 'comfortable' relationships between staff

> It's about risk: you can't be in a school that's involved in building capacity unless you are prepared to take risks, because things can get very comfortable in schools. It's about getting people to take that leap and take a look at where they are going.
>
> (Primary headteacher)

The importance of valuing and drawing on individual enthusiasms and desires and using these flexibly to create new opportunities

> Many of our best people take us to different plateaus we can't ourselves conceive of. It's not in the machine, it's more geographical: we are going to go up that track to that one, and it's right because we are being led that way but for reasons that are not always susceptible to articulation. It's the helicopter thing the Grand Canyon thing. What we ultimately want to be is on the top looking down, but we need the right guide to take us to different levels and somebody knows that area better than another and the different paths up.
>
> (Secondary headteacher)

The need for different motivators when staff vary in their commitment to personal development and enthusiasm for change

> There is a simplistic idea that everyone must move on and develop. But there is often a whole core of people who are there because they need to earn money, they are there because it is convenient, they live near to the building whatever it is. You have to keep that in mind.
>
> (Primary headteacher)

> For the last two years we have been giving teachers and support staff temporary allowances. It's nice to say to people 'You're a nice person. You are doing so well.' But they want money at the end of the day so every member of the staff has been getting one allowance point and that is very much appreciated.
>
> (Primary headteacher)

Many 'orthodox' theories of school improvement are pessimistic about the potential of individuals to make a meaningful impact on a whole school and appear almost distrustful of individualism, which has become something of a 'heresy' (Hargreaves, 1994), such is the focus on building collaborative and trusting relationships. Individuals who do not buy into collective action are often seen as if not actually limiting then certainly not contributing effectively to whole-school development. Hence, Huberman's (1993) use of the term 'lone wolf' to describe those individuals who work predominately in isolation to develop their craft, or the warnings about the dangers of fragmentation and the hot-house school where individualism leads to innovation overload and wasted effort (Hargreaves, 1995). But, in practice,

> individualism has other meanings and connotations which are not so clearly negative in character. Clearly when we speak of individualism, therefore, we are speaking not of a singular thing but of a complex social and cultural phenomenon with many meanings – not all of them necessarily negative. If we are to develop a sophisticated rather than a stereotypical understanding of how teachers work with their colleagues, and of the benefits and drawbacks of these different ways of working, then it is important to unpack this concept of teacher individualism more carefully and reconstruct it in professionally helpful ways. It is time we approached individualism in a spirit of understanding, not one of persecution.
>
> (Hargreaves, 1994: 00)

Capacity-building theorists tend not only to approach individualism with understanding; they want to know how they can use more personal motivations and individualistic forms of learning and risk-taking to help a school improve. They do not see such behaviour as a failure of a school's culture. They want leaders to recognise, and harness more effectively, the generative power of 'individualism' and also different 'types' of individuals within the process of school improvement. They are not calling for everyone to become the 'extended' professional or to enter into 'collaborative' relationships with other colleagues, or even share the same vision. Capacity theorists value individualism as much as collectivism because they believe that in certain circumstances in the 'journey' of school improvement very different types of individuals are needed to stimulate the 'dramatic learning moments' needed to move a school on.

So what kind of individualism is likely to generate more capacity? There are numerous different definitions of individualism, but Brooks (2000) in his critique of current views of modern work practices and lifestyles discusses individualism in terms of the pursuit of 'higher selfishness':

> Workers in this spiritualized world . . . are not the heroes of toil. They are creators. They noodle around and experiment and dream. They seek to explore and then surpass the full limits of their capacities . . .

Self-cultivation is the imperative. With the emphasis on self. This isn't a crass and vulgar selfishness, about narrow self-interest or mindless accumulation. This is a *higher selfishness*. It's about making sure you get the most out of yourself, which means putting yourself in a job that is spiritually fulfilling, socially constructive, experientially diverse, emotionally enriching, self-esteem boosting, perpetually challenging, and eternally edifying. It's about learning. It's about working for a company as cool as you are. It's about finding an organization that can meet your creative and spiritual needs.

(Brooks, 2000: 134)

Brooks (2000) sets this form of 'healthy' individualism within a 'healthy' organisation:

Companies today, the mantra goes, have to think biologically. They have to create lean, decentralised, informal participatory systems. They have to tear down rigid structures and let a thousand flowers bloom. The machine is no longer held up as the standard that healthy organizations should emulate. Now it's the ecosystem. It's the ever changing organic network that serves as the model to define a healthy organization, filled with spontaneous growth and infinitely complex and dynamic interconnections.

(Brooks, 2000: 125)

Brooks traces the origins of current theories about the relationship between individualism and collective development back to writers such as the anthropologist Jane Jacobs, who in her critique of overly rationalist and mechanistic urban planning campaigned for the organic and diverse nature of urban life, which grew out of the unplanned interaction of small communities, and the individuals within them. She echoes the widespread criticisms of many system-wide educational changes in her observations of the failure of so much 'top-down' urban development. Over the last forty years theories such as that put forward by Jacobs have become meshed with theories of creativity, management and environmentalism to create a singular view of 'healthy' organisations.

From Brooks's perspective the connections between people in an organisation do not arise solely because of a common professional identity, the establishment of trusting relationships, or because people buy into a shared vision. Rather it requires an organisation that sets out to support the 'higher selfishness' of individuals, their ideas of self-fulfilment and development. Recognising the power of individualism would call for many school leaders to redress the current balance they have currently struck between organisational development and individual fulfilment. This is very difficult to do when schools face rapid and multiple changes that require them to act as a corporate whole. There are, though, dangers in not sponsoring creative individualism and of overconformist cultures. A lack of creativity, variety in problem-solving approaches and insufficient criticality were all reported as problems by the headteachers we talked to.

Building up and breaking down shared norms and practices

So what new challenges for school leaders do current theories of inter-personal capacity contain? One of the main switches in emphasis arises from the recognition that, as well as building up the relationships and cultures that constitute a school community, leaders need to break these down and remake them in more flexible forms. Just as at the individual level capacity theorists are critical about the simplistic belief in the power of 'positive' relationships and the stereotyping of individualism at the inter-personal level, so they too recognise the dangers inherent in 'team-building' and the forming of communities based on 'dominant' cultures. This is because they recognise that the building of any type of community, or collective culture, inevitably results in the exclusion of some as well as the inclusion of others:

> Self-identification as a member of [a] community often occurs as an oppositional differentiation from other groups, who are feared, despised, or at best devalued. The ideal community, I suggest, validates and reinforces the fear and aversion some social groups exhibit towards other.
>
> (Young, 1990: 29)

Young's argument is that it is inevitable in the building of any form of community, political or professional, that certain individuals are excluded.

School-improvement theorists often stress the importance of building certain types of cultures because they have a greater generative capacity than other forms of communities. The greater potential of these types of communities arises from factors as varied as the psychological benefits of a shared sense of identity and belonging to the more efficient marshalling of individual efforts in pursuit of common goals. But even when the aims of these communities are inclusive they inevitably exclude some individuals because no process of community-building is ever going to dominate completely all the other sets of group identities staff live with, whether they see themselves as science teachers, members of a senior management team or as part of a key-stage team. Capacity theorists recognise this tension between different group identities and therefore stress the need to build a large degree of flexibility and permeability into the teams that are being formed.

The suggested solution to the problem of overly rigid teams and team structures is twofold. First, try to break down existing ways of working by making them as flexible as possible; it is crucial that individuals are placed in new relationships, use new tools and take on new roles within and across teams. Second, create new temporary groups with different identities that overlap with, but challenge, those already in existence. For example as members of action researcher teams or school-improvement groups teachers are not only brought into new roles and relationship but also create groups that hopefully will become new 'communities of practice'.

The development of leadership capacity is a good example of this twofold approach to interpersonal capacity-building based on both expanding existing groups and building new ones. Current theories of distributive leadership champion the use of both sets of strategies so as to encourage as wide a range of individuals as possible to take on leadership roles. They recognise the need to challenge established practices and build new norms around current ideas of what constitutes leadership and who could be described as a leader:

> The leadership in the schools described in this paper is not perceived as being inextricably linked to status or experience. It is available to all. In this way, coaching and mentoring have become important leadership qualities, designed to support individuals but also to expand leadership capacity.
>
> (Jackson, 2000: 5)

Jackson in describing how these schools developed more diffuse or distributive approaches to leadership discusses not only how the existing management group took on new roles as mentors so as to help include others within the 'management group' but by building new norms about who could be leaders, and what leadership involved, they created 'new' communities of leaders. As one headteacher observed:

> What I find interesting is the shift in emphasis away from the head at times as symbolising change, the head being the change agent to this kind of emphasis on collective competence and how you actually make the whole of your staff competent to handle and manage change. In many respects you're actually reducing the role of the head as being the 'fight them on the beaches' speech giver. As you've got more individuals capable of introducing change, any change would be far better rooted because all the individuals in the organisation are involved in the process and part of it rather [than] it being something that is done to them or adjacent to them. Broadening leadership and fostering empowerment – that is what we have really revolved around.
>
> (Secondary headteacher)

In schools committed to developing leadership at different levels what has to change is not just those who see themselves as leaders (who should consider delegating their leadership responsibilities); it is also about changing the very notion of which people can become leaders and what leadership is about. Establishing these new norms involves challenging existing ones, such as leadership being the responsibility of only certain individuals in the school, often the senior management team. Then you need to build new norms by breaking down traditional power structures and ideas about what leadership involves. In the case of the schools researched by Jackson (2000) they broke leadership away from existing ideas about status and the importance of experience. In doing so these schools created a very different type of community and leadership group. They drew in those previously excluded, because they disliked its previous approach to leadership, while building a new group of leaders. But of course this new leadership group would, in turn, exclude others and so would have to be broken down and rebuilt to draw others in.

Commentary

In terms of capacity-building, school leaders are being asked essentially to lead three processes: reculturing, restructuring and reskilling – all of which need to be carried out at the level of the individual, team and whole school. If we use the example quoted previously, in Figure 7.1 at the personal level restructuring involved changing the working patterns of individuals. Reculturing meant changing the project leader's and probably other members of the team's views of leadership, challenging their views of who are the leaders in the school – not always the senior managers – and possibly about the level of experience and skills base required of leaders. Reskilling in this instance meant not only gaining new technical skills about research and evaluation but also the personal skills required when working in different ways and dealing with how they were seen and treated by others in the school.

At the interpersonal or team level reculturing involved building allegiances to a new team, rather than the one they normally worked within, and to a new way of working. This could range from something as simple as changing how decisions were normally made to more fundamental issues around what they saw as the most worthwhile feedback and recommendations to present back to the school. Restructuring in this team involved combining research and implementation in one group as well as changes to the way in which teams normally related to senior management. The reskilling that went on within the project team encompassed not only the opportunity to develop research and project management skills but also how to work with individuals with whom they normally did not have a close professional relationship.

It is this linking of reculturing, restructuring and reskilling processes so that they generate capacity not only at the personal and interpersonal level but also at the organisational level which is the key to building whole-school capacity for improvement. A commonly used metaphor to convey the level, and type, of 'connectedness' that is required is that of 'community'. Sergiovanni discusses the importance of communities of shared responsibility in building capacity:

> Communities are efficient developers of social, academic, intellectual, professional and other forms of human capital . . . The only way to beat the complexity, uncertainty, and continuous change that schools face and still maintain order is by creating local communities of responsibility that are able to cultivate higher levels of disciplined self-management among students, teachers, heads, parents, and other members of the local school community.
>
> (Sergiovanni, 2001: 47–9)

Or, to put it more simply, individual and team development can only go so far without a supportive community, and a supportive community depends upon empowered individuals and teams. This may appear to be a rather circular argument and raises the question of where to start and how to develop capacity-building within schools, as each context will already have different existing capacities and gaps. This is another of the key challenges facing those leading the development of capacity and it is worth bearing in mind the following warning by Mitchell and Sackney:

> The capacity of first attention is probably context specific. That is whether one starts to build personal, interpersonal, or organisational capacity will depend on the needs of the people in each site . . . One word of caution: starting with the least threatening capacity is probably the most enticing entry point but is not necessarily the one that will lead to the greatest improvement. At some point school people need to tackle all three, even the ones that feel uncomfortable or risky.
>
> (Mitchell and Sackney, 2000: 14)

References

Brooks, D. (2000) *BOBOS in Paradise: The New Upper Class and How They Got There*, New York, Touchstone.

Gray, J., Hopkins, D., Reynolds, D., Wilcox, B., Farrell, S. and Jesson, D. (1999) *Improving Schools Performance and Potential*, Buckingham, Open University Press.

Hargreaves, A. (1994) 'Individualism and Individuality: Understanding the Teacher Culture', in A. Hargreaves (ed.), *Changing Teachers, Changing Times*, London, Cassell.

Hargreaves, A. (1998) 'The Emotional Practice of Teaching', *Teaching and Teacher Education*, 14(8): 835–54.

Hargreaves, D. (2001) 'A Capital Theory of School Effectiveness and Improvement', *British Educational Research Journal*, 27(4): 487–503.

Hargreaves, D.H. (1995) 'School Culture, School Effectiveness and School Improvement', *School Effectiveness and School Improvement*, 6(1): 23–46.

Huberman, M. (1993) *The Lives of Teachers*, London, Cassell.

Jackson, D. (2000) 'School Improvement and the Planned Growth of Leadership Capacity', paper presented at the British Educational Research Association annual conference, University of Cardiff.

Mitchell, C. and Sackney, L. (2000) *Profound Improvement: Building Capacity for a Learning Community*, Lisse, Swets and Zeitlinger.

Sergiovanni, T.J. (2001) *Leadership*, London, RoutledgeFalmer.

Stoll, L. (1999) 'Realising our Potential and Developing Capacity for Lasting Improvement', *School Effectiveness and School Improvement*, 10(4): 503–32.

Tschannen-Moran, M. and Hoy, W.K. (2000) 'A Multidisciplinary Analysis of the Nature, Meaning, and Measurement of Trust', *Review of Educational Research*, 70(4): 547–93.

Young, I.M. (1990) *Justice and the Politics of Difference*, Princeton, Princeton University Press.

Chapter 8

Building the leadership capacity for school improvement

A case study

Christopher Chapman

Introduction

It has become generally accepted that leadership is a key characteristic of effective schooling (Sammons, Hillman and Mortimore, 1994) and is central to school improvement (Hopkins, Ainscow and West, 1994). However, the knowledge base concerning the process of improvement in low-attaining schools is limited. This chapter responds to a call for richer descriptions of improvement and leadership in schools in challenging contexts (Maden, 2001). It focuses on the attempts by leaders in one low-attaining secondary school in England to build the capacity for improvement. A detailed insight into the complexities and tensions of school improvement over a seven-year period is presented along with an analysis of capacity-building. This chapter concludes by highlighting four major themes concerning improvement and successful leadership in schools facing challenging circumstances (SFCC).

This case study evolved out of research funded by the National College for School Leadership which explored leadership and barriers to improvement in ten schools where 25 per cent or less pupils achieved 5+ A*–C grades at GCSE in 1999 and 2000 (Harris and Chapman, 2002). Bartley Green Technology College (BGTC) was visited in addition to this group of schools as an example of an improving school with successful leadership (Ofsted, 1999) that had recently managed to break through the 25 per cent five or more A*–C barrier. Interviews with the headteacher, senior managers, middle managers, classroom teachers and pupils took place during a series of visits towards the end of the summer term 2001. Further insights were gained from dialogue with members of the senior management team and informal conversations with staff. In the autumn of 2001 a draft of this case-study report was returned to the school for comments and validation. Data were placed in matrices and analysed by the dimensions of hierarchical position and research issue (Miles and Huberman, 1992). Direct quotations were taken from selected transcriptions and used to illustrate emerging themes.

Context

BGTC is located on the western edge of Birmingham near to the M5 motorway, approximately seven miles from the city centre. Housing in the area is a mixture of modern privately owned estates and low- and high-rise council-owned property. There are pockets of very high unemployment and areas of considerable socio-economic disadvantage within the school's catchment area. A Department of Applied Social Studies and Social Research (1998) survey concluded:

> 52.4% of Bartley Green pupils live in the 40% of Birmingham Enumeration Districts with the highest proportion of the population dependent on income support . . . Around half of Bartley Green School pupils come from the Bartley Green ward, with 22.9% living in Weoley and Long-bridge. All of these wards have urban deprivation scores considerably above the Birmingham average, which itself is far higher than the national average.

The school is an 11–16 mixed comprehensive school that was awarded technology college status in 2000. There are 754 pupils on roll, of which 61 per cent are boys. Twelve point three per cent of pupils come from ethnic minorities, of which just under half are Black Caribbean. The school experiences local competition, with many parents of the most able pupils choosing other schools. There is a comprehensive all-girls school located within Bartley Green which historically had a better reputation; consequently many parents still prefer to send their daughters there, although recently this trend has become less important. There are also a number of grammar schools situated near by. These schools select the top 20 per cent most academically able children throughout Birmingham. The school also has a high percentage (42.5 per cent) of pupils with special educational needs (SEN) including 9 per cent of pupils that hold a statement for SEN. Low academic achievement is also combined with high levels of socio-economic disadvantage. Currently over 46 per cent of pupils receive free school meals. However, in the recent past the percentage has often exceeded 50 per cent placing the school in the DfES category for the highest levels of socio-economic disadvantage.

In the early 1990s, BGTC was a community school. It was under-subscribed with falling rolls, attainment was low, as was staff morale. Teachers worked very hard, but mostly in isolation and discipline issues tended to dominate the school day. The factors contributing to this situation were significant in number and the relationship between them complex. In 1994 the appointment of a new headteacher combined with a pending Ofsted inspection acted as major catalysts for change. The last eight years of the school's development have been characterised by improvement in many areas. These are most vividly reflected in changes of examination performance, pupil attendance, number of first-choice applications to the school and reductions in permanent exclusions. The school's improvement trajectory can be divided into three distinct yet overlapping phases.

1994–1996: creating the foundations for improvement

The headteacher initially focused on creating the conditions for sustainable improvement. A thorough audit of the school was conducted and much time was spent investigating what was happening in classrooms, attempting to ascertain the quality of teaching and learning within the school. This focus on teaching and subsequently learning began to create a discourse around teaching and learning which continues to evolve as the school moves forward. Strategic plans were generated; these also supported the classroom by providing purpose and direction for short- and long-term improvements. Policies were generated and implemented to impact on perceived key areas such as improving behaviour and SEN provision, a rolling three-year cycle of school-improvement planning, linked to an annual staff-development review was also introduced to support the improvement process. Structural changes were made to enhance the implementation of these policies and processes. This structural change signalled the start of the most crucial cultural change in the school's development: the establishment of an 'achievement culture where everyone could succeed'. The headteacher used key issues raised from the inspection as a further mandate for change. An HMI monitoring visit in November 1996 recognised dynamic leadership by the headteacher as a significant factor contributing to the progress made in addressing the key issues.

1996–1999: consolidation

The second phase of the headteacher's leadership focused on consolidating early achievements and developing a consistent 'Bartley Green approach' to all areas of school life. The values, ethos and vision that underpin this approach are strongly subscribed to by headteacher, staff and most pupils. It is this notion of a collegiate organisation that has shifted the culture of the school to a position where expectations of all are high and people have the confidence to take risks in order to improve. The second Ofsted inspection (March 1999) was an important event that served to validate progress the school had made and also generated further confidence within the staff. These changes were supported by the leadership's continued determination to improve the core business of teaching and learning within the school. Efforts were made to improve practice by minimising the variation in quality both within and between departments through a package of combined pressure and support to improve consistency.

Continuing professional development (CPD) played an important role in attempts to develop individuals and teams through internal and external development programmes. This focus has been recognised by the school's success in gaining the Investors in People award. Many initiatives were undertaken that aimed to improve pupils' perceptions and experiences of school life. Extra-curricular activities were important, as was University of the First Age (UFA) activity in indirectly impacting on pupil achievement at school. As the organisation evolved the leadership team developed a keen sense of the need for staff to visit other improving schools and avoid 'reinventing good practice' when it could be 'borrowed'. As the culture began to shift and confidence increased the school reached a position where it was not only data- and information-rich, but was also developing the will, knowledge and expertise to use this information in a formative way that had the power to impact on practice.

1999–present: community

The current phase of BGTC's development is intrinsically linked to a bid for and subsequent award of technology college status. BGTC has interpreted technology college status as a tool for focusing on further improvement, primarily using the extra funding to target and rectify weaknesses in ICT identified by Ofsted. It also has provided the opportunity for the school to maintain a classroom focus, further developing and refining classroom processes in relation to community, capability and capacity. Strong links have been developed with local primary schools. ICT teachers regularly visit these schools and teach collaboratively with primary colleagues. The school has made attempts to engage the local community and raise the profile of the school. Links with parents have become increasingly positive and attendance at parents evenings and events continues to rise.

Devolution of power and responsibility has contributed to improvements in the capability of staff especially at middle management level. Efforts have been made to improve the alignment of the organisation at different levels and to build interdepartmental teams, creating multiple channels of communication and relationships based on higher-level networks, rather than relying on traditional linear hierarchies. These internal networks serve to develop staff, plan for succession, share ideas and develop consistent good practice across the school. The school has planned for and is implementing further structural changes that will result in a flatter management structure and further disperse the leadership within the organisation. This is most evident through the creation of new posts. These posts often include roles and responsibilities that have previously been the preserve of the senior management team.

The development of internal capacities has been paralleled by development in external capacities. The school has forged links with educational, business and other agencies in order to support learning within the organisation and to provide alternative curricula for disaffected pupils where necessary. However, where these links have not been productive or failed to support improvement the school has been flexible enough to respond by reinvesting energies in other directions. Ideas that were being developed during phase two are now being put into practice.

Building capacity for school improvement: key themes

There are a number of themes emerging from this case study concerning the way in which the capacity for school improvement is generated and sustained.

Leadership

All of the staff recognised the important role that the headteacher had played in the development of the school and appeared to enjoy being part of the success. The most recent Ofsted inspection report gives a further indication of the nature of leadership from the headteacher. The report summary states:

> The outstanding and inspirational leadership of the headteacher gives the school clear educational direction.
>
> (Ofsted, 1999)

Much of what has been achieved to date can be attributed to the values, vision and sense of purpose created and maintained by the headteacher since arriving at the school.

The headteacher's values permeate throughout the organisation and are adopted and subscribed to by staff and an increasing number of parents and pupils. The singular most important focus of the school is to improve further. Improvement is measured in terms of raising attainment of all pupils over time. The importance of raising attainment through achievement is continually reinforced to the staff especially during meetings and briefings. It is also constantly reinforced to pupils at an individual level during day-to-day interactions, through specific strategies such as mentoring schemes and in group settings such as 'achievement-focused' assemblies. Successes are also regularly celebrated. The strength of these values and the leadership of the headteacher are evident throughout the life and work of the school. However, the headteacher does not work in isolation; she has built a strong capable senior management team that supports the shared values, vision and purpose of the school. Members of the senior management team provide the direction for the school and act as role models for the staff and pupils. The curriculum deputy clearly highlights the importance of achievement within the school:

> Achievement has got to be there all the time. You've got to reward. You've got to praise and say 'well done. That was really good'.
>
> (Curriculum deputy)

The focus on achievement is combined with recognition of the importance of people and valuing them. The headteacher and senior management team place a high level of importance on caring for and developing individuals. They recognise that people are the key to improvement and they must be valued, especially in a challenging school. As the headteacher notes:

> It is people that make the difference and once you can get a few people in then things slowly begin to change. They have a different approach and attitude that slowly begins to wake other people.
>
> (Headteacher)

And

> If you say you value staff you have to show that you value them. It's no good saying it if you don't match it. So for example, if a member of staff wants time off to see their child in an assembly you have to give it. Because they are important to you, A as a worker and, B you are saying parents should come in and watch their children do things. You can't then have a disparity about not trusting people to take advantage of you in some way.
>
> (Headteacher)

Teachers are supported and encouraged to move forward, to develop or re-engage. BGTC is a school where success is important and people have to be prepared to contribute to that success. However, if they are not prepared to, cannot meet expectations or fail to subscribe to the achievement culture, they can become marginalised. This may result in a move to a school where they feel more comfortable.

Nanus (1992: 8) describes a vision as 'a realistic, credible, attractive future for your organisation'. The headteacher claims that on appointment the aim was to make BGTC a good school. However, she could not articulate the vision beyond this. There was no clear vision of what the school would look like or what its characteristics would be:

> People talk about vision as if it comes as a ready-made thing. I did not have a vision. I did not have any vision when I came here except that I wanted it to be a good school. I did not know what that meant . . .

> Even if you could do that, if you are a million miles from it, what does it say to everybody else? What you've been doing is a load of rubbish. Here I am, I have this vision and we are going to work towards it.
>
> (Headteacher)

While the vision was vague the headteacher's motives and actions seemed to be driven by her underpinning values, again focusing on achievement and people:

> I think that it is much more about ensuring as many things as possible are done well and you work with people on that. You say this isn't going well what can we do to make this better. And it isn't only better for them out there (the individual) it is better for the staff, the children and every-body and then I think you begin to get a consensus about what sort of school you are.
>
> (Headteacher)

Entrenched in her values is the belief that leadership is a practical activity. To implement change things must be done. By tackling the smaller issues and gaining an understanding of the context, gradually a clearer vision for the school has began to develop:

> I think it was much more about the nitty-gritty things that you begin to do and then you begin to get a vision of what it should be like – I don't know that I even like the word vision because it's so dream-like.
>
> (Headteacher)

In contrast, other members of staff felt that there was a clear vision from the start provided by the headteacher and the senior team and that they knew where they were going:

> I think that she has a very clear idea of what she wants the school to be like.
>
> (Middle manager B)

> It is very clear. There is no ambiguity.
>
> (Middle manager C)

> It is clear where the school is heading and the ethos of the school. Everybody is aware that we are working towards this and everybody is working towards it, it is clear what we are aiming for . . . We are given basic data and attendance targets for the year. We are given our GCSE targets, our SATs targets.
>
> (Classroom teacher B)

For the headteacher the vision is for the school to become 'good' and for that to happen she believes that it needs to be led in an interventionist manner. This was recognised by all staff we spoke to. One middle manager noted:

> The first thing she made clear was that she is hands-on. That she was going to be involved and that she was going to lead by example. So it was a hands-on approach right from the outset.
>
> (Middle manager A)

While a classroom teacher stated:

> It is clear that achievement is very important. She expects everyone to work to the best of their ability and to get the best out of the pupils and if you don't she lets you know about it by coming to you directly.
>
> (Classroom teacher A)

This hands-on approach or practical style of leadership is very important at BGTC. By modelling behaviour of the 'leading professional' the headteacher is making a number of statements to staff (Day *et al.*, 2000). First, the head-teacher is indicating that it is possible to have such a high level of commit-ment and that this level of commitment is needed if the school is to achieve success. Second, that the headteacher will not ask a member of staff to do something that she is not prepared to do herself, whether it be a duty on Friday after school or an extra-curricular event. Third, the way the head-teacher conducts herself around school is the way that she expects staff to, whether it is praising pupils or challenging inappropriate behaviour. Fourth, the headteacher teaches. She manages her time to run the school effectively, prepare lessons and mark books thoroughly, therefore she expects the staff to be able to do so. The overarching message is: if the head-teacher can do it so can any member of staff. The standards are set clearly and, therefore, so are the expectations of staff. The senior team and middle managers mirror these standards and expectations set by the head-teacher. As the school develops over time, by staff moving on or retiring, combined with the appointment of new staff, an increasing percentage of staff reflect these standards and expectations. This further improves consis-tency of actions in the school and results in reinforcement of the shared vision within the organisation.

Over time the headteacher has created a vision that the staff can believe in. In recent years the school has experienced success. The source of this success is the vision that the school has for the future, combined with prac-tical elements of school improvement that are needed to move towards the vision. These elements are articulated and reinforced by actions of the head-teacher and the senior management team on a daily basis.

The type of leadership that builds the capacity for improvement is based on an extremely strong sense of moral purpose, a sense of responsibility to the school and wider community and a sense of deep care for children. Fullan (2001: 13) argues that 'moral purpose is about both ends and means'. At BGTC, success at the end is important, but how you get there is also crucial. As staff and pupils spend more time together at BGTC they develop and foster meaningful relationships based on trust and mutual respect.

Staff development

BGTC invests much time and energy in the selection of appropriate staff. For members of staff to be appointed they must subscribe to the school philosophy and ethos, have the commitment and potential to develop as individuals and make a valid contribution to the school community. No appointment is made at any level without the candidate being observed teaching. For management positions candidates are subjected to a range of activities including taking assemblies, group discussions, presentations and chairing meetings. Outside the interview process other methods used to secure high-quality staff include: informally networking with other colleagues within and beyond the LEA; offering flexible/enhanced packages where appropriate; building links with local universities and colleges by training student teachers and proactively recruiting strong performers during their teaching practice.

Recently, the school has attempted to anticipate the loss of staff through promotion or retirement and used additional funding from initiatives and technology college status deliberately to over-staff the school before experiencing the loss of established teachers. This innovative form of succession planning is aimed at minimising turbulence and allowing new staff to familiarise themselves with the curriculum, routines and ethos of the school. If successful the transition period should support student learning and have a positive rather than negative impact on student outcomes.

Once appointed, the school is committed to the development of staff. BGTC has placed much emphasis on promoting leadership and responsibility at all levels in order to create a team approach to school development. There is a well-structured CPD policy in place and individuals take part in a process of professional review that involves discussions between appraisee and their line manager or other chosen person, lesson observations and target-setting. The arrival of performance management has been successfully tied in to this process so that there is only one system that promotes the sharing of good practice between individuals through target-setting and action-planning:

> One of the things that performance management has added particularly when someone did their management targets [was the sharing of good

practice]. For example, one head of department wanted to know something more about running meetings more effectively. So what you do is say 'I know that X runs meetings very well, go and watch them as part of your performance management' . . . So actually performance management gives us a chance to try and tune in to what it is that people think are slightly their insecurities about their role. And say 'right, by the time we meet again in November you will have gone to watch these three people lead a meeting and reflect on what you've seen and we'll discuss it'.

(Curriculum deputy)

The senior management team is committed to increasing the amount of reflection and sharing of good practice between individuals beyond existing formal structures. Teachers are being encouraged to watch each other teach. For example inside some of the technology college departments there is a policy of 'shared teaching'. In practice this means that everybody watches others teach on a regular basis. The challenge for the school is to create the time for widespread sharing of good practice within and between all departments throughout the full ability and age range. Many teachers have visited other schools to observe and discuss teaching in a different context.

Team-building and teacher leadership

Recently at BGTC efforts have been made to develop the problem-solving skills and leadership capacity of middle management by adopting a team-building approach. This has included formal training for middle managers from external providers supported by informal interactions with members of the senior management team. The curriculum deputy was keen to focus on the role of the middle managers and their contribution to team-building:

We're doing, and have done a lot this year to put expectations on team leaders to get the most out of their teams but to hold the team leader accountable for it. So there is this sense that you are building a group of people that are working towards this common aim . . . I do think that the idea of training a group of people to look at what their team entails. And what their team is about. And what are the strengths and weaknesses inside the team. I think that those things are quite important. To recognise that team leaders are the next people to be developing their teams.

(Curriculum deputy)

The BGTC development team consists of senior and middle managers and meets on six occasions in an academic year. It is central to the school-improvement ethos and provides a forum for innovation, discussion and reflection between academic departments, systems and phases. As the headteacher noted:

> I've got heads of department that are much more reflective and aware, they have development plans. I've recently appointed a head of department that has the same view of her department as I have of the school.
> (Headteacher)

Opportunities exist for inexperienced classroom teachers to perform middle management roles. For example, an inexperienced humanities teacher, for example, took on the role of Head of Geography for the period around the Ofsted inspection. Opportunities also exist for middle management to perform senior manager roles on either a temporary or permanent basis, for example recently a head of department joined the senior management team in a strategic planning role. Another head of department has subsequently joined the senior team in a CPD coordination role. These opportunities can serve many purposes. First, they provide valuable professional development for the individuals involved and the associated experience gained from them can often result in either internal or external promotion. Second, the school can benefit from improved channels of communication as cross-hierarchical links and relationships are established by individuals working outside their traditional *modus operandi*. This often results in individuals and departments gaining an alternative perspective on colleagues and their work. In turn, the individuals' increased understanding of the organisation enhances synergy within the school and further reaffirms the school vision and ethos.

The senior management team encourages individuals to contribute ideas and share examples of good practice with other departments at development team meetings. An example of a recent change initiated by discussion at development team is the relocation of elements of the French department. Teaching rooms have been moved so that all the French classrooms are next to one another. It is anticipated that this will facilitate increased levels of peer observation and team teaching while promoting a strong collaborative ethos within the department.

In addition to the development team and the devolution of power and responsibility to middle managers, senior management have used performance data and regular monitoring strategies to hold middle managers accountable for the development of their team in relation to pupil outcomes:

> What we are trying to do with middle managers is develop their sense of accountability. It's not about them showing me they're doing it. It is

> about them taking a grip on their department and feeling that their department is doing it and they are happy and confident with that.
>
> (Curriculum deputy)

Monitoring by senior management plays a key role in departmental evolution. However, differences are recognised between departments and individual strategies matched to each department's phase of development. This form of individualised support can act as a motivating factor for individuals within teams. However, for this strategy to be successful the leadership team must possess a detailed knowledge of individual colleagues (Leithwood *et al.*, 1999). In general there is a high level of expectation and pressure placed on departments through regular monitoring of their progress but the curriculum deputy articulated the managerial flexibility within the system:

> We maintain a fairly heavy level of monitoring but there is also a fairly light touch in some departments. A department that we think is functioning very well, with a very strong team of teachers, with a very effective head of department, actually, the amount of monitoring we do of that is fairly minimal . . . If the head of department comes to me and says 'I haven't got the books of four kids [for a book review senior managers collect a sample of pupils' books for evaluation and and then provide feedback to staff] I've only got these two' I don't really care because I'm confident about what's going on. But if another member of staff came to me and said 'I've only got two' I would say 'go away and get the other two'. We adopt a different approach for different departments. What you have is more imput into some areas than others.
>
> (Curriculum deputy)

In addition to the use of different strategies to develop different departments the style of support also varies. At BGTC there is an acceptance that like schools, departments have differing needs, strengths and weaknesses. For example a new head of department with four new staff will receive a 'more supportive, less demanding' (Curriculum deputy) approach from senior managers compared to an established head of department with a team of experienced teachers. To support this individualised approach there are also more traditional methods employed to monitor departmental progress. Individual meetings between heads of department and the headteacher and curriculum deputy are used to explore departmental performance against targets and predictors. These discussions are in-depth and often focus on variations between individual teachers, classes and pupils. Points for action are then determined from these meetings and the middle manager is responsible for the implementation and monitoring of agreed strategies.

Reflections

The BGTC case study illustrates four important leadership considerations that have been central to the creation and subsequent generation of sustained improvement and leadership capacity at BGTC.

Organisational philosophy

BGTC could be described as a culturally tight and managerially flexible organisation bound together by a singular shared vision, where all stakeholders share common values. Central to these values are the core process of teaching and learning and the development and maintainence of the internal conditions to support the process. The organisation is underpinned by a strong sense of moral purpose. Staff, parents, pupils and other stakeholders are encouraged to subscribe to these organisational norms. On occasions, when individuals challenge these norms, efforts are made to adapt beliefs and behaviours of the individual. However, if these efforts fail the organisational norms are not compromised and if necessary the individual may leave the organisation in search of another post or school. BGTC then makes a concerted effort to find a suitable replacement that can subscribe to this strong organisational culture.

Leadership function

While the literature suggests that no one particular style of leadership works in challenging contexts it is clear that purely directive or prescriptive models are likely to result in failure due to being unresponsive to the demands of the leadership task presented by challenging schools (Harris *et al.*, 2001). The headteacher at BGTC is a very strong, motivated practical leader but the style could not be described as heroic or of the super-head genre. It is tenacious in nature and focuses on attention to detail. At its core is the belief that the staff in the school are the school's largest asset, therefore they must be valued and continuously developed if the school is to move forward. It is becoming clear that successful leaders in SfCC match their style of leadership to the development phase of the school. Crucially at BGTC the approach to leadership has been flexible. A more autocratic approach is used when the leadership team feels that it is necessary to move the school forward. In other situations the approach has been more democratic. The sensitivity of the leadership team to time and space has allowed an approach to emerge that has complemented the development phase of the school.

It is a leader's capacity to respond to circumstances and manage change effectively that proves to be the most important characteristic of successful leadership. Subsequently, this depends on the leadership roles and capacity for change that have been developed within the wider staff and community of the school. BGTC's success to date is a result of complex interpersonal relationships and distributed multilevel leadership that has been promoted through a commitment to CPD at both individual and team level. The head-teacher uses a range of strategies to bring out the best in her staff and is keen to provide opportunities for staff to take on extra leadership roles and responsibilities within the school.

Intrapersonal and interpersonal development

It has become widely accepted that staff development plays a pivotal role in school improvement (for example, Barth, 1990; Hopkins *et al.*, 1994; Joyce and Showers, 1995). Recent work suggests that staff development is even more crucial in schools starting from a low competency base or attainment level (Reynolds *et al.*, 2001; Harris and Chapman, 2002). The headteacher at BGTC pays considerable attention to the professional development of staff, regularly provides a range of opportunities matched to individual needs and encourages staff to take them. The culture of the school supports the development of all individuals, irrespective of position or experience. Internal CPD is valued and teachers often present or share ideas at staff meetings and training days. Support is provided to visit other schools and departments in order to share good practice. The senior team can recognise variation in performance of teachers within the school. A range of innovative strategies combining elements of pressure and support are employed to develop the lowest-performing teachers. However, the development of individuals alone can only produce limited rewards. The key is to build new (and develop existing) relationships within and between teams in order to create a professional learning community that promotes the generation and sharing of knowledge for all. Therefore, professional relationships are central to successful leadership and improvement.

Although a high level of monitoring still prevails from senior management, BGTC is developing a strong club culture (Reynolds *et al.*, 2001). As confidence rises, accountability measures have become increasingly based on informal relationships and mechanisms rather than solely relying on those created within formal structures. These relationships have developed in a culture of trust and risk-taking amongst teachers. Relationships and leadership have been fostered and maintained through a tight sense of collegial responsibility between colleagues and pupils, and ultimately this responsibility is underpinned by the strongest sense of moral purpose. Pupils recognise the staff's commitment to them and consider teachers to act professionally and in a fair manner. The leadership team has been proactive in generating positive relationships with parents and the wider community.

Staffing mix

The blend of personality, expertise, youth and experience can be an important feature of developing effective teams at all levels within the school. Patience, staff turnover, succession planning and new appointments have provided BGTC with the opportunity to create a favourable staffing mix within the school. The staffing mix helps to minimise or exaggerate the tensions between polarised positions. As an example, if one considers innovation versus consolidation within a team, it could be argued that a highly innovative team is more likely to be young and less experienced, while a team more suited to maintaining the *status quo* is likely to be older and more experienced. Unfortunately, this very simple example fails to account for the complexities of reality, as innovation and consolidation are only two of an infinite number of dimensions that leaders must attempt to understand and consider in relation to any one team. Other factors, including the school's development phase and the senior team's priorities for change, must also be included in the equation if the required balance is to be achieved.

Commentary

Researchers and academics have begun to conceptualise and develop various models of capacity and related concepts such as 'capacity-building'. BGTC is an example of a school that has been engaging in capacity-building for a long period of time. Over the last seven years the leadership team has been implementing a series of complex strategies aimed at improving the school. The success of these strategies has been underpinned by the core principle, of capacity building focusing on organisational philosophy, leadership function, intrapersonal and interpersonal development and creating an optimum staffing mix. In summary this case study supports the emerging evidence relating to leadership in challenging contexts that suggests that the autocratic 'super-head' approach that has dominated the discourse surrounding failing and challenging schools is misguided. A leadership approach that is more likely to improve our most challenging and vulnerable schools must focus on facilitating relationships and team building within and beyond the organisation.

References

Barth, R. (1990) *Improving Schools from Within: Teachers, Parents and Principles Can Make a Difference*, San Francisco, CA, Jossey-Bass.

Chapman, C. (2001) 'Ofsted and School Improvement in Challenging Circumstances', paper presented at the British Educational Research Association Conference, University of Leeds.

DASSSR (1998) Letter extract to BGTC from Department of Applied Social Studies and Social Research.

Day, C., Harris, A., Hadfield, M., Tolley, H. and Beresford, J. (2000) *Leading Schools in Times of Change*, Buckingham, Open University Press.

Fullan, M. (2001) *Leading in a Culture of Change*, San Francisco, CA, Jossey-Bass.

Hargreaves, D. (1995) 'School Culture, School Effectiveness and School Improvement', *School Effectiveness and School Improvement*, 6(1): 23–46.

Harris, A. (2001) 'Leadership in Schools Facing Challenging Circumstances', paper presented to British Educational Leadership, Management and Administration Society conference.

Harris, A. and Chapman, C. (2002) 'Democratic Leadership for School Improvement in Challenging Contexts', paper presented at International Congress for School Effectiveness and Improvement, Copenhagen, January.

Harris, A., Sinanan, M. and Chapman, C. (2001) *Leadership in Schools Facing Challenging Circumstances: An International Literature Review*, prepared for the National College of School Leadership.

Hopkins, D., Ainscow, M. and West, M. (1994) *School Improvement in an Era of Change*, London, Cassell.

Joyce, B. and Showers, B. (1995) *Student Achievement through Staff Development: Fundamentals of School Renewal*, 2nd edn, New York, Longman.

Leithwood, K., Jantzi, D. and Steinbach, R. (1999) *Changing Leadership for Changing Times*, Buckingham, Open University Press.

Maden, M. (2001) *Success against the Odds: Five Years On*, London, Routledge.

Miles, M. and Huberman, A. (1992) *Qualitative Data Analysis: An Expanded Sourcebook*, 2nd edn, Thousand Oaks, CA, Sage.

Nanus, B. (1992) *Visionary Leadership*, San Francisco, CA, Jossey-Bass.

National Commission on Education (1996) *Success against the Odds: Effective Schools in Disadvantaged Areas*, London, Routledge.

Ofsted (1999) Inspection Report: Bartley Green Community School, Birmingham LEA. Online at: www.ofsted.gov.uk/reports.

Reynolds, D. (1996) 'Turning around Ineffective Schools: Some Evidence and Some Speculations', in J. Gray, D. Reynolds, C. Fitz-Gibbon and J. Jesson (eds), *Merging Traditions: The Future of School Effectiveness and School Improvement*, London, Cassell.

Reynolds, D. (1998) 'The Study and Remediation of Ineffective Schools: Some Further Reflections', in L. Stoll and K. Myers (eds), *No Quick Fixes: Perspectives on Schools in Difficulty*, London, Falmer.

Reynolds, D., Hopkins, D., Potter, D. and Chapman, C. (2001) *School Improvement in Schools Facing Challenging Circumstances: A Review of Research and Practice*, London, DfEE.

Sammons, P., Hillman, J. and Mortimore, P. (1994) *Key Characteristics of Effective Schools: A Review of School Effectiveness Research,* London, Ofsted.

Stoll, L. and Myers, K. (1998) *No Quick Fixes: Perspectives on Schools in Difficulty,* London, Falmer.

Teddlie, C. and Reynolds, D. (2000) *The International Handbook of School Effectiveness Research,* London, Falmer.

Thrupp, M. (2001) 'Failing Schools and Social Disadvantage: An Overview of New Labour Policies and their Impact', paper presented at the British Educational Research Association conference, University of Leeds.

Part IV

Future directions and implications for leadership and school improvement

Chapter 9

Successful leadership in the twenty-first century

Christopher Day

Schools and society

> School principals will need to be 'multilingual', working within multiple and competing discourses eg. of managerialism and care, accountability and professional autonomy, competition and collaboration, personal and social education, needs of students and the narrow instrumentalism of government required 'standards'.
>
> (Gewirtz *et al.*, 1995)

This chapter focuses upon successful school leadership for the present and the future. During this time, the context for successful leadership will continue to change in the direction of more accountability, more responsibilities for creating and sustaining school and classroom cultures which are able to manage change and respond to ongoing changes in society, family, students' attitudes to formal learning and developments in technology. Indeed:

> heads and teachers will need more than ever before to nurture, not only the cognitive processes within the needs of individuals but also the social relationships and arrangements which stimulate learning, recognizing that learning is a shared responsibility by all the social partners.
>
> (Coffield, 1996: 9)

Speculating about the future of schools is a relatively recent phenomenon and it is tempting to associate this with the increasing recognition of its connectedness with politics, economics and society. This section, then, will use what some writers on schools of the future have written as 'indicators' or 'hypotheses'. We have selected writers from England, Australia, Scandinavia and America. We begin with the words of a Professor of Public Policy at George Mason University, Washington DC, writing of human nature and social order. In 'The Great Disruption', Fukuyama (1999) writes of the consequences of the shift into an 'information society' in which 'inexpensive information technology makes it increasingly easy to move information across national borders, and rapid communication by television, radio, fax, and e-mail erodes the boundaries of long established cultural communities' (3) as being not entirely positive. He points to 'seriously deteriorating social conditions in most of the industrialized world . . . the decline of kinship as a social institute' (4) and the statistical increase in crime, fatherless children, reduced educational outcomes and opportunities, decline in trust and confidence in institutions and politicians and the break-down of generalisable rules of conduct as individuals maximise personal freedom.

> Schools have traditionally not simply provided students with knowl-edge and skills; they have also sought to socialise them into certain cultural habits ultimately designed to make them better citizens . . . Schools in many instances are being asked to socialise children whose parents have failed to provide their offspring with adequate social capital and are not managing to keep up . . .
>
> (Fukuyama, 1999: 258–9)

In his classic text on post-capitalist society, Peter Drucker (1993) devoted one chapter to 'the accountable school'. In it he argues that although the technological revolution will transform schools over the next few decades from being almost totally 'labour-intensive' to highly 'capital-intensive' and embracing the new technology of learning and teaching will be a pre-requisite for national and cultural success and economic competitiveness (178), it will be the changes in the social position and the role of the school which will be the real challenge. Schools will, he believes, need to imbue students of all ages and on all levels with motivation to learn and with the discipline of continuing learning. They will become places where the emphasis is on individuals using technology to learn, freeing teachers to identify strengths, motivate, direct, encourage individuals rather than spending much of their time supervising, managing and controlling; but they will continue to be held accountable for the results they achieve. Accountability was a theme echoed only a year later by David Hargreaves who wrote that the educational challenge for schools and teachers in England in the twenty-first century is 'to raise standards of learning and per-formance of students and the standards of teaching and the performance of teachers' (Hargreaves, 1994: 4).

It is not the purpose of this chapter, or indeed this book, to discuss in detail the complex arguments which Fukuyama and others make, for they are speculating on world trends in social and economic realities and not specifically upon schooling. However, it is clear that the responsibilities of schools, and therefore their headteachers, will be defined much more sharply in terms of their roles in promoting responsible citizenship and high academic standards. In this context it is interesting to note the dismissal of notions of 'value added', so prevalent in the UK, by Fukuyama who refers to the findings of the 1966 Coleman Report supported by 'a great deal of subsequent research', that family and peers have a much greater impact on educational outcomes than the inputs over which public policy has control, like teacher salaries, classroom sizes and spending on facilities' (115). To put it a different way, teachers must teach within the constraints not only of their own expertise and with the resources and curricula provided, but also in relation to the 'luggage' carried by their students. If this luggage is changing in the ways suggested by Fukuyama, then it follows that teachers' work will become more rather than less complex. When he writes about the 'ligatures binding [individuals] in webs of social obligation [being] . . . greatly loosened' (47), we are reminded again that schools have both academic and social functions. This is particularly so in school environments which are 'disadvantaged' in terms of the socio-economic backgrounds of the students but also their diminished opportunities for high-quality education caused by problems of staff recruitment, lack of appropriately qualified specialist teachers in key areas and retention, which, it seems, have become permanent features in the landscape of many schools in England. These, combined with calls for the raising of academic standards based upon nationally measurable criteria which are not always appropriate, compound the difficulties of successful leadership. Here, then, is the abiding challenge: to reconcile external demands for student attainment when much of the curriculum is irrelevant to the needs of students in the twenty-first century and the increasing alienation of the students to traditional forms of teaching and learning with the erosion of the morale, health and job satisfaction of many teachers. Behaviour management and student disengagement from learning, once the almost exclusive preserve of secondary schools, now are an increasing concern for many primary schools too. It is not only inner-city schools that serve socially and economically deprived families which face problems of motivation, discipline and attendance. Many students from so called affluent areas are not only disengaged from school learning but also from their parents – most of whom have full-time jobs and are often disengaged from their children. They have, for one reason or another, 'checked out' of childrearing:

> They have disengaged from responsibilities of parental discipline – they do not know how their child is doing in school, have no idea who their child's friends are, and are not aware of how their child spends his or her free time – but they have also disengaged from being accepting and supportive as well. They rarely spend time in activities with their child, and seldom just talk with their adolescent about the day's events.
> (Steinberg, 1996: 188)

That many students are emotionally isolated at home and alienated from school is revealed in a survey of 14-year-olds. Although almost all agreed that schoolwork was worth doing and almost all of their parents thought that it was important to do well in school:

- over half said that most of the time they did not want to go to school;
- one in four thought that teachers were too easily satisfied;
- one in four admitted to having played truant;
- one in five denied being happy at school (NCE, cited in Hargreaves, 1994).

It is not only students who are being alienated. For many teachers, the hope, optimism and self-belief which are the vital wellsprings of successful learning and positive educational change (Hargreaves and Fullan, 1998: 1) are being eroded by the constant drip of increased accountability, student testing, school inspection, performance management and accompanying bureaucratisation by governments who pay lip service to the importance and complexity of teachers and teaching whilst continuing to increase workload in the name of raising standards.

It may be that in the latter part of the twentieth century and the beginning of this one, teachers and heads 'have been given an impossible task by an over-expectant society' (Longworth and Davies, 1996: 40).

Schools, teachers and learners

Underpinning all of the writing on schools of the future is the assertion that 'schools are one of our last hopes for rebuilding a sense of community' (Hargreaves and Fullan, 1998: 42). Among those who have written about the future nature and shape of the schooling system and how this will affect teachers in England is Tim Brighouse (2001). He has speculated on the idea of a 'colleagiate academy, a collection of urban secondary schools with the various subject faculties outside the basic core, transcending individual schools'. Here, 'interdependence and reliance on ICT would give a different rhythm to the timetable'. In these and other schools, there would be a more extensive use of para-professionals (classroom assistants and associates), freeing teachers to be researchers, to hone their teaching skills and to 'convince children that they are unique and valued . . . the precursor of the next step, which is skill acquisition or conceptual learning even when they are personally doubtful' (65). In Australia, Hedley Beare has speculated that, 'the identifiable block of buildings we now call school will disappear' along, in England, with national examinations at 16 and 18 years of age, that part of the school's formal task is 'to provide systematic "teaching" of parents so that they know how to ensure that learning-in-family, incidental learnings at home and out of school, and parent nurturing are in harmony with and reinforce the students' formal learning programme' (2001: 190), that school, 'continues to be concerned about a student's personal development, about her beliefs and values, her behaviours and her social interactions and skills', and that, 'Teachers operate not so much as single instructors but in teams whose members have interlocking and complementary skills' (190). Like Brighouse, he recognises the powerful learning influence of ICT. Like Drucker, he believes that schools will be within society, that teachers will be 'knowledge workers'. These writers recognise the process of redefining schools and teachers that is gathering speed, and that this is driven in part by cost factors.

> 'Quality teaching' for pupils is about activity, not passivity; about nego-tiation and close relationships, not distance and deference.
>
> (Morgan and Morris, 1999: 00)

Teachers will need commitment, energy and skill if they are to grapple with the immense emotional, intellectual and social demands as they work towards building the internal and external relationships demanded by such knowledge-creating schools. Although the needs are plain and the aspirations of David Hargreaves and others are not unreasonable it is as well to remember that, in England at least, the current state of morale is not high and that energy levels for many are at breaking point. Andy Hargreaves summarises the dilemma. In writing of the 'fourth age' of pro-fessionalism (the first three being pre-professional, autonomous, collegial) as being 'postmodern', he suggests:

> So we are now on the edge of an age of post modern professionalism where teachers deal with a diverse and complex clientele, in conditions of increasing moral uncertainty, where many methods of approach are possible, and where more and more social groups have an influence and a say. Whether this postmodern age will see exciting and positive new partnerships being created with groups and institutions beyond the school, and teachers learning to work effectively, openly and author-itatively with those partners in a broad social movement that protects and advances their professionalism, or whether it will witness the deprofessionalization of teaching as teachers crumble under multiple pressures, intensified work demands, reduced opportunities to learn from colleagues, and enervating discourses of derision, is something that is still to be decided.
>
> (Hargreaves, 2000: 175)

In England, it has been suggested that teachers in this century 'must help to shape the education system rather than simply functioning with it . . . modelling by team-playing, networking and supporting community . . . in order to cultivate in students the personal, moral and communal qualities that will matter in, and so be a preparation for, the knowledge society' (Hargreaves, 1998: 12).

Finally, in this all too brief tour of a selection of views of the educational future, Per Dalin (Norway) and Val Rust (America) produced a visionary view of the challenges facing society, the realities of work and leisure for children in the twenty-first century, and the implications for schools (Dalin and Rust, 1996). Like others, they place the school of the future within the context of lifelong learning in which all age groups, social classes and worker categories participate. Like others they suggest that schooling will be, 'characterized by more flexibility and diversity' (142) than has hitherto been the case, that the learner will, more than ever before, be placed at the centre and, 'be able to choose from a variety of learning opportunities and learning modes' (145); and that although teachers will continue to be important, their roles will be redefined as they increase in complexity:

> Teachers will no longer be expected to have the one and only right answer. They will be expected to stimulate the curiosity of each child, to focus on the basic issues and to help each child to discover and to work systematically.
>
> (Dalin and Rust, 1996: 145)

Interestingly, in the context of the recent history of the curriculum in English schools, they suggest that a 'detailed outline of the content of the curriculum will no longer be the primary issue' (146).

The problem is that despite their experience of change over the last two decades, most schools and school systems in general:

- do not yet really know how to respond to the changes they experience in assertive ways;
- have not yet developed systematic ways of learning about the nature and implications of the social changes around them;
- have limited and unimaginative strategies for responding to change;
- have perceptions and reactions that are dominated by conventional wisdom, with the result that they try familiar (but unsuccessful) solutions, or low-risk one-of-a-kind initiatives that have little impact on the larger system; and
- possess a weak outward-looking stance (Levin and Riffel, 1997, cited in Hargreaves and Fullan, 1998: 23).

David Hargreaves developed this theme in writing of 'knowledge-creating schools' with four interconnected characteristics:

1 Openness to the outside world:
- a strong awareness of the external environment . . . and a capacity to recognise, assimilate and exploit external knowledge
- sensitivity to the expectations and preferences of students, parents and governors.
2 A modification of the culture of the school and its organisational structures
- a culture of, a commitment to and an enthusiasm for continual improvement
- institutional planning that is coherent
- decentralisation and flat hierarchies, groups being given the responsibility for scrutinising ideas and decision-making within their sphere of action
- internal hybridisation, that is cross-functional teams and job rotation
- temporary developmental structures outside the bureaucratic maintenance structures – task forces of people who come together to solve a problem and disband after completing the task
- a positive climate with a constant and explicitly maintained tension between liberty and control, freedom and responsibility in professional work.
3 New kinds and styles of relationship which focus on:
- informality of relationships among staff who value task-relevant expertise rather than organisational status and engage in high volumes of professional talk through intensive internal networking . . .
- a recognition by managers of the specialised, expert knowledge held by teachers
- encouragement of diversity, deviant ideas being a potential seedbed of innovation
- the provision of regular opportunities for reflection, dialogue, enquiry and networking in relation to professional knowledge and practice, and a high commitment to continuing professional development.
4 Knowledge creation as a central activity of teachers:
- professional knowledge creation is not seen as the chance quirkiness of a minority of 'creative' individuals, but as a whole-school process that has to be managed
- a readiness to tinker and experiment in an ad hoc way with new ideas or variations on old ideas is encouraged and supported, in order to do things better, within a culture that does not blame individuals when things prove not to be good enough . . .
- teachers become ready to engage in alliances and networks to further such work, including networking with other schools: since no school can alone create all the knowledge needed, sharing is essential and in the interests of all.

(Hargreaves, 1998: 24–6)

Leadership for the future: challenging the performativity culture

> To cope with a changing world, any entity must develop the capability of shifting and changing, of developing new skills and attitudes: in short the capability of learning . . . the essence of learning is the ability to manage change by changing yourself – as much for people when they grow up as for companies when they live through turmoil.
>
> (de Gues, 1997: 20)

Over the last two decades the discourses of school effectiveness, efficiency and accountability (in terms of answerability) have served the demands of governments for raising standards of school performance in terms of their economic 'market-led' agendas. Whilst this has been able to be accommodated by middle-class communities, it has further disadvantaged many inner-city, migrant and socially deprived communities who not only find themselves at the lower ends of 'league tables' but also having to manage an increasing number of students who are either unable to cope with a national curriculum or who are alienated because it does not relate to their needs. In all schools, however, the net effect of these policies has been to overemphasise productivity and performativity in measurable, quantifiable terms – tempting if not causing headteachers to give priority to their management functions rather than the educational leadership of the whole community. The repositioning of schools within the marketplace, should not divert the headteachers' attention from the broader educational purposes of teaching and learning. They need still to be both 'saturated in pedagogies . . . [and] ethically involved with the ambiguities and complexities of life in [and beyond] schools' (Thompson, 2001: 19).

Although we know that school principals play a crucial role in school-wide efforts to raise standards of teaching and pupil learning and achievement, evidence-based knowledge of what makes successful leaders remains elusive. The most popular theories are located in the 'transactional' and 'transformational' models identified more than twenty years ago (Burns, 1978) and lately reinvented through such terms as 'liberation' (Tampoe, 1998), 'educative' (Duignan and McPherson, 1992), 'invitational' (Stoll and Fink, 1996) and 'moral' leadership (Sergiovanni, 1992). What is clear from these, and the effective schools literature, is that successful leaders not only set direction, organise and monitor, build relationships with the school community, and are people-centred; but they also model values and practices consistent with those of the school so that 'purposes which may have initially seemed to be separate, become fused' (Sergiovanni, 1995: 119).

The problem, however, with these theories and those borrowed or adapted from studies of business leadership is that they are based either on observation or self-report of leaders and those leaders are not necessarily all successful. Few studies have sought information from heads recognised as effective; fewer still have sought educated opinion from those who know most about them and who have experienced the realities of their leadership in times of change i.e. their students, staff, governors and parents.

In 1993, Beck and Murphy published the results of their analysis of the extensive literature on school principalship in America in which they identified metaphorical themes from the 1920s to the 1990s. These ranged from being 'Values Brokers', through 'Scientific Managers', 'Democratic Leaders' 'Theory-Guided Administrators', 'Bureaucratic Executives', 'Humanistic Facilitators' and 'Instructional Leaders'. In the 1990s, they described the conditions for principalship as being crisis in the economy, the changing nature of the social fabric and the evolution towards a post-industrial world (the information society). Like other authors, they identify the 'major metamorphosis' which schools are experiencing, the attacks on the current system and the attempts to transform education through changes in governance, curriculum, management and curriculum delivery; and like others they see the focus moving from hierarchical, bureaucratic organisational structures to more decentralised systems in which traditional patterns of roles and relationships are altered as 'maintenance of the organisational infrastructure' becomes secondary to 'the holistic development of persons' (Beck and Murphy, 1993: 187). In schools, the 'model of the teacher as a "sage on the stage" in which teachers are viewed as content specialists who possess relevant knowledge that they transmit to students through telling, is being replaced by an approach in which teaching is more like coaching, where the student is the primary performer . . . [and] the traditional dominant relationship between schools . . . and the public is being reworked in favour of more . . . partnerships . . .' (1993: 189)

The principal in these contexts, they suggest, will be a:

Leader (of transitions)

Servant (leading not from the apex of an organisational pyramid but from the nexus of a web of interpersonal relationships in which the bases of their influence is professional expertise and moral imperative rather than line authority)

Organisational architect (addressing the environmental challenges confronting schools as proponents of change)

Social Architect (designing and constructing with others an integrated social agency network to address the conditions confronting many of their pupils – and their families)

Educator (being lead learners)

Moral Agent (addressing issues of values, purpose-defining, recognizing the moral and ethical responsibilities of schooling)

Person in the Community (remembering that he or she is a person whose work as an educational leader is first, foremost and always with persons . . . who are physical, intellectual, spiritual, emotional and social beings . . . (and) building a community of learners in which all persons can flourish.

(Beck and Murphy, 1993: 190–5)

In the present decade, the conditions of the 1990s described by Beck and Murphy and others continue to prevail, and the need for headteachers to recognise their broader, more complex roles and responsibilities becomes even more urgent.

In 1998, the National Association of Headteachers, the largest in the UK, commissioned such a multi-perspective study. Twelve heads were selected from schools of different sizes, operating within different phases, located in a range of geographical, economic and socio-cultural settings. All the schools had received a 'positive' Inspection Report by Ofsted, particularly with regard to their leadership; all were performing better than average; and the heads all had a good reputation amongst their peers. Gender and experience were also factored in. All schools were visited for three days, by members of the five-strong research team, a substantial number of interviews were conducted and local documentation supplemented these. Analysis of all the data revealed a surprising consensus among the different constituencies in each school and between them. All held similar constructions of why the head in their school was successful. Their heads were:

- values-led
- people-centred
- achievement-orientated
- inwards- and outwards-facing
- able to manage a number of ongoing tensions and dilemmas.

All emphasised the sets of core personal values of the heads were based upon care, equity, high expectations, and achievement, which were clear to and shared by the overwhelming majority of the school constituencies and which were the drivers for the life of the school. All emphasised the importance attached by the heads to monitoring standards in the school, to keeping 'ahead of the game' so that their schools responded rather than reacted to new external demands, testing them against their own standards, minimising bureaucratic demands on staff; all spoke of the improvement-orientated collaborative school cultures which the heads promoted, and the emphasis upon continuing professional development which met both organisational and individual needs. All spoke of the time and care which the heads gave enthusiastically to their work; the way the heads modelled their values. The heads themselves were clearly strategic, 'reflective practitioners', exercising a range of inter- and intrapersonal skills, able to analyse, evaluate, articulate and communicate with a range of agencies locally and nationally.

Alongside these positive traits were ongoing problems. Heads worked long hours, were enabled to continue to develop partly through the unsung support of external networks of colleagues, friends, family. It was, however, both their personal values and their abilities to maintain and develop learning and achievement cultures while they managed ongoing tensions and dilemmas. Some of these dilemmas follow.

Leadership versus management

Leadership is essentially the process of building and maintaining a sense of vision, culture and interpersonal relationships, whereas management is the coordination, support and monitoring of organisational activities. To enact both roles successfully requires a careful balancing act.

> Leadership is about having vision and articulating, ordering priorities, getting others to go with you, constantly reviewing what you are doing and holding on to things you value. Management is about the functions, procedures and systems by which you realise the vision.
>
> (Infant deputy)

Development versus maintenance

> If I don't develop others, the school won't develop. So that's my priority. Other jobs can be delegated but not this one.
>
> (Primary head)

A tension exists between the amount of time and energy that heads devote to system maintenance and the amount that they devote to ensuring that staff are always competent, challenged and supported in seeking higher standards.

Internal versus external change

> The pressure is from outside, but I have to manage the pressure inside . . .
>
> (Secondary head)

An increase in external scrutiny of schools creates its own tensions. Head-teachers found themselves positioned uneasily between those forces outside schools instigating and promoting changes and their own staff who, ultimately, had to implement them. They demonstrated their leadership by the selection of which initiatives to take on; the relative support which they provide for their implementation; their knowledge of how others were tackling new initiatives and by the ways they adapted initiatives to their particular values and circumstances.

Autocracy versus autonomy

> Although we can work closely, there has to be a time when decisions are taken and she has to say whether we can or cannot do this.
>
> (Primary deputy)

In school cultures of collaboration in which decision-making is no longer the exclusive preserve of headteachers, and yet heads remain responsible and accountable for the schools' success (or otherwise), a key leadership skill that these heads displayed was their ability to manage the boundaries of autocratic and democratic decision-making.

Personal time versus professional tasks

Increasing external requirements upon schools had led many heads to commit more and more of their personal time to school-related business.

> I work at least 60 hours a week . . . it worries me because I don't know how long I can go on putting in the amount of energy.
>
> (Primary head)

Although most heads in the study had found ways of managing the demands of intensification the personal opportunity costs were universally high and, long term, potentially damaging.

Personal values versus institutional imperatives

Whilst there was little evidence in the study of opposing sets of values within the schools, tensions did arise from externally generated pressures of rationalism, and definitions of efficiency and effectiveness which were perceived as challenging strongly held people-centred values.

> He holds traditional human values – care for people and community and giving back to society the benefits of what you have been given at school. You are a better person if you achieve academically, but that is only part of being a balanced person.
>
> (Primary teacher)

Leadership in small versus large schools

Heads in small primary schools were disadvantaged on two main counts. Because they had regular, significant class-teaching responsibilities, they were unable to fulfil their strategic leadership roles satisfactorily:

> it's all the stress of planning and preparing and co-ordinating as a class teacher which is too much . . .
>
> (Primary head)

The breadth of the curriculum which needed to be addressed also provided additional demands upon the small number of staff.

Develop or dismiss

For heads who have to make decisions about teaching standards, continuing poor teaching by a member of staff creates a leadership dilemma, cutting across the heads' personal framework of values and beliefs, their ideological and educative commitments to the development of everyone in the school community.

> You can support somebody who is incompetent for as long as you like, but there comes a point where you know that it is not going to make any difference, particularly if they have been doing it for a long time.
>
> (Infant head)

Dismissing a staff member touches upon the culture of the school, staff morale, and the nature of the relationship between leader and led. The heads in the study, however, had not shrunk from taking such 'tough decisions', illustrating the clear if painful boundary that must be drawn at key times between the personal and professional relationships which are at the heart of the educational health of school communities.

Power with or power over

The basis of this dilemma is the extent to which similar and dissimilar values can be reconciled. The heads in this study sought to achieve a balance between consulting and involving staff in their decisions whilst still providing a clear direction forward, but were aware that such involvement might well lead to demands for a bigger say in the direction and that this might well challenge their right always to make the final decision.

> We are leaders in our own little domain and sometimes it's hard to
> accept the overall leadership . . . because you think you have got a
> better way of doing it.
>
> (Primary teacher)

Subcontracting or mediation

This final dilemma reflects the position of most heads in the study as they
found themselves legally responsible for the implementation of externally
imposed change, some of which challenged their own moral purposes,
sets of core values and practices, and analysis of the needs of their particular
school.

> At the end of the day the head has to have integrity and to stick to core
> values and beliefs. It is important that the head can demonstrate integ-
> rity in the face of adversity . . .
>
> (Infant head)

The heads had not become 'subcontractors', unthinking links in a chain
leading from those who developed policy to those who received it. Nor
were they subversives, attempting to undermine the authority of policy
imperatives. Rather, they managed changes with integrity and skill,
integrating them into the vision, values and practices of their schools.

In the final chapter of *Changing Leadership for Changing Times*, Leithwood
and Jantzi (1999) predict that future schools and leaders

> will face a steady stream of complex problems, a prediction that places a
> premium on continuous improvements in school staff's individual and
> collective problem-solving capacities.
>
> (Leithwood and Jantzi, 1999: 216)

They go on to suggest that school principals, therefore, need:

- openness to new ideas;
- tolerance for divergent points of view;
- tolerance for strategic failure;
- questioning of basic assumptions;
- speculative thinking;
- personal mastery;
- interconnectedness.

> Learning is the essential fuel for the leader, the source of high octane
> energy that keeps up the momentum by continually sparking new

understanding, new ideas, and new challenges. It is absolutely indispensable under today's conditions of rapid change and complexity. Very simply, those who do not learn do not long survive as leaders.

(Bennis and Nanns, 1985: 188)

At the present time, it is clear from both research and experience reported elsewhere in this book that forms of 'transformative' leadership which encourage participation, ownership and interdependence in staffrooms and classrooms and are underpinned by vision, high expectations of all, a focus upon increasing the quality of classroom learning opportunities and, alongside these, raising levels of achievement, continuing professional development, a sense of moral purpose, principles of social justice and strong community links are closely associated with successful leadership; and that successful leaders not only actively promote a wide range of formal and informal learning for all their staff but are themselves 'lead learners'. The most recent empirical European research confirms that:

1 Leadership means having a clear personal vision of what you want to achieve.
2 Good leaders are in the thick of things, working alongside their colleagues.
3 Leadership means respecting teachers' autonomy, protecting them from extraneous demands.
4 Good leaders look ahead, anticipate change and prepare people for it so that it doesn't surprise or disempower them.
5 Good leaders are pragmatic. They are able to grasp the realities of the political and economic context and they are able to negotiate and compromise.
6 Good leaders are informed by, and communicate, clear sets of personal and educational values which represent their moral purposes for the school (Day *et al.*, 2000: 165; MacBeath, 1998: 63).

One of the best-known and respected American writers has developed a model of 'pedagogical leadership' which incorporates these and which is described as that which invests in capacity-building by developing social and academic capital for students and intellectual and professional capital for teachers (Sergiovanni, 1998). He points out that within schools, professional capital is created by a fabric of reciprocal responsibilities and mutual support. Recent empirical research on successful leadership in small and medium-sized businesses in England concluded also that people-centred leadership had the most impact upon performance and profitability:

The effectiveness with which organisations manage, develop, motivate, involve and engage the willing contribution of the people who work in

them is a key determinant of how well those organisations perform . . .
employee commitment and positive, 'psychological contact' between
employer and employee are fundamental to improving performance.

(Patterson *et al.*, 1997: vii–viii)

It seems, then, that a focus upon the well-being of students and staff is a key
indicator of successful school leadership. However, at present, in many
countries:

under new public sector management, there are emerging irreconcilable
goals for schooling. On the one hand there are those who are pushing
schools to operate like businesses, and to pursue the educational
equivalent of profit maximisation. On the other hand, schools are ultimately concerned with the development of students who are not only
employable, but also autonomous, responsible, moral individuals who
are effective members of society . . . Heads who are able to model
moral leadership in the way they run their schools are more likely, in
our view, to concentrate on the ultimate goal of schooling, even
though they are constantly under pressure to do otherwise.

(Dempster and Mahoney, 1998: 137–8)

Heads, then, need also to be able to manage tensions and dilemmas
associated with managing 'irreconcilable goals'.

What is often forgotten in research and writing about leadership are the
consequences of managing this, however successfully, for the self. Indeed,
noteworthy in the Day *et al.* (2000: 58–60) study was the presence of considerable stress in the lives of successful headteachers:

The job has no boundaries so you must impose your own to maintain
your sanity.

(Primary head)

I have to tell myself that I can't be all things to all people all of the time.

(Secondary head)

Because of the amount of paperwork I have a feeling of failure because
I can't meet my own agenda and feel constrained by events.

(Secondary head)

Engaging head and heart

All researches point to the need for heads to possess qualities of strategic
thinking so that they remain 'one step ahead' of the game; moral purpose;
and emotional as well as intellectual leadership. One of the key character-

istics of successful leaders is the ability to do this, to think and reflect, to be emotionally, socially and cognitively intelligent, as well as to act strategically (seeing ahead, seeing behind, seeing above, seeing below, seeing beside, seeing beyond and, above all, seeing it through). However, this will not be accomplished by the simple adoption of a rational planning model:

> Strategies grow initially like weeds in a garden, they are not cultivated like tomatoes in a hothouse . . . These strategies can take root in all kinds of places, virtually anywhere people have the capacity to learn and the resources to support that capacity. Such strategies become organisational when they become collective, that is, when the patterns proliferate . . . pervade the behaviour of the organisation at large . . . The processes of proliferation, may be conscious but need not be; likewise they may be managed but need not be . . . Put more simply, organisations, like gardens may accept the biblical maxim of a time to sow and a time to reap (even though they can sometimes reap what they did not mean to sow) . . .
>
> To manage this context is to create the climate within which a wide variety of strategies can grow . . . and then to watch what does in fact come up . . . Management must know when to resist change for the sake of internal consistency (that is, when to do some weeding) and when to promote it (that is, when to do some manuring) . . . must sense when to exploit an established crop of strategies and when to encourage new strains to displace them. It is the excesses of either – the failure to focus (running blind) or failure to change (bureaucratic momentum) – that most harms organisation.
>
> (Mintzberg, 1994: 287–9, quoted in Beare, 2001: 00)

Brian Caldwell believes that the concept of 'educational strategist' will be pre-eminent in the leadership role for this century (Caldwell, 2000: 269). Schools need a capacity for strategic thinking as a continuous activity among leaders 'that should be widely dispersed and utilised in a range of structures and processes in which various strategic conversations should take place' (Caldwell, 2000a: 81), and this matches well to notions of 'distributive leadership' discussed elsewhere in this book. He suggests that:

> Leaders in schools that seek to become world class may start the journey through strategic conversation with their colleagues. The aim is to reach a shared understanding as far as vision and strategies for realisation are concerned.
>
> (Caldwell, 2000a: 81)

The challenge implicit in this statement is for leaders who wish to be trans-formative to see change as an opportunity for emancipation rather than increased control or manipulation. It is clear that 'thinking' is both a cognitive and an emotional process, and that living with uncertainty requires that both are nurtured:

> Although intelligence plays a part in conceptualizing a strategy in pursuit of a vision . . . emotional factors play a very important part in that the capacity to live with uncertainty is a consequence of a resilient capacity which develops from a sense of inner security. One might call this emotional maturity.
>
> (Khaleelee and Woolf, 1996: 9)

These authors claim that personality and life experience radically affect leadership capacity; and their work provides an interesting psychological perspective which suggests that the toleration of uncertainty, an inner emotional security, the capacity for honest self-assessment through self-knowledge and understanding, and a capacity for concern are attributes which underpin the performance of successful leaders over time. They also, however, recognise that even these leaders may, from time to time, experience stress, paranoia – external forces are 'out to get you' – or strong desires to operate in a world of straightforward 'either/or' decisions.

Though it is widely recognised that leadership is stressful (Cooper and Kelly, 1993) and may have negative long-term consequences for the leader (as well as recruitment and retention of leaders) unless managed, the management of self is not a central component of leadership training and development. Within this, the importance of emotions in successful leadership is now becoming widely acknowledged.

Emotional intelligence has been defined as a composite set of abilities that enable a person to manage themselves and others:

1 self-awareness, including emotional self-awareness, accurate self-assessment and self confidence;
2 self-management, including achievement orientation, adaptability, initiative, trustworthiness, conscientiousness and self-control;
3 social awareness, including empathy, service orientation and organisational awareness;
4 social skills, including leadership, influence, communication, developing others, change catalyst, conflict management, building bonds, teamwork and collaboration.

(Boyatzis, 2000: 2)

In the everyday world no intelligences are more important than the intra- and interpersonal. Sadly, at present, emotions are still usually acknowledged and talked about only insofar as they help administrators and reformers 'manage' and offset teachers' resistance to change, or help them set the climate or mood in which the 'really important' business of cognitive learning or strategic planning can take place.

(Hargreaves, 1998: 2)

As Beatty has argued compellingly, in reporting research on teacher recalled interactions with headteachers:

> The fact is that, 'emotions are not optional' (Hede, 2000). What we do with and about them may be in part a matter of choice, but denying they exist or ignoring them does not make them go away. Whether consciously acknowledged or not, they reflect and shape what we think and say and do.

(Beatty, 2001: 6)

To have a clear and well-articulated set of values, to exercise moral leadership and to understand and manage successfully the interplay of powerful intra- and interpersonal emotions in one's own life and those of teachers and other key stakeholders in the school are, in our view, fundamental to successful school leadership over the next decade of challenge to schools.

Hargreaves and Fullan (1998: 116, 119) provide six guidelines for heads:

1 Steer clear of false certainty – accept there are no ready made solutions from outside.
2 Base risk on security – trust and value colleagues so that they will feel able to take risks knowing that they are secure in doing so.
3 Respect those you want to silence – often those who speak against you or raise disturbing questions have something important to say, so beware surrounding yourself with those who are content to walk in your shadow.
4 Move towards the danger in forming new alliances – use external support, establish new relationships, 'lead the way to redefine collaboration so that it encompasses alliances with groups and individuals outside the school'.
5 Manage emotionally as well as rationally – 'structures are only as good as the relationships and know-how of the people who occupy them. Emotional management is ultimately about attending to these relationships properly'.
6 Fight for lost causes – 'a hopeful stance in the face of seemingly intractable problems is the most healthy, constructive thing that [principals] can do'.

Successful leaders of the future, then, need to:

- be continuous learners;
- promote the capacity to learn and manage change among others;
- be reflective (i.e. know themselves);
- be emotional leaders, recognising the part it plays in decision-making, attitudes, relationships and practice;
- be strategic thinkers who engage in strategic conversations with a range of stakeholders within and without the school;
- recognise that knowledge creation is the responsibility of 'teachers' and 'learners';
- be prepared to lead others in understanding the implications of ICT for modes of teaching and learning;
- demonstrate high levels of expectations;
- be seen to care and nurture;
- attend to the culture of teaching, learning and communication;
- be the standard-bearers;
- build networks for enhancing learning.

We continue to be impressed with the non-rational components of human action. We recognise that chaos and confusion are more apt to define the reality of most leaders than are predictability and reason. On the other hand, we believe that the act of leadership is, in part, an effort to impose order on chaos, to provide direction to what otherwise appears to be adrift, and to give meaning and coherence to events that otherwise appear, and may in fact be, random. (Schlechty, 1996: 153)

'Productive' leaders need, like teachers, to be 'activist professionals' (Sachs, 1997), to be active agents, engaging internally and externally in discussions of issues that relate directly or indirectly to education and schooling, as part of their 'moral' purposes. They need to lead, not from the top, but from the centre, having

> a commitment to leadership dispersal which supports the spread of leadership practices and collaborative decision-making processes;
> supportive relationships with staff (teachers and others) and students;
> 'hot knowledge' about how educational theory translates into strategic action alligned with community concerns;
> a focus on pedagogy which describes the extent to which leadership in a school is focused on improving pedagogy and views pedagogical reform as a central concern;
> support for the development of a culture of care which is supportive of teacher professional risk-taking;

a focus on structures and strategies which describes the extent to which leadership focuses on developing organisational processes that facilitate the smooth running of the school.

(Hayes *et al.*, 2000: 5)

Leadership training and development

The characteristics of successful leaders and their ability to be simultaneously people-centred whilst managing a number of tensions and dilemmas highlight the complexity of the kinds of values-led contingency leadership exercised by the successful heads to whom we referred earlier (Day *et al.*, 2000). Many studies illustrate that there are no neat solutions to situations which hold within them so many variables; that successful leadership is defined and driven by individual and collective value systems rather than instrumental, bureaucratic, managerial concerns. Leaders in the NAHT study were identified as being reflective, caring and highly principled people who emphasised the human dimension of the management enterprise. They placed a high premium upon personal values and were concerned more with cultural than structural change. They had all moved beyond a narrow rational, managerial view of their role to a more holistic, values-led approach guided by personal experience and preference. What, then, are the implications for the leadership training and development of aspiring and serving school leaders? Nations across the world are extending their provision of training and development programmes. In England, the establishment by the Teacher Training Agency of programmes for aspiring heads, new heads, and serving heads shows the importance that the government attaches to effective leadership, further underlined by the establishment of a high profile, innovative National College for School Leadership. But even the most recent training programmes fail to address the key themes which have emerged from this book.

Because values are central to successful leadership, reflection upon these must be central to training. Alongside this must be a focus upon critical thinking, emotional and cognitive development, and intra- as well as interpersonal skill development. Recognising the intimate link between the personal and the professional, between the development of the individual and the organisation is paramount. Finally, problem-solving and managing 'competing forces' must be key components of leadership training if schools are to become high-achieving learning communities. Rational models which focus upon the development of only behavioural skills and competencies are insufficient to meet the needs of those aspiring, new and experienced heads who wish to become and remain successful in the changing times and circumstances of the twenty-first century.

References

Beare, H. (2001) *Creating the Future School: Student Outcomes and the Reform of Education*, London, RoutledgeFalmer.

Beatty, B.R. (2001) 'Emotion Matters in Educational Leadership: An Analysis of Teacher-Recalled Interactions with Administrators', paper presented at the 82nd Annual Meeting of the American Educational Research Association, Seattle, 10–14 April.

Beck, L.G. and Murphy, J. (1993) *Understanding the Principalship: Metaphorical Themes 1920s–1990s*, New York, Teachers College Press.

Bennis, W. and Nanus, B. (1985) *Leaders*, New York, Harper and Row.

Boyatzis, R. (2000) 'What if Learning were the Purpose of Education? Developing the Whole Person and Emotional Intelligence', paper presented at the Third London Leadership Centre Annual Lecture at the Institute of Education, London, 26 June.

Brighouse, T. (2001) 'The Caldecote Memorial Lecture', R.S.A., 18th October, 2000, London, *RSA Journal*, 1(4): 63–5.

Burns, J.M. (1978) *Theories of Educational Management*, London, Harper and Row.

Caldwell, B. (2000a) 'Leadership in the Creation of World Class Schools', in K.A. Riley and K. Seashore Louis (eds), *Leadership for Change and School Reform: International Perspectives*, London, RoutledgeFalmer.

Caldwell, B. (2000b) 'Reinventing School Leadership for Lasting Reform', in C. Day, A. Fernandez, T.E. Hauge and J. Moller (eds), *The Life and Work of Teachers: International Perspectives in Changing Times*, London, RoutledgeFalmer.

Coffield, F. (1996) 'A Tale of Three Little Pigs: Building the Learning Society with Straw', paper presented to the European Educational Research Association Annual Conference, Seville, Spain, 27–30 September.

Cooper, C. and Kelly, M. (1993) 'Occupational Stress in Headteachers: A National UK Study', *British Journal of Educational Psychology*, 63: 130–43.

Dalin, P. and Rust, V.D. (1996) *Towards Schooling for the Twenty First Century*, London, Cassell.

Day, C., Harris, A., Hadfield, M., Tolley, H. and Beresford, J. (2000) *Leading Schools in Times of Change*, Buckingham, Open University Press.

de Gues, A. (1997) *The Living Company*, Cambridge, MA, Harvard Business Press.

Dempster, N. and Mahoney, P. (1998) 'Ethical Challenges in School Leadership', in J. MacBeath (ed.), *Effective School Leadership*, London, Paul Chapman.

Drucker, P.F. (1993) *Post-Capitalist Society*, Oxford, Butterworth-Heinemann.

Duignan, P.A. and McPherson, R.J.S. (1992) *Educative Leadership: A Practical Theory for New Administrators and Managers*, London, Falmer Press.

Fukuyama, F. (1999) *The Great Disruption: Human Nature and the Reconstitution of Social Order*, London, Profile Books.

Gewirtz, S., Ball, S.J. and Bowe, R. (1995) *Markets, Choice and Education in Education*, Buckingham, Open University Press.

Hargreaves, A. (2000) 'Four Ages of Professionalism and Professional Learning', *Teachers and Teaching: Theory and Practice*, 6(2): 151–82.

Hargreaves, A. and Fullan, M. (1998) *What's Worth Fighting For Out There?* New York, Teachers College Press.

Hargreaves, D. (1994) *The Mosaic of Learning: Schools and Teachers for the Next Century*, London, Demos.

Hargreaves, D. (1998) *Creative Professionalism: The Role of Teachers in the Knowledge Society*, London, Demos.

Hayes, D., Mills, M., Lingard, B. and Christie, P. (2001) 'Productive Leaders and Productive Leadership: Schools as Learning Organisations', paper presented to the American Educational Research Association Conference, Seattle, 10–14 April.

Khaleelee, O. and Woolf, R. (1996) 'Personality, Life Experience and Leadership Capability', *Leadership and Organization Development Journal*, 17(6): 5–11.

Lambert, L. (2000) *Building Leadership Capacity in Schools*, California, South Australian Secondary Principals Association.

Leithwood, K., Jantzi, D. and Steinbach, R. (1999) *Changing Leadership for Changing Times*, Buckingham, Open University Press.

Levin, B. and Riffel, J.A. (1997) *Schools and the Changing World*, London, Falmer Press.

MacBeath, J. (ed.) (1998) *Effective School Leadership: Responding to Change*, London, Paul Chapman.

Morgan, C. and Morris, G. (1999) *Good Teaching and Learning: Pupils and Teachers Speak*, Buckingham, Open University Press.

National Commission on Education (1993) *Learning to Succeed*, London, Heinemann.

Patterson, M.G., West, M.A., Lawthorn, R. and Nickell, S. (1997) *Impact of People Management Practices on Business Performance*, London, Institute of Personnel and Development.

Sachs, J. (1997) 'Reclaiming the Agenda of Teacher Professionalism: An Australian Experience', *Journal of Education for Teaching*, 23(3): 263–75.

Schlechty, P.C. (1990) *Schools for the 21st Century: Leadership Imperatives for Educational Reform*, San Francisco, CA, Jossey-Bass.

Sergiovanni, T.J. (1992) *Moral Leadership: Getting to the Heart of School Improvement*, San Francisco, CA, Josey-Bass.

Sergiovanni, T. (1994) *Building Community in Schools*, San Francisco, CA, Jossey-Bass.

Sergiovanni, T.J. (1995) *The Principalship: A Reflective Practice Perspective*, Boston, Allyn and Bacon.

Sergiovanni, T.J. (1998) 'Leadership as Pedagogy, Capital Development and School Effectiveness', *International Journal of Leadership in Education*, 1(1): 37–47.

Steinberg, L. (1996) *Beyond the Classroom: Why School Reform Has Failed and What Parents Need to Do*, New York, Simon and Schuster.

Stoll, L. and Fink, D. (1996) *Changing our Schools*, Buckingham, Open University Press.

Tampoe, M. (1998) *Liberating Leadership*, London, The Industrial Society.

Thompson, P. (2001) 'How Principals Lose "Face": A Disciplinary Tale of Educational Administration and Modern Managerialism', *Discourse: Studies in the Cultural Politics of Education*, 22(1): 5–22.

Chapter 10

Professional learning communities and performance training sects

The emerging apartheid of school improvement

Andy Hargreaves

In 1973, American sociologist Daniel Bell coined the term 'the knowledge society', to describe the economic shift from an industrial economy where most people were engaged in producing things to a post-industrial economy where the workforce was increasingly concentrated in sciences, ideas and communication. In the 1990s, management guru Peter Drucker (1993) extended the idea of the knowledge society beyond that of referring to particular kinds of work, to describe how knowledge increasingly characterised and permeated all parts of economic life and the very ways that corporations operated. The basic economic resource of society, Drucker says, is no longer capital or labour. Instead

> it is and will be knowledge. . . . Value is now created by 'productivity' and 'innovation', both applications of knowledge to work. The leading group of the knowledge society will be 'knowledge workers'. . . . The economic challenge will . . . therefore be the productivity of knowledge work and the knowledge worker.
>
> (Drucker, 1993: 8)

In the knowledge society, knowledge, creativity, invention and ingenuity are intrinsic to everything people do (Homer-Dixon, 2000). Robert Reich (2001), President Clinton's former Secretary of Labor, describes how profitability in the new economy depends not on old industrial economies of scale with their techniques of mass production and marketing. Rather, in a world of spiralling and capricious consumer choice, companies stay profitable and viable by inventing new products and services more quickly than their rivals. Competitive companies therefore rely on building sectures and systems of 'continuous innovation' (49) where 'speed and cleverness . . . count far more than production' (41). In this secture, 'geeks' who can invent, create, discover and take all-consuming pleasure in novelty and in seeking out new possibilities, are at a premium. So too are employees and experts who can empathise with clients' needs; who can anticipate and foresee their future desires, and who can figure out what is most likely to titillate their consumer taste buds!

All this innovation and market anticipation calls for knowledge – and the greatest entrepreneurial geniuses like Thomas Edison or today's Stephen Spielberg, says Reich (2001: 58), possess both kinds. But individual geniuses are rare. Successful corporations must therefore bring the innovators and marketers together, breaking down the old departmental divisions between marketing on the one hand, and research and development, on the other, that used to characterise corporations in the older industrial era.

The best corporations in the knowledge society therefore operate as learning organisations where innovators and marketers work in teams, enjoy ease of communication with each other, have regular access to outside knowledge and are able to generate and apply new ideas together (Senge, 1990; Nonaka and Takeichi, 1995; Leonard-Barton, 1995; Leadbeater, 2000). These organisations build their capacity to create and apply new knowledge continuously over time. As Reich (2001: 64) observes, 'mutual learning that leads to continuous innovation tends to be informal, unplanned, serendipitous'. The organisational challenge is to create the groups and sectures in which this mutual, spontaneous learning can take place.

Developing the knowledge society

The knowledge society is a learning society. Economic success and a secture of continuous innovation depend on the capacity of workers to keep learning themselves and from each other. A knowledge economy runs not on machine power but on brain power – the power to think, learn and innovate. Industrial economies needed machine workers; knowledge economies need knowledge workers (Schlechty, 1990). Drucker puts it this way.

> Knowledge workers will give the emerging knowledge society its character, its leadership and its profile. They may not be the ruling class of the knowledge society, but they are already its leading class.
>
> (Drucker, 1994: 64)

International educational change expert Michael Fullan (1993: 80) concludes that 'knowledge-creation using the world of ideas about learning' – including the best of brain research, cognitive science and so on – must be at the heart of teaching and schooling.

Leading social theorists and policy advisors of all political stripes are recognising that high quality public education is essential to developing knowledge workers and the knowledge society everywhere. Castells advises that

> Education is the key quality of labor; the new producers of informational capitalism are those knowledge generators and information processors whose contribution is most valuable to the firm, the region and the national economy.
>
> (Castells, 1996: 345)

Writers of very different ideological persuasions (e.g. Castells, 1996; Giddens, 1998) concur that a strong and improved public education system is essential to producing a vigorous knowledge economy and to enabling poorer communities and countries to participate in and not be marginalised by it.

But if the knowledge economy puts a premium on developing deep knowledge, fostering creativity, ingenuity and inventiveness, improving communication and teamwork and promoting technology, traditional 'grammars' of schooling are ill-suited to developing these essential understandings, skills and dispositions.

The integration (or non-integration) of information and computer technology into secondary schools provides a striking example of the failure of ingenuity in educational change. Unlike primary schools where computers are typically integrated into classrooms, secondary schools usually install their computers in separate laboratories. Why? Because in this way, the grammar of schooling with its one-subject, one-teacher, one-class system is left intact. Student computer-use is confined to special sessions during the week where particular classes are all timetabled into the computer lab together, or to assignments that students undertake individually after school, in their own time. The rest of the time, teaching and learning proceed as they have done for decades, and the absent computer safely locked in its laboratory provides no challenge to them.

Old traditions of teaching do little to promote teaching and learning in the knowledge society. Neither do new patterns of Western-style standardised reform which impose heavy burdens of curriculum content, subject teachers to an overexamined professional life, and squeeze the creativity out of their professional work (Hargreaves, in press). In the knowledge society, you cannot add value to learning by undervaluing the complexity and creativity of teaching. Standardised solutions can neither create nor sustain knowledge society schools.

Futures for teaching in the knowledge society

The OECD has sketched out six likely scenarios for the future of public education in the knowledge society (OECD, 2001). Two of these presume an unravelling of existing arrangements, that will lead to either more entrenched bureaucracy in school systems, or increasing emphasis on market and choice-based solutions as people's dissatisfaction with public education spreads. A second pair of options presumes a shrinkage of

public schooling either by atrophy as teacher shortages and a desperate pro-
liferation of innovations create panic and 'meltdown' in educational policy,
or by investment in other alternatives outside the school in e-learning and
non-formal learning. Just two scenarios, which the OECD labels as
Re-Schooling, assume that public schooling can be saved and improved for
the better. One of these sees the school being reinvented as a focused learning organisation that emphasises learning for the knowledge society. The
other envisions schools as focal points for broader community relationships
and networks, developing students' social capital and enabling them to live
well and work productively in the knowledge society. These last two recommendations amount to teaching for the knowledge society and beyond it.
But how can schools become learning and caring communities given everything that teachers and their systems have experienced and endured in the
past fifteen years of educational upheaval and reform?

Cultures, contracts and change

Elsewhere, I have looked at the fate of Britain's Railtrack as a metaphor for
understanding how and why public education has been going off the rails
(Hargreaves, in press). The collapse of Railtrack in a series of tragic
accidents, and a crippling set of ensuing speed restrictions along with its
record of standards, safety and security was the result, in many ways,
of the railway service abandoning a system of regulation by *cultures of
knowledge and experience* where workers knew and trusted their local
'patch' of railway, the people who worked there and the practices which
maintained and sustained it (Wolmar, 2001). Instead, Railtrack introduced
a system of regulation by *contracts of performance* where quality assurance
through mutual obligation, trusted relationships and local knowledge was
replaced by detailed performance targets imposed on a mobile, low-cost,
flexible workforce of contract labour (Figure 10.1).

Similar patterns have characterised more than a decade of public education reform. Teaching standards for students, performance standards for
teachers, an increasingly casualised teaching force, more and more contract-
ing out of professional development and other support services, and the rise
of charter schools and other private options have replaced the forms of
accountability that used to be embedded in the long-standing relationships
and experiential knowledge of local school districts.

Figure 10.1

Yet we mustn't get too nostalgic about the loss of local sectures to impersonal contracts in education. Local educational sectures can be paternalistic, even feudal in the ways they sectivate compliant loyalty among their teachers and principals. Too often they have camouflaged incompetence, moving problem teachers and headteachers around the system instead of confronting them and their unions. To say that moving from sectures of knowledge and experience to contracts of performance represents only a turn for the worse, oversimplifies the issues.

We need a more sophisticated understanding of how sectures *and* contracts can contribute to reinventing state education in the knowledge society so that it combines the mutual trust of relationships with the professional trust and accountability of performance contracts. Contract-based and secture-based regimes for regulating quality and standards can and do interact with each other in different ways to create different patterns and emphases of school reform, and different types of teaching communities. In the rest of this chapter, I want to examine two of these which are now prevalent: professional learning communities and what I call performance training sects.

Professional learning communities

Professional learning communities add contracts to secture. They put a premium on teachers working together but also insist that this joint work consistently focuses on improving teaching and learning, and uses evidence and data as a basis for informing classroom improvement efforts and solving whole-school problems.

Since the emergence of Peter Senge's (1990) influential management text, *The Fifth Discipline*, many writers have advocated that schools in complex, knowledge-using societies, should become effective learning organisations (e.g. Fullan, 1993; Leithwood and Louis, 1998). If schools were learning organisations, they would develop structures and processes that enabled them to learn in and respond quickly to their unpredictable and changing environments. They would operate as genuine communities which drew on their collective power and human resources to pursue continuous improvement. All their members would be able to see the 'big picture' of their organisation, understanding how parts and whole were interrelated (what's known as 'systems thinking'), and how actions in one domain created consequences in another. They would see the connection between their own personal learning and how the organisation learned collectively as being the key to change and success (Mulford, 1998; Cousins, 1998; Marks and Louis, 1999; Mitchell and Sackney, 2000).

Linking these ideas to the writing of Etienne Wenger (1998) on communities of practice, school-improvement advocates have gone on to recommend that effective schools do and should also operate as strong professional learning communities (Louis and Kruse, 1995; Hord, 1997; Cochrane-Smith and Lytle, 1999; Wireburg and Grossman, 2000; McLaughlin and Talbert, 2001). Professional learning communities in schools emphasise three key components: collaborative work and discussion among the school's professionals; a strong and consistent focus on teaching and learning within that collaborative work; and gathering assessment and other data to inquire into and evaluate progress and problems over time (Newmann and Wehlage, 1995; King and Newmann, 2001). Professional learning communities lead to strong and measurable improvements in students' learning (Newmann and Wehlage, 1995; Little, 2001). Instead of bringing about 'quick fixes' of superficial change, they create and support sustainable improvements that last over time, because they build the professional skill and capacity to keep the school moving (Stoll, 1999; King and Newmann, 1999). In their research on school and departmental communities, McLaughlin and Talbert found that strong communities,

> centered their work on students and shared responsibility for students' mastery of content and progress in the curriculum. They developed 'innovative' methods of instruction that achieved a better 'fit' of course work to students without compromising expectations for students' conceptual learning.
>
> (2001: 11)

A strong professional learning community brings together the knowledge, skills and dispositions of teachers in a school or across schools to promote shared learning and improvement. A strong professional learning community is a social process for turning information into knowledge. It is a piece of social ingenuity based on the principle that in Fullan's words 'new ideas, knowledge creation, inquiry and sharing are essential to solving learning problems in a rapidly changing society' (Fullan, 2001). Professional learning communities promote and presume key knowledge-society attributes such as teamwork, inquiry and continuous learning. They work best when they are combined with sectures of caring and are grounded in long-term relationships of trust, foundations of security and commitments to active care among teachers and others (Hargreaves, in press, ch. 5). Professional learning communities do not flourish in overly standardised systems which severely restrict teachers' discretion for decision-making and self-initiated change. As McLaughlin and Talbert (2001) put it,

> schools and teachers sanctioned on the basis of standardized test scores are drilling their students to pass the test even when they believe the learning is of limited enduring value and the practice is educationally unsound.
>
> (2001: 129)

To build strong learning communities, they advocate a 'shift from system policies that seek to provide standardized practice to those that aim to strengthen teachers' judgement and opportunity to learn'.

Professional learning communities exert their effects slowly, yet sustainably over time. They have clear links to improved standards of learning. Their success depends on continuing support from outside the school, compatibility with external reform imperatives, strong support in terms of instructional materials and leadership development, and a staff with sufficient levels of knowledge, competence and skill to share with their colleagues.

Professional learning communities are not an attractive improvement strategy for policy makers and school leaders who face pressures and demands for quick results in raising achievement levels. They do not fit well with standardised testing regimes or highly prescriptive curriculum frameworks when teachers or leaders do not yet have the minimal levels of expertise on which a professional learning community might be built. In these conditions, policy makers and administrators tend to turn to another reform strategy instead: what I call performance training sects.

Performance training sects

In the face of what Tom Sergiovanni (2000) calls the 'standards stampede', educational reformers have armed themselves with strongly asserted claims from parts of the educational research community that particular teaching practices are highly effective for improving student learning, and that there are proven methods to manage the educational change process effectively. Reformers have then launched a set of large-scale reform strategies which combine a strong insistence on performance standards and prescribed classroom techniques with measures to reculture teachers' working relationships more collaboratively.

The large-scale initiatives include Peter Hill's groundbreaking work with literacy reform in Catholic school systems in Australia (Hill and Crévolat, 1999); Robert Slavin's high-profile *Success For All* programme which involves more than 1,600 schools within and beyond the United States (Slavin, Madden, Dolan and Warik, 1996); the widely publicised success of New York District #2 and its superintendent, Tony Alvarado, in dramatically turning around its students' performance in reading and mathematics (Elmore and Barney, 1997); Alvarado's follow-up impact on the much larger school system of San Diego (Fullan, 2001); and England's massive National Literacy project that has legislated literacy reform in all the nation's primary schools (Barber, 2001).

Although these large-scale initiatives vary in their details, they and their advocates are tightly interlinked in networks of mutual influence and key similarities run through all of them. These include

- making instruction the central focus of improvement efforts;
- concentrating attention on high-profile areas of instruction – especially literacy and numeracy;
- setting ambitious targets for improved achievement results across the whole system that will produce large gains with rapid success;
- giving particular priority to low-achieving students in order to narrow the achievement gap between students from advantaged and less advantaged homes;
- expecting all students to achieve higher standards (with greater support for those who need extra help) – no excuses, no delays;
- providing clearly defined, closely prescribed and sometimes tightly scripted programmes of instruction for teachers to follow that ensure compliance and consistency (though the actual degree of prescription varies);
- providing intensive training for teachers in workshops and summer institutes in the core instructional priorities, to establish large-scale competence in them;
- creating a strong and generous support structure of trainers, co-ordinators and consultants to work with teachers on implementing the priorities within their schools;
- providing intensive one-to-one peer coaching support for teachers within the classroom, on the basis of the evidence that this is one of the key factors that gets more teachers to use and persist with the change over time;
- insisting that principals become instructional leaders, including being directly involved in all relevant training activities within their school;
- having teachers examine achievement data together in order to make adjustments in their instruction where necessary;
- aligning the improvements in instruction with the evaluation and testing system;
- involving parents and the community in supporting their children's learning within the selected initiative.

The emphasis throughout is on providing the pressure and support to train teachers intensively in a limited number of given instructional priorities that will deliver rapid and significant increases in measured learning performances for all students. This strongly supported, closely aligned and intensively applied strategy has already yielded key benefits for students and their teachers (Datnow and Cartellano, 2000).

First, almost all the initiatives have shown significant early success in improving student achievement results, including narrowing the achievement gap between students from different social backgrounds. Second, the reforms have led teachers and schools to treat literacy and numeracy seriously when this had not always been the case. Third, the achievement gains have challenged the views of some teachers that their poor or minority students could not learn to significantly higher standards, and for the first time, many teachers have started to believe that all their students have the capacity to learn. This breakthrough in teachers' belief systems makes them more receptive to further professional learning. Fourth, the scripted materials and strong support structures can benefit teachers beginning their careers, uncertified or underqualified teachers who work in poorer school districts, poorly paid and trained teachers in less developed countries, and other teachers whose knowledge, skills and overall expertise are weak or underdeveloped. A highly driven programme of instructional change provides these teachers with a repertoire of strategies that is inalienably theirs for life, and that can provide a strong platform for further improvement. Last, teachers who have endured years of unwanted reform, finally find themselves being offered extensive and generous levels of support and release time from the classroom to learn things that make a real difference with their students. The forceful pressure to improve is undeniable, but the support is significant too.

The regime of intensive performance training raises many problems, however. Like Railtrack contract workers who learned to repair only the rails but not the rest of the track (Wolmar, 2001), performance training might get quick results, but it is less successful in securing sustainable improvement. In December 2001, England's early gains in literacy scores as a result of its National Literacy Project suddenly reached a plateau. Tightly regulated regimes of performance training also achieve less success at the high-school level where students' learning is more complex, as is their school as an organisation. In England, improving high-school literacy is more challenging than in the case of younger children. Interestingly, the successes of Tony Alvarado in New York were achieved in a district that did not include high schools. In high schools, the instruction is more complex and, as Kathryn Riley and her colleagues' research indicates, many students' difficulties are not so much with the instruction but more with the fragmented organisation of high-school life (Riley, Rushaque andForrester, in press). When literacy skills become more sophisticated, performance training regimes have less dramatic effects.

Second, the repeated stress on literacy and numeracy in these programmes draws attention and support away from other areas of the curriculum such as social studies, arts or citizenship where critical thinking, creating and applying knowledge and other core competencies of the knowledge society are typically given greater emphasis. Regimes of performance training may therefore improve results in basic skills in the short term but imperil more complex knowledge society objectives in the long run.

Then there are the effects on teachers. Research on the impact of performance training initiatives indicates that many teachers dislike teaching highly prescriptive programmes (Datnow et al., 2002). Even when teachers acknowledge the benefits for students, they dislike losing their classroom discretion by being locked into an instructional strait-jacket. They feel less satisfied, less professional, less motivated to teach overall. As Maurice Galton (2000) has argued, even if it is effective for students, mandating instructional change by force is undesirable since it can damage teachers' long-term commitments to their work.

Of course, some teachers *do* like to have their teaching spelled out for them. But pandering to this preference runs the risk of sectivating compliance and recycling professional dependency on the external authority of bureaucrats, on scripted texts, or on the 'incontrovertible' results of research. In performance training sects, there is little opportunity for promoting continuous professional learning among reflective teachers who can exercise discretionary judgement. Over time, teachers inducted into performance training sects will lose the capacity or desire to make professional judgements and become more reflective.

The evangelical nature of performance training sects deprives teachers of this responsibility. Their job is to follow, not question. They cannot challenge the versions of literacy or other curriculum changes they are required to teach. While more reflective and challenging forms of coaching exist, performance training sects promote strictly technical coaching as unreflective practice (Hargreaves and Dawe, 1990). For all their technical complexity and their sophisticated systems of mentoring and support, performance training sects make support look more like suffocation. They put the sin into synergy!

Professional development apartheid

Professional learning communities and professional training sects each combine contracts of performance with sectures of commitment – but in different ways. There is growing recognition in the field of school improvement that 'one size doesn't fit all' (Hopkins, 2001). Different kinds of schools and systems need differing ways of tackling improvement. The same strategy will not suit all of them. In this respect, professional learning communities and performance training sects can offer complementary not competing approaches to change.

Sophisticated professional learning communities seem to work best with high-capacity teachers in high-capacity systems; where teachers are highly skilled and qualified, the schools are at least already reasonably effective, leaders are capable of motivating and engaging their teachers, and there are sufficient resources to provide teachers and schools with the time and flexibility they need to work together professionally (McLaughlin and Talbert, 2001). By contrast, improvement through performance training seems to yield results in low-capacity systems, where large numbers of teachers are uncertified and underskilled, where schools have a record of poor performance and many teachers have lost belief in their capacity to make a difference, where too many leaders see themselves as managers more than instructional leaders, and where resources have been scarce or spread too thinly across too many initiatives – the plague of projectitis, as I call it. Given the schools and the systems we've got and the differences between them, a differentiated rather than 'one size fits all' solution to school improvement and professional learning and development seems to offer an effective and pragmatic solution.

However, flexible differentiation of approaches to school improvement and professional growth can easily turn into deep-seated divisiveness between communities. In the United States, Datnow and her colleagues (2002) have found that among a range of federally approved and funded Comprehensive School Reform models of change from which districts could choose, those that operated off broad principles, guiding frameworks, and the promotion of open-ended teacher collegiality and networking tended to be adopted by schools in more affluent communities. Meanwhile, the tightly scripted, closely monitored programmes that involved intensive training in given methods were mainly adopted by poorer districts, often dealing with high proportions of minority students.

England's educational policies might generate similar divisions. Schools that are performing well according to inspection evidence and test results will enjoy 'earned autonomy' in terms of freedom to manoeuvre beyond prescribed curriculum programmes (DFES, 2001). However, because the United Kingdom has one of the most stubborn ties between educational achievement and students' social background, and still operates a competitive market system of school choice which reinforces these ties, 'earned autonomy' will be enjoyed mainly by schools and teachers in middle-class communities. Meanwhile, schools and their teachers who are categorised as failing or close to failing remain tied to prescribed programmes, endlessly intrusive monitoring and inspection, and sects of performance training in mandated methods of teaching. The definition of failing schools in raw terms of comparisons with test scores in all other schools also means that 'failure' becomes an official problem only in poor, disadvantaged communities which often have high concentrations of racial and ethnic minorities. The cruising schools with coasting teachers who ride in the slipstream of their middle-class academic achievers get off scot-free.

Separate communities, separate teachers, separate development – this is nothing less than an *apartheid of professional development and school improvement.* Schools and teachers in relatively affluent communities enjoy all the benefits of professional learning networks and communities. Their self-skilling teachers engage in professional learning teams and generate student exit outcomes *with* parents to produce self-skilling students who see the 'big picture', employ systems thinking and receive excellent preparation to work in the higher echelons and 'weightless work' of the knowledge economy (Hargreaves *et al.*, 2001).

Schools and teachers in poor communities in the desolate sprawl of housing estates or the Fourth World of less developed nations, struggle in the shadow of impending failure – watchful of test scores, fearful of intervention and with a bellyful of imposed restrictions and requirements. These teachers and schools are thrown into performance training sects where their instructional options and professional learning choices are restricted. They teach the basic skills of maths and literacy that get their students to improve up to a point in primary school only to see their achievements plateau in the high-school years. These schools prepare students to participate in very different sectors of the knowledge economy. Students learn not to create knowledge, develop ingenuity or solve unfamiliar problems in flexible formats; their destiny is to be literate and numerate enough to serve and support the 'weightless work' of their affluent superiors in restaurants, tourist hotels, health spas, and other service work where understanding instructions, communicating obsequiously and urging others to have a nice day, have far greater importance than inventiveness or ingenuity. In the name of 'one size doesn't fit all', these separate systems and forms of separate development prepare students from more and less privileged backgrounds respectively for two very different sides of the knowledge economy: those who create knowledge, and those who cater to those who create.

In Bauman's (1998) terms, students, teachers and parents in affluent, high-achieving communities become the 'tourists' of knowledge society schools who enjoy flexibility, autonomy, freedom of movement, networking and mobility as they are drawn towards magnets of excellence, opportunity and organisational learning. By contrast, students, teachers and parents in poorer, low-achieving communities become the 'vagabonds' and 'vagrants' of the knowledge society – immigrant or working-class students and their casualised, uncertified or demoralised teachers, whose mobility must be monitored and movements must be watched through endless surveillance and evaluations; whose learning is ordered, restricted, and regulated as they are left behind in the 'special education' magnets of the system.

If we want to prepare *all* young people to have the chance to be among the most successful workers within the knowledge society as well as decent citizens beyond it, this new social geography of divisive improvement that offers professional learning communities to the advantaged and imposes performance training sects on the rest is one of our most imminent and disturbing threats.

Conclusion

While standardisation and quick-fix changes seem to be throwing teaching and learning off the rails, the emergence of professional learning communities promises a way of securing longer term, sustainable improvements in our schools – serving as the sleepers and the ballast of educational change. As well as securing sustainable change, professional learning communities also exemplify and promote key knowledge-society characteristics such as learning in teams, involving all the school in the big picture, using technology to enhance everyone's learning, and engaging in systems thinking. Schools as professional learning communities also work best when they do not only process knowledge and learning effectively, but also attend to the social and emotional aspects of teaching, learning and caring, and build social capital among students and teachers as a way of strengthening community and relationships.

In reality, though, professional learning communities are hard to create. They presume and demand qualities of leadership and levels of teacher capacity that are not always available – especially in schools in poor and disadvantaged communities with long legacies of failure and hopelessness. In desperation, reformers in these poorer communities have turned to implementing tight regimes of performance training in a limited number of instructional strategies, supported by coaching, curriculum consultants, and the involvement of school leaders. These strategies have produced demonstrable gains in achievement results, changed many teachers' beliefs about their capacity to make a difference to disadvantaged students' learning, and given teachers a toolbox of techniques that is theirs for life. They have also created as many problems as they have solved.

When they are applied to all of a system's schools, performance training sects repeat all the familiar problems of micro-management and standardisation. They demand uniform loyalty and compliance, they are insensitive to the needs of different schools, they crowd creativity and inspiration out of the curriculum and they diminish teachers' capacity for professional judgement. They foster basic learning and competent teaching, but not the kinds of teaching and learning that fuel the knowledge society.

When they are applied only to districts in difficulty, these strategies perpetuate an apartheid of professional development where professional learning communities are enjoyed by schools and teachers in more affluent communities and performance training sects are inflicted on the rest. These differential strategies of improvement run the risk of creating divided strata of development where underdevelopment is associated only with and recycled among minorities and the poor – separating those who create the knowledge society from those who merely cater to it.

It is time to consider more sophisticated strategies for improvement in the knowledge society that combine elements of performance training and professional community in almost all schools – so that critical dialogue exists from the outset and prevents performance training from becoming a compliant sect. Some elements of training almost always need to be combined with those of learning community and vice versa. How this balance works and in what proportion depends on the type of school and its state of development. Critical dialogue is never something we should leave until later; it belongs at the beginning too.

However, alongside all this attention to strategies of improvement in the context of a knowledge society, is important to remember that many of the basic challenges of schools and teaching in poor communities are not due to lacking strategies of improvement, but of having to endure the scourge of impoverishment. Nations that care about including everyone in the knowledge society as a matter of economic development and social justice, and that care about averting the worst human consequences of the knowledge society, must face the challenge of fundamentally redistributing economic and social resources across the society to those who have the greatest need. We will never have a fair nor fully effective knowledge society until the poor can enjoy generously equipped schools, highly qualified teachers and extensive outside support just as much as their more comfortable neighbours.

If the public will does not yet support redistribution of support towards the public sector and the poorest groups of public schools, it is not our task to capitulate to its lesser morality. As governments, teachers and citizens, our task is to create a visionary social movement that will provide opportunity for the weak, safety and security for everyone including the privileged, and community for all of us in a more dynamic and inclusive society that harnesses the talents of all its people (Hargreaves, 1999).

The knowledge society is beckoning. It is time that everyone in education is granted their right to engage with it. Ingenuity, investment and integrity are required from all of us. Otherwise insecurity, and worse, will be all that we have and no less than we deserve.

References

Bauman, Z. (1998) *Globalization: The Human Consequences*, Oxford, Basil Blackwell.

Bell, D. (1973) *The Coming of Post-Industrial Society*, New York, Basic Books.

Castells, M. (1996) *The Rise of the Network Society*, Oxford, Blackwell.

Cochrane-Smith, M. and Lytle, S. (1999) 'Teacher Learning Communities', *Review of Research in Education*, 24: 24–32.

Cousins, B. (1998) 'Intellectual Roots of Organizational Learning', in K. Leithwood and K.S. Louis (eds), *Organizational Learning in Schools*, The Netherlands, Swets and Zeitlinger.

Datnow, A., Hubbard, L. and Mehan, H. (2002) *Extending Educational Reform: From One School to Many*, London, FalmerRoutledge.

Drucker, P. (1993) *Post-Capitalist Society*, New York, HarperCollins.

Drucker, P. (1994) 'The Age of Social Transformation', *Atlantic Monthly*, 27: 53–80.

Fullan, M. (1993) *Change Forces: Probing the Depths of Educational Reform*, London, Falmer.

Fullan, M. (2001) *Leading in a Culture of Change*, San Francisco, Jossey-Bass/Wiley.

Giddens, A. (1998) *The Third Way*, Cambridge, Polity Press.

Hargreaves, A. (1999) 'Reinventing Professionalism: Teacher Education and Teacher Development for a Changing World', *Asia-Pacific Journal of Teacher Education and Development*, 2(1): 65–74.

Hargreaves, A. (forthcoming) *Teaching in the Knowledge Society*, New York, Teachers College Press.

Hargreaves, A. and Dawe, R. (1990) 'Paths of Professional Development: Contrived Collegiality, Collaborative Culture and the Case of Peer Coaching', *Teaching and Teacher Education*, 4(2).

Hargreaves, A., Earl, L., Moore, S. and Manning, S. (2001) *Learning to Change: Teaching beyond Subjects and Standards*, San Francisco, Jossey-Bass/Wiley.

Hill, P. (2000) Guest editor's introduction – 'The Future of Public Education', *The Journal of Educational Change*, 1(4): 303–6.

Homer-Dixon, T. (2000) *The Ingenuity Gap: Can We Solve the Problems of the Future?*, New York, Alfred A. Knopf.

Hord, S.M. (1987) *Evaluating Educational Innovation*, London and New York, Croom Helm.

King, M.B. and Newmann, F.M. (2001) 'Building School Capacity through Professional Development: Conceptual and Empirical Considerations', *The International Journal of Educational Management*, 15(2): 86–93.

Leadbeater, C. (2000) *The Weightless Society: Living in the New Economy Bubble*, New York and London, Texere.

Leithwood, K. and Louis, K.S. (eds) (1998) *Organizational Learning in Schools*, The Netherlands, Swets and Zeitlinger.

Leonard-Barton, D. (1995) *Wellsprings of Knowledge: Building and Sustaining Sources of Innovation*, Boston, Harvard Business School Press.

Little, J.W. (2001) 'Professional Development in Pursuit of School Reform', in A. Lieberman and L. Miller (eds), *Teachers Caught in the Action: Professional Development that Matters*, New York, Teachers College Press.

Louis, K.S. and Kruse, S.D. (1995) *Professionalism and Community: Perspectives on Reforming Urban Schools*, Thousand Oaks, CA, Corwin Press.

McLaughlin, M. and Talbert, J. (2001) *Professional Communities and the Work of High School Teaching*, Chicago, University of Chicago Press.

Marks, M.B. and Louis, K.S. (1999) 'Teacher Empowerment and the Capacity for Organizational Learning', *Educational Administration Quarterly*, 35 (special issue): 707–50.

Mitchell, C. and Sackney, L. (2000) *Profound Improvement: Building Capacity for a Learning Community*, Downington, PA, Swets and Zeitlinger.

Mulford, W. (1998) 'Organizational Learning and Educational Change', in A. Hargreaves, A. Lieberman, M. Fullan and D. Hopkins (eds), *International Handbook of Educational Change*, The Netherlands, Kluwer Press.

Newmann, F. and Wehlage, G. (1995) *Successful School Restructuring*, Madison, WI, Center on Organization and Restructuring of Schools.

Nonaka, I. and Takeuchi, H. (1995) *The Knowledge-Creating Company: How Japanese Companies Create the Dynamics of Innovation*, New York, Oxford University Press.

OECD (2001) *Schooling for Tomorrow: What Schools for the Future?*, Paris, Organization for Economic Cooperation and Development.

Reich, R. (2001) *The Future of Success*, New York, Alfred A. Knopf.

Schlechty, P. (1990) *Schools for the Twenty-First Century: Leadership Imperatives for Educational Reform*, San Francisco, Jossey-Bass.

Senge, P. (1990) *The Fifth Discipline: The Art and Practice of the Learning Organization*, New York, Doubleday.

Sergiovanni, T. (2000) *The Lifeworld of Leadership: Creating Culture, Community, and Personal Meaning in our Schools*, San Francisco, Jossey-Bass.

Stoll, L. (1999) 'Realizing our Potential: Understanding and Developing Capacity for Lasting Improvement', *School Effectiveness and School Improvement*, 10(4): 503–32.

Wenger, E. (1998) *Communities of Practice: Learning, Meaning and Identity*, Cambridge, UK, Cambridge University Press.

Wineburg, S. and Grossman, P.L. (eds) (2000) *Interdisciplinary Curriculum: Challenges to Implementation*, New York, Teachers College Press.

Wolmer, C. (2001) *Broken Rails: How Privatization Wrecked Britain's Railway*, London, Aurum Press.

Index